POPULATING THE *BARRERA*

Spanish Immigration Efforts in
Colonial Louisiana

POPULATING THE *BARRERA*

Spanish Immigration Efforts in Colonial Louisiana

Gilbert C. Din

University of Louisiana at Lafayette Press
2014

Cover Credits:
front top, *Armas de la Provncia de la Luisiana*, Archivo General de Indias, Seville, Spain; front bottom, *Baxa Luisiana* by Jaun Pedro Walker, The Historic New Orleans Collection 1977.97; rear, *Mapa de las locaciones Del Distrito de Manchack*... by Vicente Sebastián Pintado, Library of Congress.

© 2014 by University of Louisiana at Lafayette Press
All rights reserved
ISBN 13 (paper): 978-1-935754-30-5

University of Louisiana at Lafayette Press
P.O. Box 40831
Lafayette, LA 70504-0831
http://ulpress.org

Printed on acid-free paper.

Library of Congress Cataloging-in-Publication Data

Din, Gilbert C.
  Populating the barrera : Spanish immigration efforts in colonial Louisiana / Gilbert C. Din.
     pages cm
  Includes bibliographical references.
  ISBN 978-1-935754-30-5 (paper : acid-free paper)
  1. Louisiana--Politics and government--To 1803. 2. Louisiana--Colonization--History--18th century. 3. Louisiana--Emigration and immigration--History--18th century. 4. Land settlement--Political aspects--Louisiana--History--18th century. 5. Governors--Louisiana--History--18th century. 6. Spaniards--Louisiana--History--18th century. 7. Spain--Colonies--America--Administration--History--18th century. 8. Frontier and pioneer life--Louisiana. I. Title.
  F373.D57 2013
  976.3'02--dc23
                            2013038864

Contents

	Foreword	vii
1	Early Spanish Colonization Efforts in Louisiana	1
2	Lieutenant Colonel Francisco Bouligny and the Malagueño Settlement at New Iberia, 1779	23
3	The Immigration Policy of Governor Esteban Miró in Spanish Louisiana	39
4	Proposals and Plans for Colonization in Spanish Louisiana, 1787-1790	63
5	Pierre Wouves d'Argès in North America: Spanish Immigration Commissioner, Adventurer, or French Spy?	79
6	Spain's Immigration Policy in Louisiana and the American Penetration, 1792-1803	105
7	The Irish Proselytizing Mission to West Florida	133
8	The Canary Islander Settlements of Louisiana: An Overview	153
	Bibliography	179
	Index	191

Foreword

Many decades ago, I was in Madrid as a graduate student exploring the Spanish archives for a research topic for my dissertation in Historia de América at the Universidad Complutense de Madrid. When I now look back on those days, there were countless subjects that awaited fledgling historians like me. Initially, a theme on Lower California attracted my attention. At the time King Carlos III expelled the Jesuit missionary order from the Spanish colonies in 1767, the Jesuits left behind numerous records that detailed their work. The documents for Lower California included ledgers, diaries, books, maps, and a wide assortment of manuscripts they had accumulated through the eighteenth century. Royal officials shipped them to Spain, where the records were deposited in Madrid's Archivo Histórico Nacional (AHN). I spent several days poring through the documentation before deciding against pursuing a religious topic. My secular mind warned me that missionary activity among the indigenous inhabitants of Lower California was not my cup of tea. Furthermore, hailing from southern California added to that sentiment because I craved something more exotic.

Fortunately, the AHN possessed a surfeit of documents suitable for investigation. After considering several more topics, an archivist directed me to a collection of very legible manuscripts in the Estado (State) papers called "Relaciones diplomáticas entre España y los Estados Unidos." These records deal with problems between Spain and the United States in the years after American independence in the late eighteenth century. Several of the *legajos*, or bundles of documents, in the Sección de Estado and numbering from 3882 to 3902 contain records that discuss Spain's effort to augment Louisiana's inhabitants through the acquisition of Acadians, Canary Islanders, French Canadians, Irishmen, Germans, and even American Protestants. For that purpose, Spanish authorities received proposals to bring in Louisiana Creoles, Americans, Irishmen, and assorted other foreigners. In addition, within these AHN manuscripts are those that detail James Wilkinson's notorious scheme to form an alliance with Spain through the separation of Kentucky from the United States. Another intriguing aspect was Spain's attempt to convert to Catholicism the Protestant British settlers and American immigrants in West Florida. The proselytizing labor fell to English-speaking Irish missionaries who were recruited in Spain; they were there because the Anglican British government had shut down the Catholic seminaries that trained priests in Ireland. Inasmuch as the immigration documents are tied to diplomatic themes, they incorporate letters generated at Court wherever that happened to be—Madrid, Aranjuez, San Lorenzo de El Escorrial, or San Ildefonso de La Granja. Players in the drama in Spain include the principal Spanish ministers of state and other Court officials. In the colonies they are the governors, captains general, sometimes the intendants, and to a lesser degree the Spanish diplomatic officials in New York and Philadelphia assigned to handle relations with the United States government.

The AHN documents, however, do not include the multitude of documents that originated in Louisiana, written either by the governor or by commanders at the new settlements and directed to the governor. Spanish officials evacuated these provincial records upon their withdrawal from Louisiana and West Florida in the early nineteenth century. They were housed in Havana for several score years. Eventually in the late nineteenth century, Spain transferred them to the Archivo General de Indias (AGI) in Seville, where they were labeled "Papeles Procedentes de la Isla de Cuba." To consult these documents, I took the overnight train from Madrid down to Seville several times and spent approximately four months rummaging through a good batch of legajos, taking notes and copying documents. In addition, I used whatever published materials on Louisiana the libraries of the archives and Madrid's Biblioteca Nacional (National Library) possessed. The Manuscripts Section of the Biblioteca Nacional also contains several small collections of documents that deal with Spanish Louisiana and Florida. Many of these documents are one of a kind and without copies at the AHN or AGI. The other repositories in Madrid, however, failed to yield records useful to my research.

After arranging the documents and notes in the proper order, I began composing my dissertation that became "Colonización en la Luisiana española del siglo XVIII." It focuses on Spanish policies and efforts to enlarge Louisiana's sparse population and create a *barrera* (barrier) along the Mississippi River against first British and then American encroachment on their North American possessions. The creation of settlements in Louisiana plays a far lesser degree of importance in the dissertation. This is not to say that documents on the establishment of settlements do not exist, rather they were at the AGI in very scattered legajos that made them time-consuming to consult. In addition, my research at the AGI preceded organization of the Papeles de Cuba according to chronology and authors to facilitate microfilming them in a coherent manner. In other words, the Papeles were then in a terrible disarray and required protracted time to pore through the bulky legajos that can each hold as many as two thousand documents. Besides, use of all these records would have taken untold years and produced a multi-volumed dissertation. As it was, my doctoral oeuvre still consumed four hundred pages of text. Fortunately, when I presented it at the Universidad Complutense de Madrid, a panel of professors judged my research exemplary and the dissertation "*sobresaliente*" (outstanding).

Upon returning to California, locating a teaching job became my first priority. I soon found one at Imperial Valley College. Regrettably, instructing five classes per semester, usually different history courses (United States, Western Civilization, or History of the Americas) and always two in either physical or cultural anthropology yielded negligible time for research and writing. During my residence there, I accomplished little toward preparing my dissertation as a book or even writing an article. I was especially eager to explain Gov. Esteban Miró's role in immigration. Through examination of his letters and other immigration proposals, I discovered that he was the hidden inspiration behind Spain's decision to allow American Protestants to settle in West Florida and Louisiana, a point no other historian had yet recognized. I soon moved on to Fort Lewis College, in Durango, Colorado, and Miró's immigration labors became the first article I put together and sent off to a journal. The *Southwestern Historical Quarterly* published it in 1969 in a record six months, from submission of the manuscript to the appearance of the journal article. The stars must have been smiling because no other periodical has matched the *SwHQ*'s extraordinary speed in the publication of my subsequent articles.

Furthermore, its appearance in print commenced an era when I composed one or two articles every year, many of them based on material from my dissertation. As much as I would have liked to convert the dissertation into a book, teaching new courses again consumed much of my time and writing articles was a more manageable task. By the time I got to ten published articles on immigration, I had virtually exhausted my research materials. The articles were not dissertation chapters, but information plucked from assorted chapters, reorganized and rewritten in new ways, and included secondary sources—books and articles—that were not available in Spain.

By the mid-1970s, with the dissertation articles either published or awaiting publication, I made my first visit to Louisiana and the Deep South to present a paper at the Louisiana Historical Association's annual meeting. Talks with new found colleagues convinced me to continue exploring the state's and the region's little known Spanish past. In the summer of 1975, I spent six weeks at the AGI researching how the Francisco Bouligny memoir came to be written and one week in New Orleans gathering photocopies of Bouligny's letters and his memoir, helped generously by the late Fontaine Martin, a Bouligny descendant. This research, which resulted in the publication of *Louisiana in 1776: A Memoria of Francisco Bouligny* (New Orleans, 1977), also assisted in the acquisition of documents for my last article on immigration. It was belatedly completed in 1984, after yet another trip to the AGI, and published two years later.

As I moved into new areas of research, I put the articles on immigration behind me. In succeeding years, several of them appeared in book collections of published articles, and they made me regret that my initial extended historical investigation had not produced a book. Nevertheless, I had the consolation that they had been published in various journals. But alas, articles in the academic world generally do not garner the scholarly accolades that books enjoy. Occasionally, I received suggestions to combine the immigration articles and present them in book form. Because I was always busy with other research tasks, I procrastinated. At last in March 2011, I spoke with James Wilson, associate director of the University of Louisiana at Lafayette Press. I told him about my plan to gather the articles into a book, and he agreed to consider the manuscript for publication. Therefore, I returned to the articles, chose the most significant among them, and revised portions of their texts and notes to improve the wording and update the bibliographies. Because I had designed the articles to stand alone, repetition sometimes appears in them to explain the purpose behind Spanish immigration labors or to shed light on persons involved in accelerating population growth. Some of the repetition has been eliminated, and I hope the rest will serve to remind readers of the participants in the long ago drama and clarify how various projects were intertwined and helped or hindered each other.

This briefly describes the first seven articles. The final article was written about ten years after the other articles appeared in print. At that time, I was composing a study on the Canary Islanders of Louisiana, first as a report for the National Park Service, and later as a book. I hoped the study would be of interest to historians, to descendants of those immigrants, and to a wider public curious about the *Isleños* (Islanders) who were virtually unknown even within the state. While I had gathered some information on the Canary Islanders as I researched my dissertation, the material in the eighth article extends beyond my initial investigation inasmuch as I had not examined the development of their settlements through the colonial era. Nevertheless, because the article fits in with Spanish colonization schemes and the founding of communities in Louisiana, it is included here.

To facilitate the examination of Spanish immigration work, the articles are presented more or less in chronological order. For readers who wish to follow a strict political chronology, I advise examining first chapters 1, 3, 4, and 6. The other four chapters, 2, 5, 7, and 8, explore certain aspects of Spain's immigration efforts. These chapters provide information on the founding of New Iberia, the commission of Pierre Wouves d'Argès as an immigration agent, the labors and travails that confronted Irish missionaries in West Florida and Louisiana as they tried to convert Protestant immigrants, and the hardships endured by the Canary Islanders in their first settlements in the colonial era. It is my hope that the chapters—or articles—in this book will correct errors made by early historians and explain the reasons the Spanish government shifted policy several times as it endeavored to attract settlers to Louisiana and West Florida in the late eighteenth century.

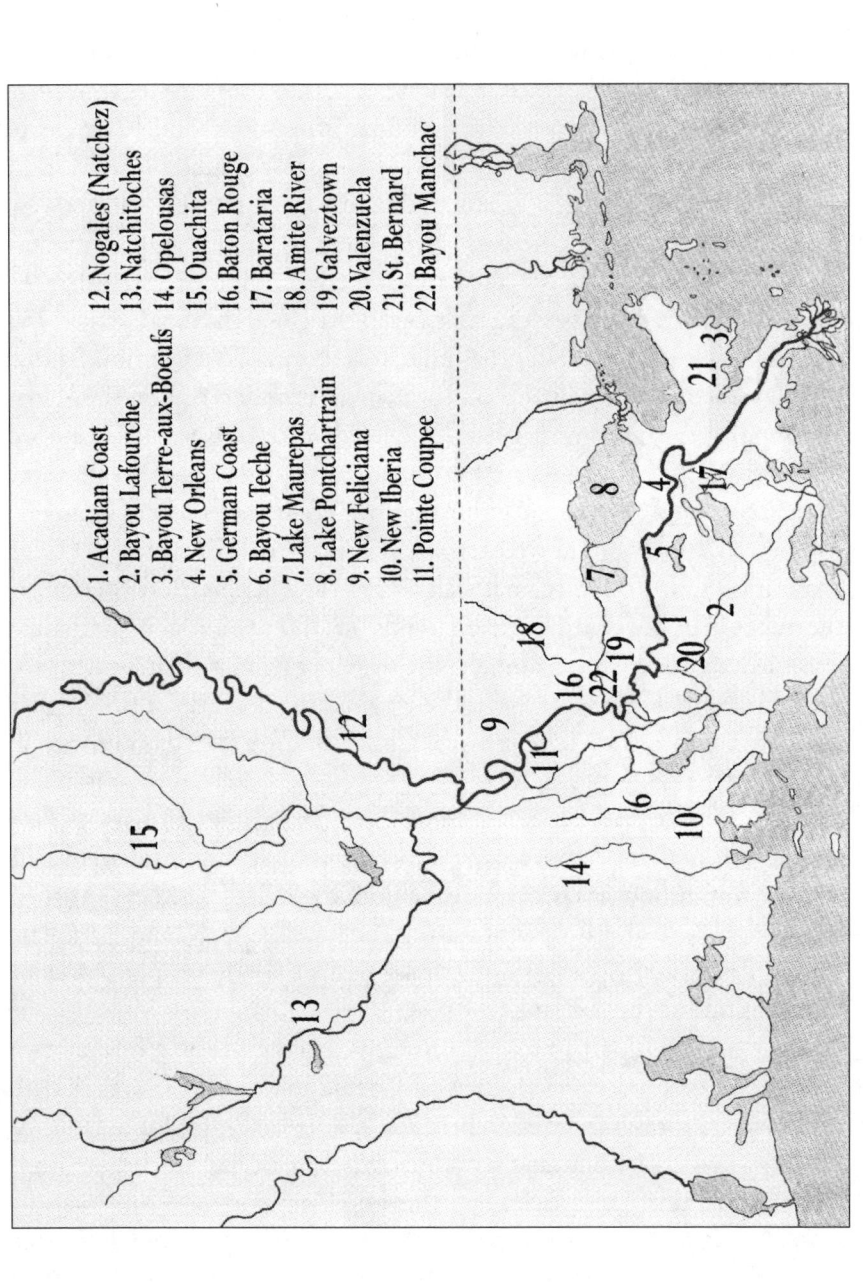

Chapter 1
Early Spanish Colonization Efforts in Louisiana

When Spain acquired Louisiana from France in 1762, its chief value was as a buffer province, or *barrera*, for the more important Kingdom of New Spain (Mexico). Colonial officials repeatedly mentioned it when they urged the Crown to develop Louisiana and augment its population. Spain, however, moved slowly in taking possession of the colony and held it weakly in the 1760s. Acceptance of Louisiana imposed a costly burden on the royal exchequer inasmuch as the colony produced almost nothing in revenue and soon consumed significant quantities of money. Since it was virtually barren of European inhabitants, Louisiana's usefulness as a buffer could only be realized if it built up a substantial population capable of resisting aggressive neighbors to the east, first Great Britain that acquired trans-Appalachia (the lands from the mountains to the Mississippi River) and West Florida in 1763 as a result of the Seven Years' War and later the United States that absorbed the British lands at its independence. To offset the dangers it faced in the early period of control over Louisiana, Spain welcomed and assisted the settlement of a mixture of immigrant groups: Acadians, French Canadians, Spaniards, and Catholics from friendly nations. For approximately twenty years, the financially insecure Iberian nation expended significant sums of money to promote colonization. By the early 1780s, however, Spain recognized the impossibility of continuing to subsidize immigration to Louisiana. The task was too formidable for Spain's limited resources and worldwide commitments.[1]

---

1. This article first appeared in *Louisiana Studies* 11 (Spring 1972): 31-49. On early European colonization efforts in the Mississippi Valley, see Gilbert C. Din, "Empires Too Far: The Demographic Limitations of Three Imperial Powers in the Eighteenth Century Mississippi Valley," *Louisiana History* 50 (Summer 2009): 261-72.

Spain acquired Louisiana, which is to say the right bank of the Mississippi River and the Isle of Orleans, that included New Orleans (Great Britain received the left bank), without knowing much about them by the Treaty of Paris in 1763 that concluded the disastrous Seven Years' War for both France and Spain. French settlement on the Gulf Coast had started in the late seventeenth century at Biloxi and Mobile before its few inhabitants trekked up the Mississippi River. French traders founded Natchitoches, the first European settlement in the colony in 1714, for trade with the Indians and Spaniards living in lands to the west. New Orleans, established in 1718 as the provincial administrative head, became the second settlement. Population growth, however, came slowly as the government dispatched few settlers until monopoly companies (Antoine Crozat, Company of the West under John Law, and the Company of the Indies) took control of the colony. Through his speculation scheme, Law induced the government or ambitious individuals to send French inhabitants, prison inmates, indentured individuals, women from work houses and orphanages, and persons deceived by his sham advertising, to the colony where many succumbed to adversity and hardship in large numbers. The same happened with African slaves. Thomas Ingersoll states that between 1719 and 1731, about 5,600 slaves arrived in the colony, and only 3,604 were alive in 1731. Fewer whites entered Louisiana and only 1,721 were then residing in 1731. The appalling death rates of both whites and blacks to 1731, when the Crown reclaimed the colony, soured the inhabitants of France who came to regard Louisiana as a charnel house of the unfortunate condemned to reside in the colony.[2] Several decades elapsed before Frenchmen again willingly went there.

France acted slowly in informing Louisiana officials of the colony's cession to Spain, and the news reached New Orleans only in September 1764. The inhabitants then waited a year and a half before the first Spanish governor of Louisiana, Antonio de Ulloa, arrived on March 5,

---

2. Thomas N. Ingersoll, "Old New Orleans: Race, Class, Sex, and Order in the Early Deep South, 1718-1819" (Ph.D. diss., University of California, Los Angeles, 1990), 47-48; Gilbert C. Din, *Spaniards, Planters, and Slaves: The Spanish Regulation of Slavery in Louisiana*, 1763-1803 (College Station: Texas A&M University Press, 1999), 4-5, 7, 239n.

1766.³ He brought only a handful of officials and approximately ninety soldiers because Spain then prioritized improving its defenses in the Caribbean following the disastrous Seven Years' War. Spain's dominion over Louisiana remained feeble from 1766 to 1768, and it became more tenuous in New Orleans when most of Spain's soldiers departed for military posts along the Mississippi in 1767.⁴ Six decades of French rule had produced a colony with only about eleven thousand inhabitants, over half of whom were African slaves.⁵ Therefore, augmenting its population became a Spanish necessity to retain its grasp on the vast western Mississippi basin. In the first phase of implementing an immigration policy for Louisiana, Governor Ulloa did little more than assist the arriving settlers.

Prior to Ulloa assuming command, a small stream of immigrants was entering Louisiana, composed mainly of Frenchmen who did not wish to live under British rule. Most of the new French settlers were Acadians, former inhabitants of Nova Scotia who had been deported by the British

---

3. John Preston Moore, *Revolt in Louisiana: The Spanish Occupation, 1766-1770* (Baton Rouge: Louisiana State University Press, 1976), and Moore, "Antonio de Ulloa: A Profile of the First Spanish Governor of Louisiana," *Louisiana History* 7 (1967): 189-218.

4. Allan J. Kuethe, *Cuba, 1753-1815: Crown, Military, and Society* (Knoxville: University of Tennessee Press, 1986), 90-91; Gilbert C. Din, "Protecting the "*Barrera*": Spain's Defenses in Louisiana, 1763-1779," *Louisiana History* 18 (Spring 1978): 188-90.

5. "Resumen General," New Orleans, Louisiana Census of 1766, manuscript 569, folio 107, Museo Naval (Madrid), lists the white population as 1,893 adult white males fit to bear arms, 1,044 white women, and 2,619 children. However, Paul LaChance, in "The Growth of the Free and Slave Populations," in *French Colonial Louisiana and the Atlantic World*, edited by Bradley G. Bond (Baton Rouge: Louisiana State University Press, 2005), 230, with documents from the French archives, lists the white population for 1766 at 5,094 and the African at 5,940. See also Martín Navarro, "Political Reflections on the Present Condition of the Province of Louisiana," in James Alexander Robertson, ed., *Louisiana Under the Rule of Spain, France, and the United States, 1785-1807: Social, Economic, and Political Conditions of the Territory in the Louisiana Purchase*, 2 vols. (Cleveland: Arthur Clark Company, 1911), 1: 240. Although Antonio Acosta Rodríguez's *La población de Luisiana española (1763-1803)* (Madrid: Gráficas Condor, S.A., 1979), has many censuses of small settlements in Louisiana, he ignores province-wide censuses.

in 1756 and dispersed through the English Atlantic colonies, Caribbean Islands, and England and France. Many of them, however, were dissatisfied with their imposed homes. Inasmuch as Louisiana was still French in 1759, they preferred to resettle there, and Acadians began moving to the colony where local authorities assisted them in settling down. Many of the immigrants found new homes along the Mississippi River north of the German Coast (so named because of its German inhabitants who entered during the early French era), and the newly settled region acquired the sobriquet of Acadian Coast.[6] In 1764 and 1765 the largest numbers of Acadians arrived, which was after Spain had acquired ownership of the colony but before Governor Ulloa reached New Orleans. Assistance to the immigrants consisted of land, rations for six months, agricultural implements, and seeds.[7]

Meanwhile, a group of French Canadians entered Upper Louisiana (the west bank of the Mississippi River), which until then had been virtually empty of Europeans. Most of the early eighteenth-century inhabitants established settlements such as Fort Chartres, Kaskaskia, and Cahokia on the river's east bank. In the Treaty of Paris of 1763, however, France ceded its trans-Appalachian region to Great Britain, and many settlers relocated to the west bank of the Mississippi that they believed was still French territory. Slightly earlier, Pierre LeClède Liguest and his stepson Auguste Chouteau established St. Louis in 1764 as an Indian trading post, and it became the second French settlement on the upper Mississippi's west bank; Ste. Genevieve was the first, and its founding dated back to the 1740s. In the early 1760s, Upper Louisiana, or Spanish Illinois as it was also called, contained very few inhabitants, and its growth in settlers remained slow.[8]

---

6. Émile Lauvrière, *Histoire de la Louisiane Française, 1763-1939* (Paris: G.-P. Maisonneuve, 1940), 412.

7. On the Acadians, see Carl A. Brasseaux, *"Scattered to the Wind": Dispersal and Wanderings of the Acadians, 1755-1809* (Lafayette, La.: Center for Louisiana Studies, 1991); and *The Founding of New Acadia: The Beginnings of Acadian Life in Louisiana, 1765-1803* (Baton Rouge: Louisiana State University Press, 1987), 20-89; John Mack Faragher, *A Great and Noble Scheme: The Tragic Story of the Expulsion of the French Acadians from Their American Homeland* (New York: W. W. Norton, 2005), 424-36.

8. Louis Houck, *A History of Missouri from the Earliest Explorations and Settlements*

After Governor Ulloa assumed direction of Louisiana, assistance to the incoming Acadians continued.[9] Ulloa accepted Louisiana's usefulness as a barrier against the English in nearby West Florida. A populated Louisiana, he contended, was infinitely more valuable than an empty colony. Consequently, he did what he could to help the immigrants, most of whom were indigent and in dire need. He allotted them full rations for a year and half rations for a second year; he also doled out tools, guns, ammunition, and medical assistance. He believed that the province would flourish if the colonists were settled easily.[10]

A financial statement written about early 1767 described the arrival of the Acadians in the colony and their settlement under conditions of privation and misery. Governor Ulloa, nevertheless, praised them and believed that if they received free transportation to Louisiana, perhaps as many as ten thousand more would come. Ulloa proposed providing them with land, food in their first year of settlement, farm tools, guns and ammunition for hunting, corn, cows, pigs, and hens. His report suggested allotting 25,000 pesos annually to assist colonists settling in Louisiana.[11]

The report convinced the Crown to implement Ulloa's suggestions.

---

until the Admission of the State into the Union, 3 vols. (Chicago: R. R. Donnelley and Sons Company, 1908), 2: 10-13; "Pierre LeClede," in *American National Biography*, 24 vols. (New York: Oxford University Press, 1999), 13:15-16. On Ste. Genevieve, see Carl J. Ekberg, *Colonial Ste. Genevieve: An Adventure on the Mississippi Frontier* (Gerald, Mo.: Patrice Press, 1985).

9. Many historians of Louisiana history have assumed that the Spaniards did not govern Louisiana until 1769, but this is untrue. Ulloa exercised authority in many areas in the province such as military affairs, taxes, finances, and commerce, among other things, and he was not challenged by the French Creole leadership based in the Superior Council. Moore, in *Revolt in Louisiana*, called it a "two-headed" government, with Charles Phillip Aubry, the acting French governor, retaining power, but Aubry was chiefly a figure-head.

10. Vicente Rodríguez Casado, *Primeros años de la dominación española en la Luisiana* (Madrid: Consejo Superior de Investigaciones Científicas, 1942), 104-105; Antonio de Ulloa, "Noticias," n.p., n.d., Archivo General de Indias (hereafter cited as AGI), Santo Domingo, legajo 2543.

11. "Governmental expenses," n.p., n.d.; Marqués de Grimaldi to Bailio Fray Julián de Arriaga, Aranjuez, May 13, 1767, both in Lawrence Kinnaird, ed., *Spain in the Mississippi Valley, 1764-1794*, 3 Parts (Washington, DC: GPO, 1949): 1: 115-19 and 68, respectively.

Officials in Madrid understood the necessity of populating the almost vacant province to create the *barrera*. On May 26 and 27, the government issued two royal orders that called for fomenting immigration to Louisiana. The Marqués de Grimaldi, the minister of state, assigned 25,000 pesos annually exclusively to building up the colony's population. Although it represented a beginning, it was still a modest sum compared to the needs of the gigantic province.[12]

Through 1767, Acadians continued to arrive in Louisiana. In May some of them were established along the Mississippi while others went to Attakapas and Opelousas (regions in the interior of the Mississippi's west bank that became known as Acadiana). In July, 211 Acadians arrived from Maryland. Governor Ulloa gave them guns, tools, and provisions and conducted them to Fort San Gabriel at Bayou Manchac. Problems soon arose with a number of these families, who grumbled about the meager help they received while Spanish officials accused them of refusing to work.[13]

In late 1767, Governor Ulloa received an inquiry from English Catholics in Maryland about moving to Louisiana. Dr. Henry Jerningham declared that he and others became interested in the colony after receiving favorable reports from former Maryland Acadians who had gone there. Jerningham wrote in November that several hundred Catholics, including many possessing property, wished to resettle if conditions in Louisiana were acceptable. In December the Maryland doctor informed Ulloa that a representative of theirs, Jacobo Walker, was going to the Spanish province, where he would spend several months gathering information about the terrain, the government, and local customs to enable him to report fully to prospective colonists. Two months later, Ulloa informed Grimaldi in Spain that he anticipated an extremely large exodus of families from the English colonies to Louisiana.[14] Contrary to his expectations, English

---

12. Joseph de Loyola to Ulloa, New Orleans, September 1767, AGI, Papeles Procedentes de Cuba, legajo (hereafter cited as AGI, PC, leg.), 109.

13. Loyola to Ulloa, New Orleans, October 22, 1767; Joseph Orieta to Ulloa, Fuerte El Ynfante San Gabriel, September 20, 1767, both in AGI, PC, leg. 109; Julián Alvarez, "Lists of the families that have come to settle in this Province of Louisiana, and are today lodged in the king's house," New Orleans, July 27, 1767, AGI, PC, leg. 114.

14. Henry Jerningham to Ulloa, St. Mary's County, Maryland, North America,

Catholics from Maryland appear not to have made the journey.

In February 1768, the English ship *Guinea* brought another 149 Acadians to New Orleans. Their settlement, too, was impeded by their complaints of insufficient rations and their refusal to devote themselves to agriculture.[15]

How many Acadians arrived during these early years is difficult to calculate. One writer has placed their number coming from the French Antilles and the English colonies at between 1,000 and 1,200, which is a reasonable estimate. Three districts where Acadians settled—Attakapas, Opelousas, and Acabannoosa—had 874 whites in the 1769 census. Other districts, meanwhile, held additional Acadians.[16]

Governor Ulloa also attempted to increase the population of Spanish Illinois. An advocate of sound morals, he wanted orderly and decent inhabitants. He proposed that the Spanish government send orphan girls of a marriageable age to Upper Louisiana if the region lacked women, and he ordered the commandant at St. Louis to create more settlements for the newcomers.[17]

Only a month before he was removed as governor by the Creole French rebellion of October 1768, Ulloa developed second thoughts about immigration. He complained to Spain about the funds spent to establish colonists and speculated that perhaps future settlement costs could be limited or terminated altogether. He suggested that hereafter newly arriving Acadians might be helped by their own people who

---

November 18, 1767, Kinnaird, *Spain in the Mississippi Valley*, 1: 36-37; Jerningham to Ulloa, n.p., December 14, 1767, ibid., 1: 39; Ulloa to Grimaldi, New Orleans, February 11, 1768, no. 2, ibid., 1: 40-42. See also Clarence E. Carter, ed., "A Projected Settlement of English Speaking Catholics from Maryland in Spanish Louisiana, 1767, 1768," *American Historical Review* 16 (January 1911): 319-27; and Mattie Austin Hatcher, "The Louisiana Background of the Colonization of Texas, 1763-1803," *Southwestern Historical Quarterly* 24 (January 21, 1921): 170.

15. Loyola to Ulloa, New Orleans, February 8 and 11, 1768, AGI, PC, leg. 109; Casado, *Primeros años*, 107.

16. Kinnaird, *Spain in the Mississippi Valley*, 1: 196, Census of Louisiana. The Acadian Coast in 1769 had 486 inhabitants while Attakapas and Opelousas in 1771 had 444 settlers.

17. Houck, *History of Missouri*, 1: 291-92.

had settled earlier. Many families were already present, and they could multiply and in time create a substantial population.[18]

To restore Spanish authority in Louisiana following the 1768 rebellion and the ouster of Governor Ulloa, Gen. Alejandro O'Reilly arrived in the colony the next year with a formidable army to regain control and punish the leaders of the insurrection. He remained in Louisiana about seven months, during which time he imposed Spanish power thoroughly throughout the colony.[19] Henceforth, the Crown showed slightly more interest in the province than it had earlier.

A group of thirty-four Acadians and forty Germans, who were all Catholic, hired a vessel, the *Britain*, on December 12, 1768, at Port Tobacco in southern Maryland, to take them to New Orleans for settlement in the colony. The ship's commander, Philip Ford, deceived the passengers about its seaworthiness, his ability as a pilot of the Gulf waters, and his clandestine intentions. The ship landed in Texas, where Spanish authorities seized the passengers and the vessel that had deteriorated completely; they suspected that Ford intended to engage in contraband trade. The sailors and immigrants, perhaps numbering eighty-nine, traveled overland to Natchitoches in Louisiana while Rafael Martínez Pacheco, commandant of San Agustín de Ahumada in Texas, purchased Ford's merchandise. The travelers, meanwhile, arrived in Natchitoches on October 24. Four days later, Césaire Borme, head of the local militia, sent four immigrants who lodged complaints against Ford and the sailors to New Orleans, where they arrived twelve days later. O'Reilly, then temporarily in charge of the colony, permitted the Germans to settle at Iberville (Bayou Manchac) and the Acadians in Natchitoches. The latter, however, quickly protested their assignment away from fellow Acadians,

---

18. Ulloa to Grimaldi, New Orleans, October 6, 1768, no. 4, in Kinnaird, *Spain in the Mississippi Valley*, 1:75-76.

19. Herbert Eugene Bolton, *The Spanish Borderlands: A Chronicle of Old Florida and the Southwest* (New Haven: Yale University Press, 1921), 240-49; Bibiano Torres Ramírez, *Alejandro O'Reilly en las Indias* (Seville: Escuela de Estudios Hispano-Americanos, 1969); and David Ker Texada, *Alejandro O'Reilly and the New Orleans Rebels* (Lafayette, La.: Center for Louisiana Studies, University of Southwestern Louisiana, 1970).

and eventually they resettled at Opelousas.[20] An unenthusiastic report, perhaps written by O'Reilly, described the families as expensive to colonize; he generally projected a negative attitude toward immigrants. Nevertheless, he helped the new arrivals with land, tools, and money.[21]

The danger of war erupting between Spain and Great Britain over possession of the Malvina (Falkland) Islands in the early 1770s again roused a concern about developing Louisiana's population. At that time the British increased their troops in neighboring West Florida; they also sent more colonists to the east bank of the Mississippi.[22] The British activities caused a stir in Louisiana, where Col. Luis de Unzaga governed following the departure of O'Reilly. Unzaga feared for the safety of Louisiana and Mexico. He predicted that British merchants and soldiers would "bring commerce in time of peace, and arms in time of war."[23] He recommended that the captain general of Cuba place a numerous population in the colony or reinforce it with forts to enable him to greet "force with force."[24] As it turned out, English settlement in West Florida proved modest; but contraband trade flourished between Louisiana planters and English merchants along the Mississippi River. Merchants sold the planters slaves, tools, and other indispensible items at bargain prices. While Unzaga made no measurable effort to prevent the illegal traffic inasmuch as the goods were essential, the sales drained Louisiana

20. Alejandro O'Reilly to Arriaga, New Orleans, December 10, 1769, no. 21, Kinnaird, *Spain in the Mississippi Valley*, 1: 135-36; Natchitoches, October 27, 1769, "List of German and Acadian families who went by an English vessel to New Orleans to Settle," Ignacio Ramón de Ezpeleta, New Orleans, December 14, 1769, ibid.; Carl A. Brasseaux and Richard E. Chandler, "The *Britain* Incident, 1768-1770: Anglo-Hispanic Tensions in the Western Gulf," *Southwestern Historical Quarterly* 87 (April 1984): 357-63.

21. Kinnaird, *Spain in the Mississippi Valley*, 1: 144-48; O'Reilly to Arriaga, New Orleans, December 29, 1769, ibid.

22. (Captain general of Cuba) to Luis de Unzaga, Havana, March 4 and 20, 1772, AGI, PC, leg. 1146; Unzaga to the Marqués de la Torre, New Orleans, April 18, 1772, no. 23, ibid.; John Walton Caughey, *Bernardo de Gálvez in Louisiana, 1776-1783* (Berkeley: University of California Press, 1934), 44-45.

23. Unzaga to (the captain general of Cuba), New Orleans, February 27, 1772, AGI, PC, leg. 1146.

24. Ibid.

of nearly all the specie in the colony.²⁵

Nonetheless, the English presence in West Florida caused the Spanish government to renew its effort to attract more settlers. By the royal order of May 26, 1774, the Crown instructed the governor of Louisiana to bring in Germans, Acadians, Frenchmen, or Irishmen, who were Catholics and not merchants. The Crown preferred workers and artisans as settlers and sought to prevent trade with the English.²⁶ These measures attempted to build up the *barrera* of Louisiana against potential foes across the river. While the province now opened up to receive more nationalities as colonists, it is questionable if many came at their own expense during these years. The next major attempt to enhance the colony's population would soon occur in Spain.

In the summer of 1776, Capt. Francisco Bouligny of the Louisiana battalion presented a lengthy memorial to the Crown in which he commented on conditions in Louisiana.²⁷ His memorial informed the government of the need to increase the colony's population, stimulate agriculture and commerce, and convert the province into an effective barrier for the defense of New Spain. He further warned of the danger and the growing strength of the English in West Florida. Bouligny believed it wiser and more economical to augment Louisiana's population than build up its military defenses. He proposed establishing clusters of families along the Mississippi River at intervals. The costs to the

---

25. Julia C. Frederick, "Luis de Unzaga and Bourbons Reforms in Spanish Louisiana, 1770-1776" (Ph.D. diss., Louisiana State University, 2000), 205-14; and Robin Fabel, *The Economy of British West Florida, 1763-1783* (Tuscaloosa, Ala.: University of Alabama Press, 1988).

26. "Royal Order to the Governor of Louisiana," (Yndice), May 26, 1776, AGI, PC, leg. 174B.

27. Francisco Bouligny, "Noticia del estado actual del Comercio y Población de la Nueva Orleans y Luisiana Española"; J. Horace Nunemaker, "Francisco Bouligny's Absence from Louisiana," *Research Studies* 10 ([Pullman]: State College of Washington, 1942), 198-201. Excerpts of Bouligny's memorial are in Alcée Fortier, *A History of Louisiana*, 4 vols. (New York, 1904), 2:25-55. The complete memoir is translated in Gilbert C. Din, *Louisiana in 1776: A Memorial by Francisco Bouligny* (New Orleans: Louisiana Collections Series, 1977). For a biography of Bouligny, see Gilbert C. Din, *Francisco Bouligny: A Bourbon Soldier in Spanish Louisiana* (Baton Rouge: Louisiana State University Press, 1993).

government could be recovered slowly from the harvests of the settlers, and they could provide soldiers when needed, thus reducing Louisiana's defense expenses. Bouligny asserted that soldiers for the colony could be obtained in the Spanish provinces of Valencia and Murcia. He advocated developing hemp and flax as crops because the Crown needed both commodities. He further recommended establishing schools to teach the Spanish language, religion, and rudimentary knowledge. For defense, he suggested that all eighteen-year-old men serve two to three years in the military, after which they would become citizen-soldiers in the militia.[28]

The captain's memorial had an effect on Spanish policy since the government adopted several projects he recommended. Most important was the Crown's renewed attempt to increase Louisiana's population. This new effort coincided with a different governor, Bernardo de Gálvez, assuming direction of Louisiana in January 1777. He received lengthy instructions that included the promotion of immigration and acceptance of all Spaniards and Catholic foreigners who entered Louisiana. The Crown, however, barred Englishmen, Dutchmen, and other Europeans from nations hostile to Spain. New settlers were required to take oaths of fidelity and vassalage and agree to remain permanently in the colony. They would receive lands in proportion to the acreage they could cultivate and enjoy all the privileges Spaniards possessed. The welcome, however, did not extend to vagrants and indolent individuals.[29]

After eleven years in Louisiana, Spain could show some success in boosting the colony's population. The same year Gálvez became governor—1777—a census pointed out that the inhabitants had grown to 17,923. Of this number 8,381 were white, 8,461 were African slaves, 545 were mulatto slaves, 263 were free blacks, and 273 were free mulattoes.[30] The colony's inhabitants had increased by more than six thousand since the 1760s, which represented a more than 50 percent rise. While it was not spectacular, it was sizable when compared to dawdling demographic

28. Din, *Louisiana in 1776*, 43-93.

29. "Ynstrucción reservada al Colonel Bernardo de Gálvez para su dirección en el Gobierno en la Provinica de la Luisiana," n.p., n.d., AGI, PC, leg. 174B; Caughey, *Bernardo de Gálvez*, 60.

30. "Census of Louisiana," (New Orleans), May 12, 1777, AGI, PC, leg. 2351.

increase during the French era.

Governor Gálvez also attempted to add to Upper Louisiana's population. He instructed Francisco Cruzat, who in 1775 replaced Pedro Piernas as lieutenant governor, to attract French and Canadian families who were living on English lands. In answer to Gálvez's order of June 6, 1777, Cruzat described the Canadians as poor; however, with financial assistance, they could be induced to cross over to Spanish territory. He claimed that they despised the English who made them fight the "Bostoneses." When the Spanish government learned that French Canadians could be easily acquired, it ordered Louisiana officials to bring them in. However, Gálvez, in anticipation of the order, had already issued instructions to commandants to admit French, Italian, and German immigrants who were Catholic or Spanish subjects. They were to be located near settlements that they could reinforce when danger threatened. Families were to receive five arpents of river front by forty deep, rations for a year, implements, poultry, and other indispensable items, with which they could "begin and easily establish a settlement capable of rendering sustenance and perhaps even make them a fortune."[31]

The following year Cruzat informed the government that flax and hemp could not be grown in Upper Louisiana as the government had ordered. He also commented on the scarcity of inhabitants in that area. Consequently, he suggested that slaves be sent to the colony and sold on credit so that they could develop suitable crops.[32] Early in 1778, Capt. Fernando de Leyba became lieutenant governor of Upper Louisiana. Governor Gálvez instructed him to attract Irish, Canadian, German, and Acadian Catholics who had been living among the English. He was to offer the settlers lands, work implements, and rations until they brought in their first harvest. Gálvez further insisted that Leyba submit a yearly list of new inhabitants and another of the goods and rations they received.[33]

---

31. Francisco Cruzat to Bernardo de Gálvez, San Luis de Ilinueses, December 8, 1777; Bernardo de Gálvez, New Orleans, February 10, 1778, "Instruction to Capt. Fernando de Leyba assigned to command (Spanish) Illinois"; both in AGI, PC, leg. 2358; Houck, *History of Missouri*, 1: 303-306.

32. Houck, *History of Missouri*, 1: 303-306.

33. Bernardo de Gálvez, New Orleans, March 9, 1778, reserved, "Particular instruction that Capt. Fernando de Leyba, chosen Lieut. Gov. of the Establishments

Desiring to employ yet other means to gain immigrants, Gálvez instructed French ships sailing to the Caribbean Islands to disseminate news that Spain welcomed Catholic colonists in Louisiana. Furthermore, they would receive assistance in settling.[34] However, these efforts were scarcely productive; if settlers came, they were few.

After the American War for Independence began, Spain sought to add a second battalion, about seven hundred men, to the soldiers already in Louisiana and create the Fixed Louisiana Infantry Regiment in anticipation of the coming conflict with Great Britain.[35] That effort added the first sizeable contingent of Spanish settlers to Louisiana. In early 1778, Lt. Col. Andrés Amat de Tortosa in Santa Cruz de Tenerife in the Canary Islands received orders to obtain seven hundred recruits and their families. From October 1778 to February 1779, five ships departed Santa Cruz filled with recruits and their families. Then Spain went to war with Great Britain in June 1779, which disrupted shipping, and another group of recruits did not leave the Canaries until May 1780. Only one of these three ships reached Havana.[36]

In New Orleans, Governor Gálvez, who expected soldiers, glowered at the families that Amat de Tortosa had sent. He alleged that too many recruits had families with numerous children. The soldiers could not support them with their meager pay of twelve reales (one and a half pesos) per day. Consequently, Gálvez employed the married recruits as settlers and not as soldiers.[37] He placed many families along the Mississippi

---

of [Spanish] Illinois, dependent on this province of Louisiana of my command, should observe," in Kinnaird, *Spain in the Mississippi Valley*, 1: 258-60.

34. Caughey, *Bernardo de Gálvez*, 78-79.

35. For Spanish military activities in West Florida during the American War for Independence, see Albert W. Haarmann, "The Spanish Conquest of British West Florida, 1779-1781," *Florida Historical Quarterly* 39 (October 1960): 107-34; Eric Beerman, *España y la independencia de los Estados Unidos* (Madrid: Editorial MAPFRE, 1992), 43-65; and Thomas Chávez, *Spain and the Independence of the United States: An Intrinsic Gift* (Albuquerque: University of New Mexico Press, 2002).

36. Gilbert C. Din, *The Canary Islanders of Louisiana* (Baton Rouge: Louisiana State University Press, 1988), 17-19.

37. Bernardo de Galvéz to José Navarro, New Orleans, October 26, 1778, AGI, PC, leg. 1232; Andrés Amat de Tortosa to Bernardo de Gálvez, Santa Cruz de Tenerife,

River at Barataria, Tierra de Bueyes (Terre aux Beoufs), Galveztown, and Valenzuela. Spanish military policy aimed to settle immigrants at strategic locations for the defense of Lower Louisiana and New Orleans. Gálvez gave the Isleños lands, food rations, farm implements, and even money in the hope that assistance would end with the harvest of their first crop. Assistance, however, continued much longer because the colonists encountered numerous obstacles on the thorny road to self-sufficiency. The governor also established some Canary Island families in Galveztown, a settlement originally begun by Americans who fled from British territory when the American rebellion began. About 400 Isleños, in 112 families, made their homes there. Unfortunately, an epidemic hit the settlement and killed about 150 Spaniards within a few months.[38]

Nevertheless, not all the Canary Island families suffered in this manner. At Tierra de Bueyes, later called San Bernardo and located south of New Orleans, 160 Spanish families and some French settlers, about 800 persons in all, were established under district commandant Pierre Marigny de Mandeville. Marigny built a church and aided the colonists with rations, tools, houses, and livestock. From the beginning San Bernardo thrived and the settlement soon supplied New Orleans with food. In November 1782 and August 1783, more Canary Islanders settled there. In May 1779, Gálvez had placed 113 families at Valenzuela (Bayou La Fourche), situated about forty miles northwest of New Orleans. However, this settlement was unable to support itself, and four years later, the Valenzuela settlers were still receiving rations.[39]

An effort to establish a number of Isleño families at Pensacola in the early 1780s failed. In 1782, thirty-six Canary Islander families were sent

---

February 19, 1779, AGI, PC, leg. 119.

38. (Captain General of Cuba) to Bernardo de Gálvez, Havana, July 27, 1779, AGI, PC, leg. 1232. Of the 1,582 Canarians who arrived at this time, 153 were bachelor recruits and 329 were married recruits with approximately 1,100 dependents.

39. Pedro Marigny to Manuel Gayoso, n.p., February 4, 1789, reserved, AGI, PC, leg. 1393; "Libro Maestro para sentar el cargo a las familias de la Nueva Población de Tierra de Bueyes," September 30, 1779, AGI, PC, leg. 568; "Libro para sentar particular y efectos que reciben las familias isleñas procedentes de la Havana llegadas a esta Provincia en Agosto de 1783, y destinadas a la Población de Sn. Bernardo alias Tierra de Bueyes por el Sr. Dn. Martín Navarro, Ynte. Gral. de esta Provincia," ibid.

there from Cuba to replace the English inhabitants who had recently departed after Spain conquered the post. Unfortunately, the settlers could not adjust to life there. Two years later, Commandant Arturo O'Neill recommended removing the families to Escambé, a region with soil more fit for agriculture, and supplying them with farm implements and livestock. He said that in Pensacola the families had not become self-supporting. But O'Neill's recommendation was not followed, and in 1785 the families petitioned the government to allow them to leave because of the food shortage in Pensacola. Before the year ended, the families departed for Havana as they had requested.[40]

Spanish documents fail to reveal the exact number of Canary Islanders who came to Louisiana during these years. To July 7, 1779, it is known that 1,582 had arrived.[41] After this time several more shiploads of settlers came to New Orleans from Havana. Many were interrupted in their journey by the war, and the immigrants often spent months or even years in Cuba. Archival documentation only reveals some of the ships and their voyages. The *Sagrado Corazón* reached Havana before the end of July 1779 with 423 passengers, and the *Suárez* came in 1780 with about 100 more persons.[42] In 1783, the frigate *Margarita* carried 156 settlers from Havana to New Orleans while another 304 persons remained in Cuba.[43] Adding these settlers to the earlier arrivals, they total over 2,500 persons, but undoubtedly the figure is incomplete. The acquisition of this number of people represented a sizable increase in Louisiana's population, and, aside from soldiers, it was the only large influx of Spanish civilians into the colony.

---

40. "Libro Maestro para sentar el cargo a las Familias de la Nueva Población de Valenzuela," n.p., May 5, 1779, AGI, PC, leg. 568; Caughey, *Bernardo de Gálvez*, 80.

41. Arturo O'Neill to Martín Navarro, Pensacola, March 28, 1783, AGI, PC, leg. 614A; Bernardo de Gálvez to O'Neill, Guarico (Cap Français), October 26, 1782, ibid.; Martín Navarro to José de Gálvez, New Orleans, July 27, 1784, AGI, PC, leg. 595A, no. 241; Arriaga to O'Neill, Havana, October 24 and 25, November 15, 1785, both in AGI, PC, leg. 85.

42. (Captain General of Cuba) to Bernardo de Gálvez, Havana, July 27, 1779, AGI, PC, leg. 1232.

43. José de Gálvez to the governor of Louisiana, San Lorenzo, November 27, 1779, AGI, PC, leg. 174A.

Because of Bouligny's memoir of 1776, a small number of families from Granada and Málaga, Spain, came to Louisiana for the purpose of growing flax and hemp. In May 1778, the brigantine *Santa Theresa* transported to New Orleans a number of Granada families, who were allegedly skilled in raising the crops and who probably totaled fewer than one hundred persons. They brought with them several boxes of seeds to be used in planting experiments. For the next two years, the families tested the seeds without achieving favorable results. Intendant Martín Navarro followed their progress without enthusiasm. He labeled the families as worthless, lacking industry, and inflicting considerable expense to the treasury. When the report reached the minister of the Indies, José de Gálvez, he ordered the intendant to return them to Spain after the war. Governor Gálvez, however, insisted that efforts to develop flax and hemp in the province continue. In 1784, ten families of forty-one persons returned to Spain; but several other Granada families elected to remain in Louisiana as settlers.[44]

A third group of Spaniards who were from Málaga went to Louisiana during these years. Before leaving Spain, the Malagueños negotiated a contract with the government that detailed the assistance they would receive until they were self-supporting. The government hired the brigantine *San Josef* to transport them to the colony. However, eighteen sick passengers left the ship at Cádiz and thus only sixty-seven continued the voyage in July 1778. Those who remained in Cádiz soon followed on the merchant frigate *Princesa de Asturias*.[45] When the Malagueños arrived in New Orleans, Governor Gálvez ordered Lieutenant Colonel Bouligny, who had returned to Louisiana from Spain, to select a site for their settlement west of New Orleans, despite the fact he had never been

---

44. Francisco Varela, Havana, July 23, 1783, "Noticia del número de Familias y Personas venidas de Yslas Canarias qe. con destino a la Provincia de la Luisiana se hallan depositadas en esta Plaza en el día de la Fecha;" Francisco Varela, Havana, June 25, 1783, "Lista de familias enviadas a Nueva Orleans"; both in AGI, PC, leg. 1393.

45. Joseph de Gálvez to the governor of Louisiana, San Ildefonso, August 24, 1778; Francisco Manxar to Joseph Navarro, Cádiz, August 9, 1778; both in AGI, PC, leg. 174B; José de Gálvez to the intendant of Louisiana, El Pardo, March 8, 1781, AGI, PC, leg. 360; Juan Ygnacio de Unzaga to Martín Navarro, Havana, April 15, 1784, AGI, PC, leg. 601.

to that region of the colony.⁴⁶

He selected Bayou Têche, and before taking the first group of settlers there, Bouligny hired sixty slaves and several artisans to construct houses for the colonists, lay out boundaries for farms, begin planting, and help the settlement get started in other ways. In January 1779, Bouligny began the journey, taking the hired slaves and laborers with only a small contingent of settlers. By February he had selected a site on Bayou Têche, which he named New Iberia, and started work. Bouligny purchased livestock from neighboring farmers to distribute among the families. He wanted them to become self-sufficient before the end of the year. In the spring, additional families arrived in New Iberia. But soon heavy rains caused the rivers to rise. The waters inundated the settlement with six to eight feet of water, and the colonists fled to shelters on higher ground. Bouligny quickly relocated the settlement to land he purchased seven or eight leagues upstream. He constructed two giant sheds as temporary shelters for the colonists. Slaves worked the fields to bring in a crop before the growing season ended; Bouligny placed heavy emphasis on raising food crops so that the Malagueños would quickly become self-sufficient. In June the waters receded sufficiently to allow more settlers to be sent from New Orleans.⁴⁷

Bouligny did not remain much longer at New Iberia. In August he learned that Spain was at war with Great Britain. Since he wanted to participate in Governor Gálvez's Mississippi campaign against the British in West Florida, he raised troops from among his settlers and African slaves and left New Iberia to join the Spanish expedition. Following the successful conquest of the British posts on the river, Bouligny returned to New Orleans where Gálvez asked that he provide an accounting of the work completed at New Iberia. To this time, the settlement had cost 31,150 pesos and 5 reales. Gálvez considered the expenditures excessive since money was scarce due to the war. In reply Bouligny explained that expenses would soon be reduced considerably, and he advised paying each family a flat sum of money so that they could build their own houses or buy

---

46. José de Gálvez to the governor Louisiana, San Ildefonso, August 7 and 24, 1778, both in AGI, PC, leg. 174B.

47. Bouligny to Bernardo de Gálvez, New Orleans, June 23, August 4, and November 12, 1778, all in AGI, PC, leg. 2358.

them from the Acadians. The news that families were still without homes shocked Gálvez, and he inquired how the slaves had been employed. Bouligny explained that they had been used in agricultural work to make the families self-sustaining as quickly as possible.[48] Because of the war Bouligny did not return to New Iberia, and Nicholas Forstall succeeded him as commandant of the settlement. Assistance to the Malagueños did not end in 1780, although government opinion of them had declined. Intendant Navarro described them as lazy, probably because assistance to them continued for several more years.[49]

New Iberia did not become a large and flourishing settlement. The number of Málaga families was small and accounted for fewer than ninety persons. In 1779, counting Germans and a few other people who settled down alongside the Málaga immigrants, the total population came to less than a hundred persons. The census of 1785 listed only 125 inhabitants at the settlement.[50]

The arrival in Louisiana of the Isleños, Granadinos, and Malagueños all occurred at approximately the same time. They came to the province after the Spanish government had already spent considerable sums of money to assist the first Acadians in settling. The cost of establishing the Spanish immigrants was also substantial, and it convinced colonial authorities as well as the Crown that less expensive settlers would have to be found for Louisiana. Moreover, the colony produced only a pittance in revenue. Costs for immigration are known only for some of the years. In 1778, a royal order gave the *ramo* (branch) of Population and Indians a budget of 40,000 pesos, which was repeated the next year. By this time many settlers were arriving in the colony, and instead of 40,000 pesos,

---

48. Bouligny letters to Bernardo de Galvez, New Orleans, January 14, 1779; a league from [Achafelaya], February 7, 1779; New Iberia, February 18, March 17, and April 21, 1779, all in AGI, PC, leg. 2358; New Iberia, March 22, June 25, and July 28, all in AGI, PC, leg. 600.

49. Bouligny to Bernardo de Gálvez, New Iberia, August 25, 1779; (Bernardo de Gálvez to Bouligny), New Orleans, October 26, 1779; Bouligny to Bernardo de Gálvez, New Orleans, October 28 and November 3, 1779, all in AGI, PC, leg. 600.

50. Bouligny to Bernardo de Gálvez, New Orleans, November 3, 1779, AGI, PC, leg. 600; intendant of Louisiana to José de Gálvez, New Orleans, n. d., no. 16, AGI, PC, leg. 93, paquete A.

costs for them soared to 128,568 pesos. Probably similar or even larger sums were expended in the next few years when more numerous colonists came. Amat de Tortosa's commission in the Canary Islands was very expensive. In Santa Cruz de Tenerife alone he received 111,562 pesos and 4 reales; in Louisiana the Isleño families required even more assistance.[51] In 1784 Intendant Navarro stated that 61,617 pesos and 3 reales had been expended in the area of Population and Indians, a decrease that reflected the smaller number of immigrants then arriving. Navarro added optimistically that "the greater part of the expenses and work of this last branch (Population and Indians) should cease when the colonist families have settled and return to the King the expenditures for their establishment."[52] However, the intendant voiced his expectation too soon. Several more years elapsed before royal assistance to the colonists ended completely. Moreover, there is no evidence that they repaid the Crown for their settlement costs.

Quite unexpectedly one final influx of immigrants came from France in 1785. They were Acadians who had been expelled from Nova Scotia and had gone to France, where they lived wretchedly on a dole provided by the French government. As early as 1775, they had requested to be sent to Louisiana, but until 1784 the French government denied them permission. At that time the Spanish Crown agreed to transport them to Louisiana and provide them with implements, housing, and rations until they could care for themselves. Thus in the summer of 1785, seven ships carried some 1,598 Acadians to New Orleans, where the first vessels arrived unannounced.[53] Nevertheless, Intendant Navarro took steps to

---

51. Charles Gayarré, *History of Louisiana*, 4 vols. (New Orleans: Armand Hawkins, 1885), 3: 170. Caughey, in *Bernardo de Gálvez*, 31, states that about 500 settlers from Málaga came to Louisiana in 1779. My research in the Spanish archives fails to substantiate his claim.

52. Martín Navarro to Esteban Miró, New Orleans, January 19, 1785, AGI, PC, leg. 85; Marqués de Sonora (José de Gálvez) to the intendant of Louisiana, El Pardo, February 14, 1787, AGI, PC, leg. 2317. See also Charles H. Cunningham, ed., "Financial Reports Relating to Louisiana, 1766-1788," *Mississippi Valley Historical Review* 6 (December 1919): 381-97; and Jack D. L. Holmes, "Some Economic Problems of Spanish Governors of Louisiana," *Hispanic American Historical Review* 42 (November 1962): 521-30.

53. Martín Navarro to (José de Gálvez), New Orleans, August 18, 1784, "Documentos de la Luisiana," vol. 3, f. 76, Sección de Manuscritos, Biblioteca Nacional, Madrid.

see that they were cared for, given equipment and food, and settled on the land. In August Anselmo Blanchard conducted 150 persons to Manchac, where in a short time another 59 families joined them. In October 237 more people were settled at Valenzuela. Soon passengers from another ship joined them. The last of the Acadians settled at Bayou de los Ecores, or Thompson Creek, located near Baton Rouge.[54]

Even before these last immigrants arrived, Louisiana officials had been grumbling about the heavy expenditures made for incoming settlers and their failure to become self-sufficient quickly. The Acadians similarly required considerable assistance. In 1785, some 80,000 pesos were requested to be used for their rations, and the cost of their settlement was estimated at 200,000 pesos. Moreover, Louisiana was then in a financial crisis. Because of the war the colony had not received its full subsidy since 1779.[55] Despite Navarro's request for funds from Spain for use on the immigrants, none had come. The local authorities had no recourse but to print more paper money which further decreased in value the paper currency already in circulation. Finally, the Acadians aggravated the situation by not becoming self-supporting quickly. In 1787 Navarro complained about their laziness and stated that he would terminate assistance to them shortly.[56] It was not done, however, and as late as 1789, they were still receiving some governmental help.

The Acadians from France were the last immigrants brought

---

54. Martín Navarro to José de Gálvez, "Estado que manifiesta los nombres de los Barcos, número de Familias, y personas Acadianas existente, desde 29 qe llegó la primera Expedición hasta el día de la fecha," December 12, 1785, AGI, PC, leg. 2360; Fernando Solano Costa, "La Emigración acadiana a la Luisiana española (1783-1785)," *Cuadernos de Historia Jerónimo Zurita* 2 (1954): 85-125; "Report on the Acadian Immigrants who came to Louisiana from France in 1786," De Aspres, "Provision for Transportation of Acadians from France to Louisiana," Nantes, May 12, 1785, both in Kinnaird, *Spain in the Mississippi Valley*, 2: 169, and 2: 127-31, respectively.

55. Martín Navarro to the Conde de Gálvez (Bernardo de Gálvez), New Orleans, August 2, 1785, AGI, PC, leg. 85; (Martín Navarro) to José de Gálvez, New Orleans, September 9, 1785, no. 332, AGI, PC, leg. 595, Packet A; intendant of Louisiana to Sonora, New Orleans, February 22, 1786, no. 363, ibid.

56. Martín Navarro to the Conde de Gálvez, New Orleans, December 14, 1785, no. 23, AGI, PC, leg. 85; intendant of Louisiana to José de Gálvez, December 22, 1785, no. 247, AGI, PC, leg. 593.

Early Spanish Colonization Efforts in Louisiana 21

across the Atlantic Ocean at government expense and helped in their settlement. Since the authorities could no longer afford to subsidize immigration, Spanish policy was already in the process of change. Almost at the same time these last settlers arrived in Louisiana, Spain agreed to permit the Anglo-Saxon residents of the conquered British colony of West Florida, most of whom were Protestants, to remain on their lands, but with the condition they take oaths of allegiance to Spain and not practice their Protestant religions publicly. Soon this modification in immigration policy was relaxed even more to permit Protestants from the United States to settle in Louisiana and West Florida under similar conditions.[57] Esteban Miró, who became provisional governor of these two provinces in 1782 (and the royally appointed governor in 1785), convinced the Court that by allowing American immigrants to settle in West Florida and Louisiana at no cost to the Crown, the colony could be developed and made militarily stronger. He believed that in time the Americans could be assimilated.[58]

Spain's record of achievement in building up Louisiana's population in its first twenty years of dominion over the colony was significant. From about 11,000 inhabitants at the time Spain obtained the province, the population rose to 31,433 in 1785, which included West Florida. While natural increase accounted for a part of its rise, at least five to six thousand more Europeans settled in Louisiana at the expense of the Spanish government. Royal expenditures, however, were considerable. It possibly amounted to as much as two million pesos spent on transporting and settling the immigrants. Considering that Spain had a world-wide empire and diverse commitments, the accomplishment was truly remarkable. Nevertheless, after this time the Crown assumed an inflexible position and decreed that money was no longer to be applied to immigration. That decision ended one period in Spain's effort to augment Louisiana's population and build up the *barrera*, and it started another as Spanish officials in the colony now searched for settlers elsewhere.[59]

---

57. Intendant of Louisiana to Sonora, no. 407, New Orleans, July 22, 1786; (Martín Navarro) to Antonio Valdés, no. 4, New Orleans, October 10, 1787, both in AGI, PC, leg. 593.

58. See the following chapter in this book.

59. Gayarré, *History of Louisiana*, 3: 170.

Chapter 2
Lieutenant Colonel Francisco Bouligny and the Malagueño Settlement at New Iberia, 1779

The founding of New Iberia in 1779 was part of the Spanish effort of the late 1770s to build up Louisiana's scant population and augment its defenses. In response to Great Britain pouring soldiers, colonists, and commercial activity into neighboring West Florida, Spain liberalized its immigration policy for Louisiana and allowed Catholic Acadians, Germans, Frenchmen, and Irishmen to establish themselves in the colony. With the outbreak of the American War for Independence, Spain took additional steps to bolster Louisiana for its own sake and as a barrier for the more important colony of New Spain. Much of the Spanish government's activity of the late 1770s resulted from the memorial presented in Spain in 1776 by Capt. Francisco Bouligny of the Fixed Louisiana Infantry Battalion.[1]

Bouligny, a native of Alicante, Spain, had arrived in the province in 1769 as the adjutant in Gen. Alejandro O'Reilly's expedition to put down the French Creole rebellion of the year before.[2] He elected to remain in

---

1. This article first appeared in *Louisiana History* 17 (Summer 1976): 187-202. The most complete study of Francisco Bouligny is Gilbert C. Din, *Francisco Bouligny: A Bourbon Soldier in Spanish Louisiana* (Baton Rouge: Louisiana State University Press, 1993). See also Fontaine Martin, *A History of the Bouligny Family and Allied Families* (Lafayette, La.: Center for Louisiana Studies, 1990). Vicent Ribes has written extensively about the Bouligny family, Francisco's brothers, in Alicante. See his *Comerciantes, esclavos y capital sin patria* (Valencia, Spain: Artes Gráficas Soler, 1993). In it he publishes Bouligny's 1776 memoria in Spanish.

2. A sketch, but with some errors, of Bouligny is in Jack D. L. Holmes, "*Dramatis Personae* in Spanish Louisiana," *Louisiana Studies* 6 (Summer 1967): 161-67. Bouligny was born in Alicante on September 4, 1736, and died in New Orleans on November 25, 1800. He was described as rather tall, slight, and with a "noble military bearing." Benjamin Franklin French, ed., *Historical Collections of Louisiana*, 5 vols. (New York:

Louisiana and serve in its battalion. After six years, Bouligny departed in May 1775, allegedly to attend to family matters in Spain and France. His main purpose, however, was to obtain a license to introduce African slaves in Louisiana, which was a lucrative business. He failed in that respect, but Minister of the Indies José de Gálvez was then looking for recent information on Louisiana, where he soon assigned his nephew Bernardo, first as head of the troops and later as governor. At San Ildefonso, the royal family's summer retreat in the Guadarrama Mountains northwest of Madrid, Bouligny presented Minister Gálvez with a lengthy memoir emphasizing economic and military conditions in the colony on August 10, 1776.[3] He strongly recommended the need to increase Louisiana's population, stimulate commerce and agriculture—particularly the twin crops of flax and hemp—and reinforce the military defenses of the province against a potential British threat from neighboring West Florida. In the settlement of families, Bouligny suggested establishing groups of fifty families along the Mississippi River in two-league intervals. He added that families from Valencia and Murcia in Spain were available as immigrants.[4]

Lamport, Blakeman and Law, 1846-1853), 5: 182-83n. Bouligny's service record is included in Jack D. L. Holmes, *Honor and Fidelity: The Louisiana Infantry Regiment and the Louisiana Militia Companies, 1766-1821* (Birmingham, Ala.: by the author, 1965), 98.

3. J. Horace Nunemaker, "Francisco Bouligny's Absence from Louisiana, 1775-1777," *Research Studies of the State College of Washington* 10 (1942): 198n. Bouligny's name was originally Italian, Bolognini, and not French. In the seventeenth century, the family moved from Milan to Marseilles, where the name acquired its French form, before they migrated to Alicante, Spain.

4. Ibid., 202. The Historic New Orleans Collection in New Orleans has acquired two collections of Bouligny family papers. Several copies of the Bouligny memoir have survived, with the original at the Historic New Orleans Collection, which has on it: "Presented to the hand of His Excellency Señor Don Josef de Gálvez, Minister of the Indies, by the author on August 10, 1776, at San Ildefonso." Other copies are at the library of Washington State University, in the manuscripts collection at the library of the University of Texas, Austin, and at the Biblioteca Nacional in Madrid. Alcée Fortier, in *A History of Louisiana*, 2 vols. (Baton Rouge: Claitor's Book Store, 1966 rpt.): 2: 25-55, summarizes much of it. The document, with a lengthy introduction explaining how it came to be written, is in Gilbert C. Din, *Louisiana in 1776: A Memoria of Francisco Bouligny* (New Orleans: Louisiana Collection Series, 1977).

Royal decrees that shortly followed bore the captain's imprint as indicated by the similarities between them and his suggestions. By 1777 the Crown had instructed the newly appointed governor of Louisiana, Bernardo de Gálvez, to promote immigration and permit Catholic foreigners to settle in the province, with the exception of citizens of enemy nations. Bernardo de Gálvez responded by attempting to lure Frenchmen and Canadians as well as German and Italian Catholics from English colonies. These settlers would receive lands, tools, and rations until they produced their first harvest.[5] More importantly, Bernardo de Gálvez urged creation of a second battalion for Louisiana, and the Crown chose to recruit volunteers in the Canary Islands. It also permitted married men to enlist and authorized dispatching them with their families to Louisiana. As a result numerous Canary Islanders went to the colony where they founded several settlements in Lower Louisiana commencing in 1778.[6] However, from peninsular Spain, and probably in response to

5. John Walton Caughey, *Bernardo de Gálvez in Louisiana, 1776-1783* (Berkeley: University of California Press, 1934), 68-69, 78-79; (Bernardo de Gálvez) to Fernando de Leyba, New Orleans, March 9, 1778, in Lawrence Kinnaird, ed., *Spain in the Mississippi Valley, 1765-1794*, 3 Parts (Washington, DC: GPO, 1946-1949), 1: 259; Bernardo de Gálvez to José de Gálvez, New Orleans, January 27, 1778, in Louis Houck, ed., *The Spanish Régime in Missouri*, 2 vols. in 1 (1909; repr., New York: Arno Press and New York Times, 1971): 1: 152-53. Governor Gálvez on February 19, 1778, issued a decree to post commandants that immigrant families were to be placed in proximity of each other so that they could render aid in case of need; each family was to receive five arpents of river front with the "customary depth" (forty arpents); during their first year of settlement they would be aided with food, farm implements, and animals. Ibid. In Bernardo de Gálvez to José de Gálvez, New Orleans, June 9, 1778, he writes that acting with the royal order of February 25, 1778, he had provided for the settlement of French Catholics and other immigrants from Spain, Italy, and Germany, who arrived without government assistance or are sent from Spain. Some Acadian families in Attakapas and Opelousas had already received help. Ibid., 155. See also Mattie Austin Hatcher, "The Louisiana Background of the Colonization of Texas, 1763-1803," *Southwestern Historical Quarterly* 24 (January 1921): 171.

6. Holmes, *Honor and Fidelity*, 24-25; Gilbert C. Din, "Early Spanish Colonization Efforts in Louisiana," *Louisiana Studies* 11 (Spring 1972): 40-42; Caughey, *Bernardo de Gálvez*, 79-81. Lists of Canary Island immigrants are in Sidney Louis Villeré, *The Canary Islands Migration to Louisiana, 1778-1783* (Baltimore: Genealogical Publishing Company, 1972), and Gilbert C. Din, *The Canary Islanders of Louisiana* (Baton Rouge: Louisiana State University Press, 1988).

Bouligny's memorial, came flax and hemp workers from Granada and still other families from Málaga.[7] Bouligny employed the Malagueños in the founding of New Iberia.

From July 1777 to June of the next year, authorities in Spain recruited approximately eighty-two persons in sixteen families in Málaga to journey to Louisiana as settlers. In the contracts they signed with the Spanish government, the king agreed to assist them liberally in their settlement until they harvested their first crop.[8] In Málaga the Crown hired the brigantine *San Josef* to transport the families to New Orleans, and they sailed from that port in early June 1778. Illness, however, forced eighteen Malagueños to disembark at Cádiz on June 13. In July, sixty-seven of the Malagueños continued their voyage on the *San Josef*. The ship stopped first at Puerto Rico, where more of the immigrants disembarked, so that only forty of the original party continued to Louisiana. Those who remained behind in Cádiz departed on August 13 aboard the merchant frigate *Princesa de Asturias*.[9] The documentation does not reveal how many of the Malagueños eventually arrived in New Orleans, but the number seems to have been over sixty.

Meanwhile, Francisco Bouligny had returned to Louisiana in April

---

7. Caroline Maude Burson, in *The Stewardship of Don Esteban Miró, 1782-1792* (New Orleans: American Printing Company, 1940), 72-73, mentions the royal orders of 1777 to promote the growing of flax and hemp in Louisiana. By October of that year the government determined that experienced growers of these crops should be sent to the colony with treatises on how to cultivate them. These experts were in Louisiana by July 1778, and sent out to different parts of the colony to experiment with growing the crops. Bernardo de Gálvez mentioned the arrival of the brigantine *Santa Theresa* with farm families skilled in the cultivation of flax and hemp and with boxes of seed. Bernardo de Gálvez to José de Gálvez, New Orleans, March 24, 1778, Archivo General de Indias (Seville), Papeles procedentes de Cuba, legajo (hereafter cited as AGI, PC, leg.), 1. See also Bryan E. Coutts, "Flax and Hemp in Spanish Louisiana, 1777-1783," *Louisiana History* 26 (Spring 1984): 129-39.

8. The contracts are reproduced in Maurine Bergerie, *They Tasted Bayou Water: A Brief History of Iberia Parish* (New Iberia: By the author, 1962), 106-26.

9. Joseph de Gálvez to the governor of Louisiana, San Ildefonso, August 24, 1778; Francisco Manxar to Joseph Navarro, Cádiz, August 9, 1778; both in AGI, PC, leg. 174B; "List of Persons who from Málaga Boarded the brig *St. Joseph*," Capt. Antonio Caballero, New Orleans, November 15, 1778, AGI, PC, leg. 576, and published in Bergerie, *They Tasted Bayou Water*, 105.

1777, as the lieutenant governor in charge of settlements, Indian affairs, and commerce, and in August Minister Gálvez rewarded him for his memoir by promoting him to brevet lieutenant colonel.[10] The next year, in anticipation of the arrival of the Málaga families, Governor Gálvez placed him in charge of their settlement. Bouligny initially selected Ouachita as the ideal location for their settlement, although he had not personally visited the site, and based his selection on descriptions four Frenchmen provided.[11] The great distance of 103 leagues from Ouachita to New Orleans caused Governor Gálvez to question the prudence of establishing the Malagueños in such a remote location and among barbarous Indians. Instead, Gálvez, who was then in Galveztown, suggested the Iberville River (Bayou Manchac) as a more suitable site since the colonists would be closer to other settlements and they could assist in the defense of New Orleans, if necessary. However, for the present he left the decision up to Bouligny and authorized him to visit the proposed site.[12] Bouligny, nevertheless, tried to alleviate Gálvez's doubts about Ouachita by stressing that it had excellent water communications with New Orleans and that the distance could be covered in six days in a heavily loaded *bateau*.[13] The lieutenant colonel, however, did not reconnoiter Ouachita because of the sudden arrival of the Malagueños. In December, Gálvez consented to their settlement, not in Ouachita, but on Bayou Têche in the Attakapas district of southwestern Louisiana. Relations between Gálvez and Bouligny at that time were tense because the governor had deprived Bouligny of his position as lieutenant governor of Louisiana, stating that the commission he possessed read merely "lieutenant governor in charge

---

10. Nunemaker, in "Bouligny's Absence," 201-202, states that Bouligny returned to Louisiana in April 1777. On April 11, Governor Gálvez issued letters announcing Bouligny as the lieutenant governor of the province. Holmes, in *Honor and Fidelity*, 98, provides August 3, 1777, as the date Bouligny became a brevet lieutenant colonel, a rank that became permanent on July 13, 1785.

11. Bouligny to Bernardo de Gálvez, New Orleans, June 23, August 4, and November 12, 1778; all in AGI, PC, leg. 2358. Bouligny's letter to Governor Gálvez of November 13, 1778, contains much information as to what transpired before the Malagueño families arrived in Louisiana.

12. Bernardo de Gálvez to Bouligny, Galveztown, November 22, 1778, ibid.

13. Bouligny to Bernardo de Gálvez, New Orleans, December 23, 1778, ibid.

of settlements, Indians, and commerce."[14] Although thoroughly incensed by the governor's arbitrary decisions (he was then favoring his father-in-law Gilbert Antoine de St. Maxent), Bouligny attempted to make the best of the situation. He carried on with the settlement project and secured Gálvez's approval for the expenditures needed. He dispatched Juan Bautista Grevemberg to reconnoiter lands and explore the Gulf Coast.[15] Moreover, he obtained permission to settle Irish, German, and French colonists among the Malagueños.

With formal approval given, Bouligny negotiated contracts to get the requisite labor needed to start the settlement. The Malagueños were indeed fortunate in not having to hack their homes out of the wilderness or turn the soil on their farms for the first time. For these arduous tasks Bouligny hired seventy-five African slaves for one year, overseers, rowers, and boats to transport the colonists, and other skilled laborers. He planned the purchase of farm implements, foodstuffs, and livestock. For his initial expenses, the lieutenant colonel requested 8,000 pesos from the governor. Gálvez approved the settlement plans and on January 12, 1779, ordered Bouligny to depart as soon as possible for the proposed site.[16]

Within a few days Bouligny left New Orleans, taking with him only four Malagueño families and four bachelors, plus a discharged soldier who also wished to become a colonist. With Bouligny went the

---

14. Ibid. On the clash between Bouligny and the governor, see J. Horace Nunemaker, ed., "The Bouligny Affair in Louisiana," *Hispanic American Historical Review* 25 (August 1945): 339-63. It contains documents on Bouligny's removal as lieutenant governor of Louisiana and the cancelling of his proposed settlement at Ouachita in favor of that of New Iberia. Bouligny's letters often refer to a river named "Theis," which is Bayou Têche. Teche, according to George Rippey Stewart, in *American Place-Names: A Concise and Selective Dictionary for the Continental United States of America* (New York: Oxford University Press, 1970), 475, is "probably a French rendering of Deutch, the name by which the German colonists of the area would have named their stream." But Bergerie, in *They Tasted Bayou Water*, 6, states that Teche comes from "Tenche," an Indian word about a legend of a huge snake that entered the Attakapas district.

15. Holmes, "*Dramatis Personae*," 166.

16. Bouligny to Bernardo de Gálvez, New Orleans, January 8 and 14, 1779, both in AGI, PC, leg. 2358, with the second letter published in Bergerie, *They Tasted Bayou Water*, 126-27.

slaves, overseers, rowers, and a handful of soldiers.[17] The journey up the Mississippi was arduous due to the winter season, rains, and the swollen river. About February 7, the weary travelers reached a point four leagues west of Plaquemine. Despite the hardships endured by the families, morale remained high.[18] Four days later, Bouligny's party entered Bayou Têche where he commenced to search for the best location for the settlement.

Southwestern Louisiana at that time consisted of many bayous or rivers and wooded lands, but more prominent were the prairies that were nearly vacant of European inhabitants except for some very scattered Germans and Acadians. Thirty years after Bouligny first entered this part of Louisiana, Henry Marie Breckenridge described it probably much in the same way the Malagueños saw it in 1779:

> The whole country is chequered by the woody margin of streams, called bayoux, though different from the refluent waters of the river. ... The fringes of wood on the borders of the bayoux seldom exceed a half mile in width, and consist of live oak, magnolia, &c. and on the wet parts, of cypress. The rivers Teche and Vermilion have the largest tracts of timbered land, and are consequently the best settled parts of the prairies. ... The distance of my journey was forgotten while I gazed with delight upon the waving surface of these meadows, now covered only by the horizon, in others by skirts of wood, dimly appearing as in some distant isle of the sea; while a thousand brilliant and odoriferous flowers shed their perfume upon the air.[19]

However, on seeing the region for the first time in 1779, the landscape confused Bouligny. He had to decide quickly where to settle

---

17. Bouligny to Bernardo de Gálvez, January 14, 1779, AGI, PC, leg. 2358; "Notice of the Málaga families who go with me on this occasion to settle themselves on the Teche ... ," Francisco Bouligny, New Orleans, January 14, 1779, ibid. The four families were the Romero, Villatoro, Aponte, and Ortiz. The four bachelors, who were counted as four families, were Francisco Balderas, Joseph Lagos, Francisco Segura, and Joseph de Porras.

18. Bouligny to Bernardo de Gálvez, one league from Atchafalaya, February 7, 1779, ibid.

19. Henry Marie Brackenridge, *Views of Louisiana* (1817; repr., Chicago: Quadrangle Books, 1962), 159, 170-71.

the colonists. After examining several locations on the Têche, he chose what he considered the most advantageous spot on the right bank. The settlement received the name New Iberia. But the first selection for New Iberia soon proved less than ideal. The immediate region was not completely uninhabited inasmuch as some Indians, several Acadians, and two freed blacks lived there. A local Frenchman, a Mr. Declouet (probably Alexandre de Clouet), drove out one of the blacks from the district. For fifteen pesos Bouligny purchased two cabins from the Indians, which apparently were not in the best of condition, and for an additional hundred pesos, he bought their friendship. The money made the chief so happy, Bouligny averred, that he provided the Spaniards with fifteen Indian rowers. After staking out the settlement, the lieutenant colonel marked out farms of six arpents of river front with the usual forty arpent depth for each family.[20]

By March the families and workers were busily engaged in the construction of houses and in agricultural chores. For the settlers of New Iberia, Bouligny purchased through Mr. Declouet a considerable number of animals: 32 pairs of oxen, 20 cows, 12 horses, and 6 mares, in addition to numerous pigs and chickens. He believed that in the future the New Iberia cattle herd could expand to 500 or 1,000 head, which could then be used to supply new settlements. He had already found another site twelve leagues up the Têche, a prairie he judged adequate to accommodate another two hundred families. For now, however, each family would receive a pair of oxen that could cultivate eight to ten arpents of land and ensure the family a harvest that year of corn, rice, and even tobacco. The oxen not distributed to the families were to be used in the preparation of additional land for planting wheat, barley, flax, and hemp when the proper time arrived and in hauling wood from a nearby cypress stand. Slaves performed the arduous work of felling trees and sawing logs into boards for house construction. Bouligny also invited the poor farmers of Opelousas and Attakapas to join his settlement under the same terms as the Malagueño families.[21] During March and April, thirty

20. Bouligny to Bernardo de Gálvez, New Iberia, February 18, 1779, AGI, PC, leg. 2358. Bouligny described the location as a two-day journey from the Gulf of Mexico and a quarter league from a lake.

21. Bouligny to Bernardo de Gálvez, New Iberia, March 17, 1779, ibid.

more Malagueños, composed of those who had remained behind in New Orleans, arrived at New Iberia.[22] The infant settlement was beginning to show signs of acquiring permanence.

Unfortunately, April brought not only showers but inundations to Lower Louisiana. Bayou Têche rose precipitously, at a rate of fifteen to sixteen inches per day, until six to eight feet of water deluged the tiny settlement. Confronted with an appalling situation, Bouligny abandoned the first site of New Iberia and led his settlers and workers seven or eight leagues upriver, where he bought new lands that were thirty by eighty arpents in size for 400 pesos from a Monsieur "Colete" (François Prévost, *dit* Collet). The new location was part of an extensive prairie approximately two leagues across where several Acadians were already settled. Bouligny's first concern was to build a temporary shelter for his people; therefore, he ordered the construction of two sheds, each sixty feet long, to house the families and slaves. He also ordered the colonists to begin work immediately planting corn, rice, and other crops so they could still produce food for themselves that same year.[23]

In June, when the flood waters had receded, nine more Malagueños joined the settlement. At the end of that month Bouligny explored a route to the sea. When he learned about the waterway, Gálvez in New Orleans felt certain that merchants trading in New Iberia would soon cause it to flourish.[24] Meanwhile work on the settlement progressed so

---

22. Bouligny to Bernardo de Gálvez, New Iberia, March 22 and April 21, 1779, in AGI, PC, legs. 600 and 2368, respectively. The March list of Málaga families is published in Bergerie, *They Tasted Bayou Water*, 134-35.

23. Bouligny to Bernardo de Gálvez, New Iberia, April 21, 1779, AGI, PC, leg. 2358.

24. (Bernardo de Gálvez) to Bouligny, New Orleans, June 7, 1779, AGI, PC, leg. 600. Gonsoulin's (Jean-Baptiste Grevemberg's) diary in French of the journey to the gulf is in AGI, PC, leg. 2358. Bouligny requested reimbursement for the expenditures occasioned by three voyages of exploration along the Gulf Coast in 1779, but Gálvez denied it because the voyages were not related to the settlement of families. From the documents contained in "Reconocimiento de Nueva Iberia," Biblioteca Nacional, Sección de Manuscritos, 19,248, ff. 136-41, see Bernardo de Gálvez to Bouligny, New Orleans, July 30, 1779; "Account of the Expenses Occasioned by Three voyages . . . ," Juan Bauta. Grevember[g], New Iberia, August 25, 1779; and Martín Navarro to the Marqués de Sonora (José de Gálvez), New Orleans, October 31, 1786. See also Robert

slowly that in July Bouligny employed some of the local Acadians to build houses for the colonists. By then it appeared likely that not all the settlers would have individual homes by winter. Bouligny described some houses under construction as being fifteen by twenty-eight feet in size and raised nine feet above the ground. Floodwaters would not again wipe out New Iberia. The houses also had covered balconies in front and in back.[25]

Work on New Iberia continued in August when news arrived of Spain's declaration of war on Great Britain. The settlement could not remain uninvolved as virtually every able-bodied man in Lower Louisiana was needed for defense against a possible British attack from West Florida. As a lieutenant colonel in the Fixed Louisiana Infantry Regiment, Bouligny immediately offered his service to the governor, along with that of fifteen Malagueños, five soldiers, two repentant deserters, three or four Germans, and twenty-five of the youngest slaves. He notified Governor Gálvez that unless he received instructions to the contrary he intended to take his men and go where he could be useful. No contrary orders arrived because Gálvez was then in the midst of planning his campaign to seize the British posts of Manchac, Baton Rouge, and Natchez in West Florida. Some time before the end of August, Bouligny left New Iberia with his contingent of soldiers, militia, and slaves.[26] The men who remained behind continued to work on the settlement although at a slower pace since the more robust workers were now absent. Bouligny's departure ended his direct involvement with New Iberia. He did not serve there again.

After the successful military campaign in September and early October against the British posts on the Mississippi, in which Bouligny and the men of New Iberia participated, the Spanish army returned to New Orleans with its prisoners.[27] With the exigencies of war over for

---

S. Weddle, *Changing Tides: Twilight and Dawn in the Spanish Sea* (College Station: Texas A&M University Press, 1995), 91-99, which discusses Bouligny, the topography of the New Iberia region, and its early settlers.

25. Bouligny to Bernardo de Gálvez, New Iberia, July 28, 1779, AGI, PC, leg. 600.

26. Bouligny to Bernardo de Gálvez, New Iberia, August 26, 1779, ibid.; Bouligny to Bernardo de Gálvez, Plaquemine, Casa de Campaña, September 3, 1779, in Bergerie, *They Tasted Bayou Water*, 146-48.

27. Holmes, *Honor and Fidelity*, 29-31; Caughey, *Bernardo de Gálvez*, 150-61; and

the moment, Governor Gálvez demanded that Bouligny provide him with an accounting of his work at New Iberia and the money spent.[28] When the costs rose to 31,150 pesos and 5 reales, an irritated Gálvez described them as excessive. Only 40,000 pesos had been budgeted that year for the establishment of colonists, and many others, in addition to the Malagueños, were being settled concurrently. The governor then inquired how much more New Iberia would cost until the settlement was completed and the measures needed to finish the work in the shortest time possible.[29]

Bouligny replied to the governor's queries by saying that he was uncertain about additional expenses for the families at New Iberia. To reduce costs, he suggested that each family be supplied with rice and corn or be given money so that it could maintain itself in the coming year. Costs could also be diminished by not building a church at New Iberia since one was present only three leagues away, an inconvenience the truly faithful would not mind. However, a priest was needed. Bouligny believed that in November, at the end of the harvest, all assistance to the settlers could be suspended except to the family of the widow Ybáñez, and, at the end of the year, salaried persons with the exception of the surgeon could be discharged. The great expenditure made at New Iberia, the lieutenant colonel contended, had resulted from the high cost of living and from the inundations that spring. Furthermore, the contracts made in Spain with the families to maintain them until their first harvest had obliged him from the start to employ a substantial number of slaves in agricultural chores to assure that the colonists would harvest a crop in their first year on the land. Despite the many reversals Bouligny encountered, it had been achieved, and it would save a considerable sum

---

Albert W. Haarmann, "The Spanish Conquest of British West Florida, 1779-1781," *Florida Historical Quarterly* 39 (October 1960), 109-14. In less than a month Gálvez seized 3 forts, about 550 regular soldiers, 8 ships and their crews, and 500 armed settlers and their slaves. Holmes, in *"Dramatis Personae,"* 162, states Bouligny fought in the campaign against Fort Bute at Manchac and at Baton Rouge. Natchez surrendered without a battle.

28. (Bernardo de Gálvez) to Bouligny, New Orleans, October 26, 1779, AGI, PC, leg. 600.

29. Bouligny to Bernardo de Gálvez, New Orleans, October 28, 1779, ibid.

of money. He recommended giving the families still without housing 200 or 300 pesos, depending on their size, to build their own homes, as the families themselves wanted, or to purchase the houses from Acadians residing nearby. Bouligny pledged that when the contracts with the slave owners expired on January 17, all additional work could be terminated. This included finishing the harvest, gathering the lumber that had been made, and building homes in New Iberia for the carpenter, blacksmith, cobbler, and surgeon.[30]

Bouligny had endeavored to provide the most optimistic report possible to the governor, who, however, received it in the worst possible light. Undoubtedly the discord of the previous year still rankled Gálvez. He described himself as speechless when he learned that certain families at New Iberia were still homeless, and again he inquired how the slaves had been employed.[31]

In his second reply to the governor, Bouligny provided new information about what had gone on in New Iberia. The families, it seems, had shown little enthusiasm for tilling the soil, knowing that assistance to them would terminate with the harvest. Only when the lieutenant colonel informed them that anyone who did not tend the crops planted on his land would receive no help after the harvest, did the Malagueños demonstrate a greater diligence in farming. Bouligny prepared a lengthy list that detailed the many projects the slaves had worked on. They plowed, planted, and cared for seventy-five arpents of corn at the new site and thirty-five at the old, twenty-five arpents of rice, and four or six arpents of potatoes, as well as some with tobacco. They built houses for the blacksmith and the families of the Artache, Prados, Migas y Vida, and Ybáñez; two houses for the Germans and two for the soldiers; and houses for Monsieur Flamand (François Grevenberg) and Mr. Henderson who also built a warehouse. The slaves constructed a royal warehouse, a great shed in which bricks and lime were made, and a large enclosure for the oxen. They looked after the livestock. Finally, they made lumber out of the trees they felled and transported to the settlement. All this was done before Bouligny departed New Iberia in August, at which time he left

---

30. Ibid.

31. Bouligny to Bernardo de Gálvez, New Orleans, November 3, 1779, ibid.

Mr. Henderson and Mr. Berwick (possibly Thomas Berviquet) in charge of the slaves, who continued to work building the settlement. Bouligny ended his report by stressing his need to return to New Iberia with the slaves he had with him to terminate the establishment of the families.[32]

Somewhat mollified by Bouligny's detailed report, the governor now accepted it without further criticism. Gálvez, however, denied Bouligny permission to return to New Iberia. War had taken priority over the settlement of colonists, and the shortage of Spanish officers made the lieutenant colonel's service indispensible. Thus Gálvez ordered Bouligny to take charge of his company. He merely requested that Bouligny supply him with an accounting of the expenses incurred at New Iberia; the governor also terminated all contracts previously negotiated to employ the workers and slaves at the settlement.[33] He further appointed Nicholas Forstall as the new commandant at New Iberia, a position he apparently acquitted with distinction.[34]

Despite Gálvez's steps to cut short expenditures at New Iberia, the cost of the settlement did not end immediately. In the next year, 1781, expenses for the colonists continued, and Intendant Martín Navarro believed that they would cease at harvest time. The Malagueños' alleged lackadaisical attitude toward toil displeased the hard-nosed intendant; he noted that their lazy behavior did not correspond to the arduous work the land required and that the families felt entitled to ask for whatever

---

32. Ibid.

33. (Bernardo de Gálvez) to Bouligny, New Orleans, November 6, 1779, ibid. While Holmes, in *"Dramatis Personae,"* 167, charges that Gálvez relieved Bouligny as commandant of New Iberia because of irregular conduct, the documentation reads that it was because of the war against Great Britain. Nevertheless, it is true that little affection existed between the two. Holmes cites Bernardo de Gálvez to José de Gálvez, no. 255 reserved, New Orleans, March 2, 1779, AGI, PC, leg. 233B, as proof, and a split that occurred in the New Orleans cabildo.

34. Nicholas Forstall was present at the November 26, 1779 meeting of the New Orleans cabildo but was absent at the next meeting on December 17. *Acts of the New Orleans Cabildo*, 5 vols. (on microfilm), 2: 4, 7. For his services as commissary at New Iberia, Bernardo de Gálvez appointed him as political and military commandant for the Attakapas district. But he seems not to have been confirmed in that post. Conde de Gálvez (Bernardo de Gálvez) to Esteban Miró, Havana, April 6, 1785, in Kinnaird, *Spain in the Mississippi Valley*, 2: 124; Bergerie, *They Tasted Bayou Water*, 12.

they wanted because of the generous contracts they had negotiated in Spain.[35] Navarro, however, erred in prematurely anticipating the end of assistance to the families. Persistent floods and severe winters forced the government to continue supporting them for several more years.[36]

After 1779 New Iberia grew at only a modest pace as it failed to attract many new settlers. In its first year of existence, counting the Malagueños, the Germans, and the few others who joined them, less than one hundred persons resided there. The census of 1785 revealed only 125 inhabitants; of these 70 were Malagueños. In 1788 New Iberia's total population had increased to 190.[37] It was far short of the nearly 500 Malagueños that John Caughey stated had established the settlement in his otherwise able biography of Bernardo de Gálvez in Louisiana.[38] Careful examination of

---

35. Intendant of Louisiana (Navarro) to José de Gálvez, New Orleans, 1778, AGI, PC, leg. 593, Pacquete A.

36. Navarro to Miró, New Orleans, January 19, 1785, AGI, PC, leg. 85; Sonora (José de Gálvez) to the intendant of Louisiana, El Pardo, February 14, 1787, AGI, PC, leg. 2317.

37. François-Xavier Martin, *The History of Louisiana, from the Earliest Period* (1827-29; repr., New Orleans: James A. Gresham, 1882), 240, 251; Charles Gayarré, *History of Louisiana*, 2nd ed., 4 vols. (New Orleans: Armand Hawkins, 1885), 3: 170, 215; "Report of Individuals who comprise the new settlement of New Iberia, 1785," Antonio Martínez, AGI, PC, leg. 600.

38. The question how Caughey, in *Bernardo de Gálvez*, 81, came to the conclusion that "almost five hundred settlers from Málaga arrived in 1779," whom Bouligny settled on Bayou Têche and where they founded New Iberia, poses an interesting historiographical problem. It probably stems from reading the published literature. Martin, in *The History of Louisiana*, 226, states that in 1779 families from Málaga arrived in Louisiana and they were treated similarly to the Canary Island immigrants. Some years later Gayarré, in his *History of Louisiana*, 3: 119-20, altered slightly Martin's statement to say that on January 14, 1779, 499 Canary Islanders arrived at royal expense who were given lands, animals, rations, and money. Bouligny transported them to Attakapas and on Bayou Têche they found New Iberia. Lastly, Fortier, in his *History of Louisiana*, 2: 60, states that on January 5, 1779, Bernardo de Gálvez mentioned that Canary Islanders also arrived in New Orleans, and then: "These four hundred ninety-nine men were sent under the command of Bouligny to form, on Bayou Teche, in the Attakapas country, a settlement, which was called New Iberia." It appears certain that these statements gave rise to Caughey's assertion that 499 Malagueños were responsible for the founding of New Iberia in 1779. Nevertheless, archival documentation clearly reveals that fewer than one hundred Malagueños were involved.

the documents in the Spanish archives failed to substantiate Caughey's assertion, and the censuses of 1785 and 1788 confirm that New Iberia did not begin with a large number of settlers. Bouligny had hoped that the cultivation of flax and hemp would flourish here but it did not. After a brief effort at agriculture, many inhabitants abandoned crops to tend livestock on the vast prairies that surrounded their settlement. Only with time did the populace return to agriculture that is now common in that part of Louisiana.[39]

As for Francisco Bouligny, after his work at New Iberia ended, he proceeded to enjoy a long and successful career with the Spanish government in Louisiana. His earlier difficulties with Governor Gálvez apparently did not hinder his advancement in the army. In the war against Great Britain, Bouligny served with distinction and demonstrated his valor at Mobile in 1780 and at Pensacola in 1781, where he led his grenadiers under enemy fire and captured a British outpost. As his service record noted, he possessed talent, zeal, and the ability to command. Because of his excellent personal qualities, he attained the rank of permanent lieutenant colonel in 1785, brevet colonel four years later, and permanent colonel in 1791. About the same time, he became the commandant of the Fixed Louisiana Infantry Regiment.[40] Upon the death of Gov. Manuel Gayoso de Lemos in 1799, Bouligny temporarily served as the military administrator of the colony.[41] He was promoted to the rank of brigadier of his regiment in 1800, but sadly death intervened before he received the commission. When Louisiana passed from Spanish hands and became a part of the United States in 1803, the Bouligny family remained under the new flag, so identified had it become with this land. Twenty-four years after Francisco Bouligny's demise, his eldest son Dominique achieved one of the highest offices possible for a Louisianan, that of United States senator.[42]

---

39. Martin, *The History of Louisiana*, 266; Fortier, *History of Louisiana*, 2: 60.

40. Holmes, *Honor and Fidelity*, 98.

41. Jack D. L. Holmes, *Gayoso, The Life of a Spanish Governor in the Mississippi Valley, 1789-1799* (Baton Rouge: Louisiana State University Press for the Louisiana Historical Association, 1965), 266.

42. Fortier, *History of Louisiana*, 2: 24.

Chapter 3

The Immigration Policy of Governor Esteban Miró in Spanish Louisiana

From 1785 to 1791 Spanish immigration policy in Louisiana, in an attempt to accommodate itself to changing conditions, departed from its traditional role of excluding Protestants. Unable to secure Spanish or European Catholics at little or no expense with whom to develop and protect the colony, Spain at last turned to the nearest available source for settlers, the United States. Esteban Miró, governor of Louisiana and West Florida during these crucial years, was at the center in the formulation of this policy. The influence he exerted both directly and indirectly on the Spanish Court to modify and determine Louisiana's immigration policy has not been previously recognized.[1]

Spanish immigration laws in Louisiana before Miró's governorship already displayed increasing flexibility. From the time Spain acquired Louisiana following the Seven Years' War, it recognized the value of this border colony as a buffer zone to protect Mexico, and it endeavored as best a declining empire could to fill the vastness of Louisiana with a loyal and Catholic population. From the 1760s, Spain allowed the entry of Acadians into Louisiana and assisted them in their settlement.[2] In the

---

1. This article first appeared in the *Southwestern Historical Quarterly* 73 (October 1969): 155-75. While Miró and immigration efforts have previously been studied, his role in determining royal policy has been overlooked. To cite two examples, Arthur Preston Whitaker, in *The Spanish American Frontier: 1783-1795* (Boston: by the author, 1927), 97-107, attributes immigration policy to the Conde de Floridablanca, the principal Spanish minister of state, in the belief that policy in an absolutist monarchy always originated at the top. Mattie Austin Hatcher, on the other hand, in "The Louisiana Background of the Colonization of Texas, 1763-1803," *Southwestern Historical Quarterly* 24 (January 1921): 169-94, provides an early survey that does little to trace the development of policy.

2. Vicente Rodríguez Casado, *Primeros años de la dominación española* (Madrid:

1770s, the Court permitted and encouraged the settlement of Acadians, Frenchmen, French Canadians, Germans, and Irish who were Catholic.[3] At the end of the decade, in order to secure recruits for the Fixed Infantry Battalion in Louisiana, Canary Islander families were settled there at royal expense. At the same time and under similar conditions, smaller numbers of families came from Granada and Málaga in Spain to promote the growing of flax and hemp.[4] In 1784 the Crown accepted the proposal of Henri Peyroux de la Coudrenière to transport and settle in Louisiana the Acadian families then living in France, and this was accomplished in 1785 at an exorbitant cost.[5]

It was the prohibitive expense of conveying families across the Atlantic and their failure to become self-sufficient within a short period of time that terminated projects of this kind. Spain lacked the financial resources to underwrite the acquisition of colonists in Europe, and to have attempted it en masse would have meant bankruptcy long before

---

Consejo Superior de Investigaciones Científicas, 1947), 104-106; Lawrence Kinnaird, ed., *Spain in the Mississippi Valley, 1765-1795*, 3 Parts (Washington, DC: GPO, 1949), 2: xxiii; Joseph de Loyola to Antonio de Ulloa, September 1767, Archivo General de Indias (Seville), Papeles procedentes de Cuba, legajo (hereafter cited as AGI, PC, leg.) 109.

3. *Yndice*, May 26, 1774, (the royal order is missing); "Reserved instruction for Colonel Bernardo de Gálvez for his direction in the Government of the Province of Louisiana," (n.d.), both in AGI, PC, leg. 174A.

4. Andrés Amat de Tortosa to Bernardo de Gálvez, (Santa Cruz de Tenerife), February 17, 1779, AGI, PC, leg. 119; Martín Navarro to José de Gálvez, New Orleans, March 24, 1778, AGI, PC, leg. 1232. See also Bryan E. Coutts, "Flax and Hemp in Spanish Louisiana, 1777-1783," *Louisiana History* 26 (Spring 1984): 129-39.

5. Fernando Solano Costa, "La emigración acadiana a la Luisiana española (1783-1785)," *Cuadernos de Historia Jerónimo Zurita* 2 (1954), 85-125. A total of 1,598 persons came from France. Navarro to José de Gálvez, "Statement that manifests the names of the Ships, number of Families, and Acadian persons present, from the 29th when the first ship arrived, until today," New Orleans, December 12, 1785, AGI, PC, leg. 2360, copy attached to Navarro's letter to José de Gálvez of the same date in AGI, PC, leg. 85. See also two works by Carl A. Brasseaux, *The Founding of New Acadia: The Beginnings of Acadian Life in Louisiana, 1765-1803* (Baton Rouge: Louisiana State University Press, 1987), and "*Scattered to the Wind*": *Dispersal and Wanderings of the Acadians, 1755-1809* (Lafayette, La.: Center for Louisiana Studies, University of Southwestern Louisiana, 1991).

the Louisiana "desert" was populated. Colonial officials continued to regard an augmented population as the best defense for the province, but, after the era of trans-Atlantic migrations, settlers needed to come from a less expensive quarter.[6]

Further changes in immigration policy came during the governorship of Esteban Miró. In 1782, in the absence of Gov. Bernardo de Gálvez, Miró, the senior army official in Louisiana, became the acting military and civil governor. As such, he assumed the task of implementing the provisions of the 1783 peace treaty that ended the state of war between Spain and Great Britain. Under the terms of the Treaty of Paris, British residents in West Florida received eighteen months to terminate their affairs and depart. In 1784 several British ships entered the Mississippi River to remove the British subjects. However, not all chose to leave.[7] After an extension of four months had expired, the remaining British residents in West Florida petitioned Governor Miró for permission to remain on their lands under the same terms as they had been living since the Spaniards assumed control.[8]

The West Florida residents had settled in the years after 1763, when Great Britain acquired the colony, while a smaller group of Americans came in mostly during the Revolutionary War. In West Florida these immigrants settled down in Mobile, Pensacola, Manchac, and especially in the Natchez District where they were most numerous. Under normal conditions they would not have qualified for residence in the Spanish

---

6. For example, John Walton Caughey, in *Bernardo de Gálvez in Louisiana, 1776-1783* (Berkeley: University of California Press, 1934), 81, states that in 1779, Spain spent 128,568 pesos on immigration costs when only 40,000 had been budgeted. See also Charles H. Cunningham, ed., "Financial Reports Relating to Louisiana, 1766-1788," *Mississippi Valley Historical Review* 6 (December 1919): 385; and Jack D. L. Holmes, "Some Economic Problems of Spanish Governors of Louisiana," *Hispanic American Historical Review* 42 (November 1962): 521-43.

7. Alejandro de Cantillo, *Tratados, convenios y declaraciones de paz y de comercio... desde el año de 1700 hasta el día* (Madrid: Alegría y Charlain, 1843), 587-88; Caroline Maude Burson, *The Stewardship of Don Esteban Miró 1782-1792* (New Orleans: American Printing Company, 1940), 24-25.

8. Memorial of Harris Alexander *et al.* to the Conde de Gálvez (Bernardo de Gálvez), New Orleans; Bernardo de Gálvez to Miró, Mexico City, October 20, 1785; both in AGI, PC, leg. 2352.

colony because immigration laws limited entry to Catholics, and most of them were Protestants. Those who remained after the evacuation were destitute, and Governor Miró feared that, if forced out by land, they would resettle nearby on the edge of the province, where others would join them, and together they would threaten the colony's security.[9]

It was at this point in 1785 that Miró unveiled a plan that would reappear elsewhere and be presented by others in the next two years. Concluding that the interests of the colony demanded that the Anglo-American residents remain, the governor proposed a way by which the Protestant settlers might be converted and assimilated through the use of English-speaking Irish missionaries. Since the Spanish conquest of West Florida (1779-1781), Catholicism had been instituted as the official religion of the province and the only one accorded public worship. In this situation Miró suggested using Irish missionaries to proselytize among the adults and require their children to be baptized and instructed in the Catholic faith. Public schools would teach the children to become Spaniards, and in time, the governor hoped, they would forget their British Protestant origins. Those not willing to submit to these conditions would be required to quit the colony, and, if necessary, the Crown would defray their transportation expenses. Miró sent his suggestions to Bernardo de Gálvez, who was now viceroy in Mexico, and he forwarded them to Spain.[10]

In Spain on March 14, 1786, the Supreme Council accepted the proposal of Governor Miró on how to handle the West Florida Anglo-American families. Those persons wishing to accept the conditions to permit them to remain in the colony were required to pledge fidelity and obedience to the Spanish government; otherwise they had to leave by sea at their own expense, or at royal cost if they were impoverished. The Council instructed Miró to devise a plan for the establishment of parishes and schools in Natchez and other places and staffed with Irish priests.

---

9. Miró to Bernardo de Gálvez, New Orleans, September 5, 1785, Archivo Histórico Nacional (Madrid), Estado (hereafter abbreviated as AHN, Est.), leg. 3888bis, no. 2. A census of the Natchez District in 1784 revealed a population of 1,619. AGI, PC, leg. 116.

10. Conde de Gálvez to José de Gálvez, Mexico City, October 27, 1785, AHN, Est., leg. 3888bis, no. 56.

The Immigration Policy of Governor Miró 43

The Council also informed the bishop of Salamanca to find suitable Irish priests in Spain to be sent as missionaries to West Florida. Eventually he located four who agreed to go, and they sailed early the next year.[11]

By February 10, 1787, Miró had worked out a scheme for the creation of the parishes. He felt that the Natchez District required two parishes: one to serve both Santa Catalina (Catherine) Creek and Second Creek, and a second parish for Cole's Creek. Each parish would have a church and residence for a priest, but at Cole's Creek there would also be a residence for a military commander and a barracks for a small detachment of troops to administer justice and prevent illicit trade and the entry of undesirable persons. The priests would be charged with teaching Catholicism and reading and writing in Spanish. Miró considered it imperative to establish these two parishes, but he also suggested a third for Tinzas, a settlement fifteen miles above Mobile, where fifty-nine Anglo-American families resided.[12]

The governor soon dispatched his plan to Spain for approval. The four Irish missionaries, however, reached New Orleans in August 1787, before a reply came. Since the Spanish Court had still not authorized expenditures for the creation of the parishes, Miró and Intendant Martín Navarro delayed until two mails had arrived without bringing instructions before proceeding with the implementation of the governor's plan.[13]

While these events were taking place in 1786 and 1787, the governor contemplated means to increase Louisiana's scant population. Quite possibly even before the summer of 1786, Miró considered the feasibility of allowing Americans from their western settlements to enter

---

11. Royal order to the Conde de Gálvez, palace, April 5, 1786; royal order to the bishop of Salamanca, palace, April 5, 1786; Andrés, bishop of Salamanca, to the Marqués de Sonora (José de Gálvez), Salamanca, September 28, 1786; all in AHN, Est., leg. 3888bis.

12. Miró to Sonora, New Orleans, February 10, 1787, and June 1, 1787, both in AHN, Est., leg. 3888bis. In 1785 the inhabitants numbered by families as follows: Second Creek, 55; Cole's Creek, 40; and Santa Catalina Creek, 180. The Natchez District then had about 1,100 whites and 900 slaves. Jack D. L. Holmes, *Gayoso: The Life of a Spanish Governor in the Mississippi Valley, 1789-1799* (Baton Rouge: Louisiana State University Press for the Louisiana Historical Association, 1965), 20.

13. Jack D. L. Holmes, ed., *Documentos inéditos para la historia de la Luisiana, 1792-1810* (Madrid: Ediciones José Porrua Turanzas, 1963), 29-30, n.20.

Louisiana under the same conditions that governed the Anglo-Americans in the Natchez District. By means of additional Irish missionaries, these immigrants from the United States could, like the others, be converted and assimilated, and they would increase the colony's population and bolster its security. It was an ambitious plan fraught with risk, but the retention of Louisiana with only meager resources demanded a bold approach. Miró realized this very well, but his extreme caution prevented him from recommending it to the Court until September 1787, and then he did so indirectly. Before that time, however, he appears to have discussed the plan with visitors in New Orleans, one of whom was Pierre Wouves d'Argès.

In August 1786, d'Argès passed through New Orleans from Kentucky on his way to France. The middle-aged chevalier of the Order of St. Louis and late captain of grenadiers in the American Revolutionary War had lived for two years near the Falls of the Ohio (Louisville) where he received land, but ultimately war between the Americans and Indians prompted his departure. While in New Orleans he spoke with the governor and the intendant about conditions in Louisiana and the American West. The Frenchman later asserted that he presented Spanish officials with a petition from 1,582 families, most of them German or of German descent and resident in Kentucky, who wished to settle in Louisiana if they received lands and freedom of religion. Since Spanish policy prohibited freedom of religion and the entry of Protestants, the officials responded that the conditions the Protestants sought exceeded their instructions, but they urged him to present his petition to the Conde de Aranda, Spain's ambassador in Paris.[14] Neither Miró nor Navarro in 1786 reported to Spain their conversations with d'Argès, and the governor later denied that the Frenchman presented his petition.[15] Nonetheless, there can be no doubt that d'Argès, whether he had a petition or whether he alone conceived the idea of permitting Americans to settle in Spanish territory, espoused the governor's method by which such immigrants

14. "Memorial of Pierre Rezard de Wouves d'Argès," Paris, March 18, 1787, AHN, Est., leg. 3889, expediente 6. For other accounts of d'Argès, see Whitaker, *Spanish American Frontier*, 78-89, and Charles Gayarré, *History of Louisiana*, 4 vols. (New Orleans: Armand Hawkins, 1885), 3: 197-201. See also Chapter 5 below.

15. Court *minuta*, AHN, Est., leg. 3899, exped. 6.

could be admitted. His subsequent proposal to the ambassador in Paris revealed this very clearly.

By February 1787, the chevalier was in Paris where he informed Aranda of his petition. The ambassador was intrigued by the proposal. Over the next month, the Frenchman related news from the Mississippi Valley and enlarged upon details for increasing Louisiana's population and promoting its security. Thus the initial step was taken in the process that revolutionized Spanish immigration policy in Louisiana, and although it was not done by Miró, he was indirectly responsible through the information and ideas that d'Argès acquired in New Orleans.

The d'Argès proposal reflected Miró's impressions, and it is doubtful that the chevalier added anything original. To the ambassador he stated that American colonists in Louisiana would provide a defensive force and develop the province economically. Spain's expense in their settlement, a consideration of no mean importance, was limited to providing an English-speaking military commander. D'Argès reasoned that the colonists, assured of their property and free commerce, would adhere to a government that dispensed such advantages. As for religion, and there can be no mistaking Miró's thoughts here, the Frenchman felt that the use of Irish missionaries and a policy of employing only persons of the king's faith in civil and military positions would soon bring about the settlers' conversion.[16]

In forwarding his correspondence with d'Argès to Spain on April 2, Aranda praised the chevalier and advised that he be heard personally at Court. Already a strong advocate of strengthening the province's defenses, the ambassador heartily endorsed the enterprise. He considered these settlers twice as valuable once they were relocated in Louisiana since the province would be made stronger and the American West simultaneously weakened. To Aranda the Natchez defense perimeter required not merely a garrison but an agricultural population as well that was disposed to take up arms. He reflected that the prospect of living in peace and with the ability to export their produce, conditions absent in the middle Ohio Valley, would soon lure numerous settlers to Louisiana,

---

16. D'Argès to the Conde de Aranda, Paris, February 18, 1787; "Memorial of d'Argès," both in ibid.

an opinion Spanish officials entertained for several years.[17]

On the thorny point of religion, Aranda urged that orthodoxy should not be stressed. A worse fate for the empire than lack of religious orthodoxy among its settlers would be the loss of the colony to the same people who might have relocated to the province as vassals committed to its defense. Establishing them along the Natchez frontier would remove them from the principal Catholic settlements downstream. While Catholicism would remain the official religion and the only faith allowed public worship, the Protestant settlers would not be molested in religious affairs, but they could not have their own ministers or religious meetings, conditions that already existed among the Anglo-American residents. Aranda was optimistic about their conversion. Denied government posts, they and their children would be drawn to the official faith in order to gain advancement. Schools staffed with Irish, German, or French priests, who were models of conduct, would teach religious doctrine and the Spanish language. Within a short time these people would forget their origins. The ambassador drew the analogy that in North Africa Spain already utilized companies of Moorish soldiers to defend Ceuta and Oran. In North America Protestants could be employed in a similar capacity.[18]

At the time the d'Argès proposal reached the Spanish Court, royal policy regarding the closure of the Mississippi River to Americans, as well as Spanish-American relations in general, came under review. After two years of hesitation, Spain closed the river in 1784 in the expectation that its loss as an outlet for their produce would destroy American settlements upriver. Such was not the result, and the settlements flourished while Louisiana's population advanced lethargically. Likewise, Spanish efforts to secure treaty recognition of its fluvial rights were steadfastly rejected by the United States government, and similar efforts to obtain a boundary settlement and a commercial treaty equally frustrated the negotiations of Diego de Gardoqui, Spain's emissary to the United States. Beginning in 1786 the Spanish government became aware of growing disaffection among certain Anglo-Americans in Kentucky and Tennessee; but, while it wished that the West could be useful in protecting Louisiana, Spain

---

17. Aranda to the Conde de Floridablanca, Paris, April 2, 1787, ibid., no. 574.
18. Ibid.

continued to act without much regard to this movement.[19]

By the middle of 1787, the Spanish Court was prepared to alter its policy of keeping the Mississippi River closed. Western American resentment against Spain, as well as against the United States government, was widespread. Seizure of American goods in Natchez in 1786 resulted in the reprisal destruction of Spanish merchandise by George Rogers Clark in Upper Louisiana. Increasingly, denying Americans use of the Mississippi River grew as a reason for the invasion of the province. Thus the d'Argès proposal seemed to offer an alternate solution on how to cope with the discontented western people: employ them rather than resist them. The chevalier's timely proposal in 1787 coincided with a modification of Spanish policy in Louisiana.[20]

In Aranjuez the Conde de Floridablanca, the principal minister of state, consulted José de Gálvez, the minister of the Indies, about Aranda's suggestion to interview d'Argès. Recent correspondence from North America was reviewed and a search was made to determine if Louisiana officials had mentioned the Frenchman in their dispatches.[21] Since nothing could be learned about the chevalier, Gálvez agreed that it might be useful to hear him, and he was invited to Spain. By the end of July d'Argès had arrived in Madrid.[22]

At the Spanish Court d'Argès succeeded beyond his wildest expectations. Floridablanca, now following the counsel of Antonio Valdés, who replaced the recently deceased José de Gálvez, consented to virtually every proposal made by the Frenchman. The chevalier received permission to return to North America and conduct his 1,582 families to Louisiana. Furthermore, Americans in general were now authorized to settle in Louisiana and permitted the private exercise of their religion, but in all other respects they were required to obey Spanish law and to swear an oath of allegiance. The wording of Valdés in his memorandum

---

19. Whitaker, *Spanish American Frontier*, 80, 104-107.

20. Ibid.

21. Floridablanca to Sonora, Aranjuez, May 10, 1787; *Minuta*, Sonora to Floridablanca, Aranjuez, June 2, 1787; both in AHN, Est., leg. 3889, exped. 6.

22. Sonora to Floridablanca, Aranjuez, June 2, 1787; royal order to Aranda, Aranjuez, June 28, 1787; both in ibid.

to Floridablanca was ambiguous, and the subsequent royal order based on it seemed to imply that the Spanish government was granting the Americans complete religious freedom.[23] Both Miró in New Orleans and Gardoqui in New York interpreted the royal order of August 23, 1787, in this fashion. If this was the Court's intent, it was never stated specifically and, in any event, Miró quickly abridged the order to make it conform to his program. The establishment of the parishes ministered by Irish clerics was again included.

In an effort to quiet the anger of western Americans on the issue of trade, Floridablanca agreed to permit them to send their produce to the Spanish province on payment of a 25 percent duty. In Spain royal officials had not considered that such a policy might impede the expected immigration to Louisiana. The question of how much land each colonist was to receive was deferred to the judgment of the governor. As for an English-speaking commander for the Natchez District, the search culminated in the appointment of Lt. Col. Manuel Gayoso de Lemos, who arrived in Louisiana in 1789.[24]

Fearful of possible repercussions, the Spanish government chose to disguise the real purpose behind d'Argès's travels. Officially, d'Argès was to be a commissioner to examine and transmit to the Spanish Court complaints of the American backwoodsmen against the government and to reconnoiter western lands prior to the fixation of boundaries. In order to demonstrate the benevolence of the Spanish king pending final determination of the boundary, American westerners could send their produce downstream to Natchez and New Orleans paying the 25 percent tariff. However, Floridablanca, lacking faith in the comparatively unknown Frenchman, took steps to circumscribe his behavior because d'Argès's demands for greater authority after receiving his appointment had raised Spanish suspicions. The first minister of state obliged him to act only in concert with Gardoqui or Miró, who were to exercise vigilance in dealing with both d'Argès and his enterprise lest the settlers be lost. In a note to Gardoqui, Floridablanca expressed belief that the

---

23. Royal order to the governor of Louisiana, San Ildefonso, August 23, 1787, no. 38, ibid.

24. Ibid. Holmes's biography of *Gayoso* is very favorable to the Spanish official.

new commercial policy for the Mississippi might be useful in furthering negotiations with the United States; therefore, the declaration that the river was open subject to a tariff was to be delayed until such time as he could obtain a *quid pro quo*.[25]

Late in January 1788, the royal mail packet *Galveztown*, after a stormy crossing, blew into New York harbor to disembark its passenger, the chevalier of the Order of St. Louis. No sooner had d'Argès landed than he besieged the Spanish envoy with a barrage of demands. He wanted public recognition for himself as a Court-appointed commissioner to hear complaints and to reconnoiter boundaries; and, if denied this, then the alternative would be an immediate declaration that the Mississippi River was open, subject to a 25 percent duty. He debated with Gardoqui on virtually every issue: he proposed a change in his route to the West although he had chosen it himself; he insisted that he select his own companion to travel with him to Kentucky; and he haggled about his salary payments. In short, the Frenchman expressed interest in almost everything except his primary purpose—to recruit colonists for Louisiana.[26]

Gardoqui displayed little patience with d'Argès. Having been engaged for several years in efforts to secure a treaty with the United States, he was now frustrated that no government existed with which he could negotiate, particularly at a moment when the Spanish Court appeared disposed to concede terms. Furthermore, since 1786 he had been involved in conversations with James White about a separatist movement in the American West that might be useful to Spain, and the envoy perhaps hoped for a positive accomplishment in this area. But with the arrival of d'Argès, he saw in the unbridled Frenchman a threat to his ambitions and was determined to resist him. Gardoqui refused to proclaim the river open because, as he explained, it was Spain's intent to derive some advantage from it. He also argued that many potential emigrants might prefer to pay the import duty rather than move. Moreover, he believed that granting religious toleration was sufficient to attract large numbers

---

25. Royal order to Diego de Gardoqui, palace, September 5, 1787, AHN, Est., leg. 3889, exped. 6.

26. D'Argès to Gardoqui, New York, January 19, 27, and 31, 1788, all in ibid.

of settlers without making further concessions. Gardoqui also hinted to the Court that d'Argès was possibly a French agent and a speculator in western lands. At length, when the two reached an impasse, the Spaniard proposed that since it was winter d'Argès should journey to New Orleans by sea and begin his project from that point in the spring. Vanquished, the chevalier reluctantly consented.[27]

In New Orleans in early July 1787, when Governor Miró still awaited instructions on the establishment of the parishes, the former brigadier general James Wilkinson floated down the Mississippi River bringing barges loaded with merchandise and initiated the misnamed "Spanish Conspiracy."[28] His notorious plan to detach the American West and gain an alliance with Spain has overshadowed a second proposal concerning immigration that he included in his memorial. Scholars have long regarded the second proposal as Wilkinson's without giving it additional attention. However, in this writer's opinion, Governor Miró was solely responsible for this suggestion. Rather than approach the Court directly, he chose Wilkinson's opportune visit to advance his plan. A close examination of Wilkinson's immigration design reveals that it contained many features identical to those propounded by Miró in his suggestions for the conversion and assimilation of the Anglo-American families, as well as the ideas presented by d'Argès in Europe.[29] There can

---

27. Gardoqui to d'Argès, New York, February 1, 1788; Gardoqui to Floridablanca, New York, February 16, April 18, July 25, 1788; all in ibid.

28. The extensive literature on James Wilkinson includes William R. Shepherd, "Wilkinson and the Beginnings of the Spanish Conspiracy," *American Historical Review* 9 (April 1904): 490-506; Whitaker, *Spanish American Frontier, passim*; Manuel Serrano y Sanz, *El Brigadier Jaime Wilkinson y sus tratos con España para la independencia del Kentucky* (Madrid: Tip. de la "Revista de arch., bibl. y museos," 1915); James Ripley Jacobs, *Tarnished Warrior: Major-General James Wilkinson* (New York: Macmillan, 1938); and the more recent Andro Linklater, *An Artist in Treason: The Extraordinary Double Life of General James Wilkinson* (New York: Walker Publishing Company, 2009). Spanish historians Juan Navarro Latorre and Francisco Solano Costa, in *¿Conspiración española? 1787-1789: Contribución al estudio de las primeras relaciones históricas entre España y los Estados Unidos de Norteamérica* (Zaragoza, Spain: Editoriales Librería General, 1949), show that Americans, not Spaniards, initiated the mis-named "Spanish Conspiracy."

29. "Memorial of James Wilkinson," New Orleans, September 3, 1787, AHN, Est.,

be no doubt that Miró was the common inspiration for all of them.

Wilkinson's immigration scheme was not conditional upon the acceptance of his first proposal and could be acted upon independently. The plan called for admitting people from Kentucky into Louisiana, a process that Wilkinson, or more properly Miró, did not regard as detrimental because the colony possessed sufficient Spanish troops to prevent turmoil. Immigrants with property were preferred since their wealth could be confiscated if they misbehaved. The Kentucky families were required to take the oath of allegiance to Spain and, while they were not to be disturbed in religious matters, Catholicism remained the only public form of worship. English-speaking Irish priests who were knowledgeable in the prevailing customs would evangelize and educate the younger generation. Wilkinson, in his irrepressible prose, offered assurances that, over a period of time, these immigrants, enjoying their property and without the necessity of paying import duties, would become tied to Spain in both interest and affection. The success of the first arrivals would induce others to join them, and together they would develop the wealth of the province and increase its importance in the Spanish Empire.[30]

In their celebrated dispatch Number 13 of September 25, 1787, that supported the Wilkinson memorial, Miró and Navarro expected the Irish missionaries to be successful in their work. They explained that additional expenses caused by bringing in more priests could be recouped through increased revenue collected from the expected rise in agricultural exports. They advised placing new settlements on both banks of the Mississippi and not confining them to the eastern bank. Miró and Navarro employed their strongest argument for the admittance of Americans by stating that no force could restrain these settlers if they wished to enter the colony, which in effect cogently summarized the reasons for their settlement on Spanish soil.[31] Unknown to the governor, at the moment he was urging the Crown to permit American Protestants to settle in Louisiana, the

---

leg. 3888bis, no. 52.

30. Ibid.

31. Miró and Navarro to the Spanish Court, no. 13 reserved, New Orleans, September 25, 1787; Whitaker, *Spanish American Frontier*, 103-106.

Court was in the process of forwarding a royal order to this effect and under the same conditions he had expounded, with the exception of those dealing with commerce.

After sending the Wilkinson memorial and their dispatch Number 13, Miró and Navarro began what amounted to a lengthy wait before the Court responded. When a royal order arrived bearing news of the d'Argès appointment, it appeared as if all was lost. The governor soon protested to Spain since the appointment probably meant the demise of the Wilkinson project. He argued that if Wilkinson's project were adopted, he could also act as an immigration agent, and that it was preferable to have a solitary person engaged in delicate affairs. However, because Miró believed that the chevalier was already in Kentucky and soon would come down the rivers with his immigrants, he issued instructions to Commander Carlos de Grand-Pré in Natchez to expect the settlers.[32]

In April 1788, however, new twists and turns suddenly rescued the Wilkinson enterprise, when d'Argès unexpectedly disembarked in New Orleans. The Frenchman had come from New York by sea and had not yet commenced his commission, nor would he, as the governor was resolved to detain him until the Court acted on Wilkinson's memorial. In May 1788, with immigration from Kentucky expected momentarily to get underway, Miró requested a clarification of the duties colonists should pay on entering the province. According to the royal order of July 14, 1787, free entry was authorized for tools and implements brought by settlers for their private use. Miró, however, questioned if duty should be exacted on goods which the immigrants acquired from the sale of their lands and other properties. D'Argès brought with him the news that trade was to be allowed and the import duty placed at 25 percent, but Miró wanted it reduced to 6 percent on the surplus goods of the immigrants out of fear that the higher rate would impede the flow of propertied settlers to Louisiana. Otherwise, the colony might receive only the indigent with no duties to pay.[33] In this manner the governor kept the chevalier cooling his heels in New Orleans while he impatiently

---

32. Miró to Antonio Valdés, New Orleans, January 8, 1788; Miró to Carlos de Grand-Pré, New Orleans, February 2, 1788; both in AHN, Est., leg. 3888bis.

33. Miró to Valdés, New Orleans, May 15, 1788, ibid.

awaited instructions concerning Wilkinson.

Court delay on the Wilkinson proposal probably stemmed from the desire to hear Intendant Navarro's opinion in Spain and to await the results of other projects, particularly the d'Argès project and Gardoqui's private conversations. In May 1788, months after the brigadier submitted his memorial, the intendant retired from service and departed for Spain. There in November he gave his observations on Wilkinson's plans and essentially reiterated what dispatch Number 13 had previously stated. Navarro, who years earlier had counseled closing the Mississippi River in order to destroy American settlements upstream, now recognized the ineffectiveness of that policy. Instead he said that these people, poor but industrious and self-sacrificing, should be used, and that with their assistance Louisiana could be developed and strengthened. Navarro rejected the d'Argès commission in order to make way for Wilkinson's better and more extensive plans. He added that the d'Argès proposal was one which "could have been for some time carried out by Governor Miró and me had we known a way, or believed that the Court would have set aside the essential point of religion."[34]

On December 1, 1788, the Supreme Council instructed Miró on how to proceed. It, together with the royal orders sent the previous year on the d'Argès project, constituted the two most important statements of immigration policy issued during Esteban Miró's governorship. The government, while setting aside Wilkinson's first proposal until Kentucky became independent, adopted his second proposal on immigration. The conditions for entry of settlers were similar to those stated at the time the chevalier became Spain's immigration official in North America, and thus were now reissued with minor modifications. The duty on goods belonging to non-colonists was further reduced from 25 percent to 15 percent, and the governor was authorized to lower it even more for "notables." While the Crown instructed Miró to use d'Argès in some suitable manner, the order confirmed the governor's choice of Wilkinson as his principal immigration agent.[35]

In Louisiana d'Argès waited uneasily for Court instructions and

---

34. Navarro to Valdés, Madrid, November 11 and 20, 1788, ibid.

35. Royal order to the governor of Louisiana, palace, December 1, 1788, ibid.

suspected that more was afoot than just the commercial proposal Miró said that Wilkinson had presented on his visit to New Orleans. In June the chevalier sent word to Col. Richard Anderson in Kentucky that the families could begin their journey down river, and in August he attempted to gain the governor's permission to go himself. Because he was denied permission to travel to Kentucky and had been thwarted in his immigration efforts, d'Argès then decided to employ his free time attending to family matters on the island of Martinique. Delays and lack of transportation postponed his departure from New Orleans until February 1789.[36]

Soon after he left, the long overdue reply to Miró's dispatch Number 13 arrived on February 25, 1789, and a week later the governor wrote to d'Argès offering him the rank of lieutenant colonel with the salary of 100 pesos monthly and command of the post at l'Ance à la Graisse, near the mouth of the Ohio River. There the governor intended to build a settlement similar to that at Natchez with a church, housing for a priest and a military commander, barracks, and other necessary structures, and he appealed to Wilkinson to send a few families to establish themselves at l'Ance à la Graisse. D'Argès, who was then in Santo Domingo, rejected the offer because of his age, but made the counter proposal that working out of New Orleans and with the rank of colonel, he could visit the families periodically.[37] Thus with his characteristic demand for additional consideration ended the d'Argès commission.

Between 1787 and 1790, a number of persons in New Orleans and New York presented programs on how to increase the movement of people to Louisiana.[38] Spain, of course, readily accepted proposals from

---

36. D'Argès to Richard Anderson, New Orleans, June 15, 1788, AHN, Est., leg. 3889, exped. 6; Miró to Floridablanca, New Orleans, August 17, 1788, AHN, Est., leg. 3888bis; d'Argès to Miró, New Orleans, August 12, 1788, ibid.; Miró to Valdés, New Orleans, September 30, 1789, AHN, Est., leg. 3889, exped. 6.

37. Miró to d'Argès, New Orleans, March 4, 1789, AHN, Est., leg. 3888bis; Miró to Wilkinson, New Orleans, March 1, 1789, AGI, PC, leg. 174A; Miró to Valdés, New Orleans, February 12, 1789; AHN, Est., leg. 3889, exped. 6.

38. Among persons presenting immigration proposals were Agustín Macarty, William Fitzgerald, Mauricio Nowland, Bryan Bruin and his son Peter Bryan Bruin, James Kennedy, William Butler, and Peter Paulus. Much of the documentation can be

persons who offered to bring in colonists without special consideration and at no expense to the exchequer. But the Spanish government refused to entertain projects involving expenditure of huge sums of money. It also denied the prospective immigration impresarios the right to sell land for personal profit, to guarantee freedom of religion, and to provide extensive privileges of self-government. Of the various schemes only that of Col. George Morgan will be discussed here to illustrate the demands made and the reasons why Spanish policy was in opposition to them.[39]

In September 1788, soon after the United States government rejected his claims to western lands, Morgan sent a memorial to Gardoqui in New York in which he discussed the creation of a settlement on the Mississippi River. Because the colonel projected a positive impression, the Spanish official expected royal acceptance of the project and granted him permission to visit Louisiana to select a site for his colony. By early 1789 Morgan, who was then in Upper Louisiana, had selected l'Ance à la Graisse, which he renamed New Madrid, for his projected settlement, circulated word in the American West that the Spanish government had given him an extensive land grant, and began the sale of lots of 320 acres at forty-eight dollars each. It was only after he had started his settlement that he wrote about his plans to Governor Miró in New Orleans.[40]

Miró learned of Morgan's unauthorized activities even before

---

found in AHN, Est., legs. 3888bis, 3889, 3893bis, and 3894. Similar material in AGI, PC, however, is very scattered. Hatcher, in "Louisiana Background," concludes that because several persons were commissioned as immigration agents, they introduced large numbers of settlers. My own investigation has revealed otherwise.

39. The literature concerning George Morgan is extensive. See Max Savelle, "The Founding of New Madrid, Missouri," *Mississippi Valley Historical Review* 19 (June 1932): 30-56, and *George Morgan, Colony Builder* (New York: Columbia University Press, 1932); Fernando Solano Costa, "La fundación de Nuevo Madrid," *Cuadernos de Historica Jerónimo Zurita* 4-5 ((1956): 91-108; and Louis Houck, *A History of Missouri from the Earliest Explorations and Settlements until the Admission of the State into the Union*, 3 vols. (Chicago: R. R. Donnelly, 1908), 2: 108-29.

40. Morgan to Gardoqui, New York, August 30, 1788; "George Morgan Plan for Settlement," n.p., September 1788; Gardoqui to Valdés, New York, October 4, 1788; all in AHN, Est., leg. 3894; Morgan to Miró, New Madrid, April 14, 1789 AHN, Est., leg. 3888bis; E. G. Swem, "A Letter from New Madrid, 1789," *Mississippi Valley Historical Review* 5 (December 1918): 342-46.

the colonel wrote and was aghast at the extent of them. Many reasons prevented Miró from accepting Morgan's project. The governor saw no reason to allow the American to enrich himself by selling land the Crown freely gave away; and Morgan's self-governing settlement was contrary to Miró's principles since it would never engender an inclination on the part of the settlers to abide by Spanish laws and customs, and at the slightest jurisdictional dispute or attempt by the governor to exercise authority over them, they would declare themselves independent. Freedom of religion was also against Spanish interests because the new colonists would never become Catholic. When Morgan arrived in New Orleans in May, the governor categorically rejected all his plans and termed his project as equivalent to the creation of a "republic," which in fifty years would be independent. Miró's own plan for admitting Americans was a cautious attempt to develop the province with the only settlers available at no cost, but to have endorsed Morgan's enterprise would have been tantamount to giving Louisiana away.[41]

Still the governor did not wish to alienate the colonel, and he hoped to use him to gain immigrants, but only under the existing regulations. He approved the land grants Morgan made to the persons who followed him to New Madrid, offered him employment as an agent to conduct families to New Madrid, and assured him that the Spanish government would reward him liberally for his services. Morgan, on his part, apologized for his previous behavior and accepted the offer. When he returned to the United States, he published a brochure describing the New Madrid settlement in glowing terms. The colonel, however, resented Miró's refusal to entertain his project, and he blamed Wilkinson and the enmity between the governor and Gardoqui for its failure. It is probable that Morgan accounted for few settlers going to Spanish territory because he soon abandoned his role as immigration agent.[42]

---

41. Miró to Valdés, reserved, New Orleans, May 20, and June 12, 1789, both in AHN, Est., leg. 3888bis.

42. Miró to Morgan, New Orleans, May 23, 1789, ibid.; "Commission from Stephen Miro to Col. George Morgan," New Orleans, May 29, 1789, in Louis Houck, ed., *Spanish Régime in Missouri*, 2 vols. (Chicago: R. R. Donnelley, 1909), 1: 308-309. A pamphlet on New Madrid is in AGI, PC, leg. 2361, and a brochure is reproduced between the pages 206-207 of Savelle's book *George Morgan*. New Madrid's population

In addition to what Morgan had proposed, Governor Miró received a number of other projects from persons offering to bring in colonists, and he commissioned some of them to act as agents under the established laws. Unfortunately, not one of them was responsible for many settlers arriving in Louisiana, and, certainly, those settlers who came did so in fewer numbers than the horde that Spanish officials anticipated. The agent Miró favored from the time he submitted his first memorial in 1787 was Wilkinson, and yet as the governor's chosen representative the former brigadier was not devoted to the concept of emigration from Kentucky because he believed it was contrary to his other scheme of separating the West from the United States.

After Wilkinson's departure from New Orleans in September 1787, Miró inundated him with reminders to send colonists. In August 1788, the governor advised him to instruct the settlers to bring with them a year's supply of food because Louisiana's harvest was expected to be small that year. After receiving the royal order of December 1, 1788, that accepted Wilkinson's second proposal, in early March 1789, Miró informed the brigadier to commence sending the families immediately. In order to make Louisiana more attractive and to promote better relations with the American settlements, the governor instructed his agent to advertise the new low duty of 15 percent, and he added privately that he could reduce that sum for the "notables."[43]

Meanwhile, Wilkinson was filled with jealousy and suspicion of any possible rival and worked only halfheartedly for immigration. After learning of Morgan's project and the d'Argès commission, Wilkinson maligned them both in letters to Miró; and later he included Benjamin Sebastian, whom he had previously recommended to the governor, in his vitriolic attacks. Wilkinson insisted that immigration worked against the larger enterprise of securing the independence of the West. He was also against lowering the duty on imports to Louisiana because it created the false assumption that it was a prelude to the removal of all trade

---

as of December 31, 1795, was 587. AGI, PC, leg. 2364. In a census report of December 1, 1797, the population was given as 615. "Statistical Census of New Madrid of 1797," in Houck, *Spanish Régime*, 2: 393-397.

43. Miró to Wilkinson, New Orleans, August 6, 1788, and March 1, 1789, in AGI, PC, legs. 2372, and 174A, respectively.

restrictions, and because the settlers would prefer to wait rather than emigrate.[44]

In New Orleans the governor patiently urged his agent to send settlers. He dismissed the notion that emigration from Kentucky injured the other project. In 1789 he wrote to the brigadier: "And thus, my friend, I only add that you will do a great service to His Majesty, if you induce a large number of families to come down the river, who have some property, and who do not need additional help, other than land."[45] He refused to believe that only poor families would come because of the 15 percent import duty. He added optimistically that a number of colonists had already arrived with slaves, and that others, too, had been established without cost to the government. While their numbers were still modest, he retained hope they would increase.[46]

In April 1789, goods belonging to the brigadier arrived in New Orleans, followed by Wilkinson himself who presented fresh ideas. By that summer, he had adopted the position that it was preferable for Kentucky, once independent, to establish a formal connection with Spain rather than to come directly under Spanish dominion. His views concerning trade and immigration were more pessimistic. He argued that by restricting trade in Kentucky to only a few persons the Spanish government could promote secessionist fervor there, and he stated that the new tariff hurt immigration because many people would prefer to pay it rather than leave Kentucky, so that he recommended withdrawing the 15 percent duty. But realizing that Miró was committed to encouraging immigration, Wilkinson produced an alternate solution: he would send confidential agents to spread the news of the favorable advantages of living in Louisiana, and, at the same time, they would attempt to convert the notables to the separatist cause. He calculated that the project would cost 7,000 pesos. Another alternative was to increase the government purchase of tobacco to 10,000,000 pounds annually.[47]

---

44. Wilkinson to Miró, Lexington, February 12, and 14, 1789, and February 6, 1791, the first two letters in AHN, Est., leg. 3888bis, and the last in AGI, PC, leg. 2374.

45. Miró to Wilkinson, New Orleans, April 11, 1789, AHN, Est., leg. 3.888bis.

46. Miró to Valdés, New Orleans, April 11, 1789, AGI, PC, leg. 177A.

47. "Wilkinson Memorial of 1789," New Orleans, September 1789, AHN, Est., leg.

The flaw in Wilkinson's proposals was that they required money, and the governor adamantly rejected spending unnecessary money. Since Miró refused to loosen the purse strings, the brigadier pleaded excessive expenditures in his operations and thus managed to pry loose the 7,000 pesos. But Miró outlined his immigration policy more concretely, reiterated that no costs were to be incurred, and avowed his certainty that if information were dispersed throughout the West of the reception and the advantages that the colonists would receive in Louisiana they would be sufficiently motivated to come. Although Wilkinson accepted these conditions, on his return to Kentucky he continued to demonstrate little enthusiasm for this unremunerative assignment.[48]

Wilkinson's attitude had greatly disillusioned Miró by the end of 1790, when he realized that the plans were not progressing as rapidly as earlier anticipated. Not only was the conspiracy in Kentucky producing no results, but nothing was changed in respect to immigration. The governor complained to Capt. Gen. Luis de Las Casas in Havana that Wilkinson ceased to mention the families and that he merely proffered advice where it was not needed.[49]

Soon after that in a letter to Spain, Las Casas expressed concern about the policy of permitting Americans to enter Louisiana. He was one of the first officials to question its wisdom. He considered the Americans in Louisiana to be too close to their own territory and hinted that since they retained their language, customs, and religion, the consequences could prove fatal. The captain general suggested instead that these families be interspersed with Spanish settlers. He recognized that it was costly and that it would reduce Spain's population, but it had the merit of promoting tranquility in the province and helping to ensure its permanence to Spain.[50]

In December 1790, Wilkinson sent Miró a letter detailing the

3889, exped. 1.

48. Miró to Wilkinson, New Orleans, September 18, and 22, 1789, both in ibid., exped. 6.

49. Miró to Capt. Gen. Luis de Las Casas, New Orleans, December 7, 1790, AHN, Est., leg. 3898.

50. Las Casas to the Conde de Campo de Alange, Havana, February 17, 1791, ibid.

reasons for the lack of immigration. He confessed that for the last two months it was completely stopped and doubted if it could ever be started. But in February 1791, he suddenly became optimistic and conjectured that the obstacles to emigration would soon vanish when the people learned the genuine nature of the king's goodwill.[51] The next month he declared to the governor of Natchez, Manuel Gayoso, "It is with the most sensible pleasure I can assure you that Emigration begins again to rear its languid head." Moreover, he claimed that he, too, thought of going to Louisiana soon. Still he persisted in recommending closure of the river to Americans mainly because Spain's purchase of American tobacco would injure immigration.[52]

Contrary to the brigadier's expectations, the "languid head" of emigration refused to "rear" itself, and the flow of colonists remained a trickle rather than the expected torrent.[53] Furthermore, the friendship between the Spaniards and Wilkinson waned considerably as the year 1791 drew to a close and with it Miró's tenure as governor. By now the governor saw little likelihood of the West's defection, but he continued to cling to the prospect that American colonization in Louisiana, under the system he outlined years earlier, was the possible salvation of the province, and more importantly, of Mexico. In a report made in Spain in 1792 upon his return, he emphasized that it was preferable to permit Americans to settle peacefully in the colony in supervised establishments with priests and military commanders rather than to resist them. He pointed out that geographically the Americans were already within the confines of the province since the drainage of the vast Mississippi basin constituted a unified region and that no bulwark could restrain them if they chose to descend on the colony.[54]

51. Wilkinson to Miró, Lexington, February 14, and 17, 1791, AGI, PC, leg. 2374.

52. Wilkinson to Manuel Gayoso, Lexington, March 17, 1791, ibid.

53. A census of June 14, 1792, showed that the Natchez District had approximately 4,691 inhabitants, but the next year the population dropped to 4,446. In 1796 Gayoso placed the district's residents at 5,318. Holmes, *Gayoso*, 116. By way of comparison, Kentucky's population leaped from 73,677 in 1790 to 220,955 in 1800, while Tennessee in the same period grew from 35,691 to 105,602. *World Almanac* (1968 centennial ed., New York, 1967), 260.

54. Miró to the Conde de Campo de Alange, Madrid, August 11, 1792, in Holmes,

The principal hope for Spanish retention of Louisiana was that Americans could be built into a barricade against more of their kind in the United States. Governor Miró cherished the belief that those within Spanish territory could eventually be assimilated, but an ambitious project of this magnitude required time, and time was not on Spain's side. His successor, the Baron de Carondelet, in order to protect the colony, revived the conspiracy of separating the American West, intrigued with Indians, and preferred Europeans to Americans in his immigration policy. Officially, Americans could still enter the province, but they were not given the encouragement they had received previously when Miró was governor.[55]

Perhaps Miró's greatest contribution in devising an immigration policy for Louisiana was his foresight in resisting the temptation of conceding land in large grants to immigration agents who pledged themselves to introduce sizeable numbers of colonists. It was this practice that Miró avoided which a generation later caused Mexico so much sorrow in Texas. He recognized the impossibility of acquiring colonists elsewhere and sought, through a wise effort of assimilation, to use Americans to create a buffer province. Because of Spain's worldwide commitments, limited resources, and the turmoil resulting from the French Revolution, this plan was not developed as thoroughly as it might otherwise have been, and the projected Hispanization achieved only limited results. Had Spain retained Louisiana and implemented Miró's proposals, the outcome might well have been considerably different from the Mexican experience of American colonization in Texas.

Documentos inéditos, 26-27. Miró also stated that, although immigration had not developed as had been anticipated, Louisiana's population had increased by 25,000 during his ten-year administration. In 1782 it was 20,000, and by 1792, it had passed 45,000. Ibid., 24.

55. Baron Francisco de Carondelet to Aranda, reserved, New Orleans, June 10, 1792, AHN, Est., leg. 3898. For views regarding the unwillingness of Americans to emigrate and the assimilation and loyalty of those who did, see Whitaker, *Spanish American Frontier*, 157-62; Holmes, *Gayoso*, 196-97, 272; and Andrew McMichael, "The Kemper 'Rebellion': Filibustering and Resident Anglo American Loyalty in Spanish West Florida," *Louisiana History* 43 (Spring 2003): 136-38.

Chapter 4
Proposals and Plans for Colonization in Spanish Louisiana, 1787-1790

Populating the vast and empty colony of Louisiana was a problem for Spain from the time it was acquired in 1763. But the task did not assume a measure of urgency until after the American War for Independence. During the 1780s, at a time when Louisiana's population growth seemed almost stagnant, American colonists in large numbers began pouring into the western settlements of Kentucky, Cumberland, and on the Holston River in Tennessee. Alarmed at the situation, Spanish authorities in North America urged their government to change its policy for admitting immigrants into Spanish territory in order to build up Louisiana's defenses and development. Spain responded to its precarious predicament in the Mississippi Valley by permitting Americans to settle in Louisiana and West Florida with the royal order of August 23, 1787. Even before this date, sensing a new direction in policy, prospective immigration agents appeared before Gov. Esteban Miró of Louisiana and Diego de Gardoqui, Spain's *chargé d'affaires* to the United States, and offered proposals on how to augment Louisiana's population. Inundated with many requests for the introduction of immigrants and for land grants, Spanish officials believed that Louisiana and West Florida would quickly be filled with tens of thousands of new settlers. After a few years, however, disillusionment set in because the influx of immigrants failed to fulfill Spanish expectations.[1]

Esteban Miró, governor of Louisiana and West Florida during these years (1782-91), was influential in formulating the immigration policy for the two colonies. Before he became acting governor in 1782, Spanish immigration laws permitted only European Catholics to enter these provinces. As relatively few settlers came voluntarily and at their

---

1. This article first appeared in *Louisiana History* 11 (Summer 1970): 197-213.

own expense, the Spanish government in the late 1770s and early 1780s introduced several thousand Acadians, Canary Islanders, and Malagueños in an effort to build up Louisiana's population. But soon the prohibitive costs of transporting colonists from Europe and settling them in Louisiana forced the abandonment of this practice.[2] Meanwhile the emptiness of the province contrasted sharply with the growing American settlements west of the Appalachian Mountains. Both Miró and the Spanish government were keenly aware of the threat those settlements posed to Louisiana. Spain ordered the Mississippi River closed to Americans in 1784 in an attempt to discourage their growth. However, it soon proved ineffectual. Spanish authorities argued that the securest means of defense for Louisiana was an augmented population. Inasmuch as no other colonists were available with whom to counter-colonize Louisiana against the expanding American menace, Miró came to favor the admittance of American Protestants. He regarded it as futile to continue to deny them entry in the colony, considering it preferable to have them established in supervised settlements in Spanish territory. Although done indirectly, it was Miró who first suggested the use of Irish missionaries to work among the Protestant immigrants in order to gain their conversion to Catholicism and to work for the cultural assimilation of their children. He believed that American settlers would be useful in the economic development of Louisiana and West Florida and assist in their military defense, even against other Americans. The Spanish Crown accepted Miró's point of view in 1787.[3]

Diego de Gardoqui, the Spanish chargé d'affaires to the United States in New York, also labored to acquire colonists for Louisiana.[4] Because his primary assignment was to secure a treaty with the United

---

2. See Gilbert C. Din, "Early Spanish Colonization Efforts in Louisiana," *Louisiana Studies* 11 (Spring 1972): 31-49.

3. Gilbert C. Din, "The Immigration Policy of Governor Esteban Miró in Spanish Louisiana," *Southwestern Historical Quarterly* 73 (October 1969): 155-75, discusses these events.

4. On Diego de Gardoqui, see Manuel Ballesteros Gaibrois, "La Misión Gardoqui," (Ph.D. diss., Universidad de Madrid, 1930); Michael A. Otero, "The American Mission of Diego de Gardoqui, 1785-1789" (Ph.D diss., University of California, Los Angeles, 1949).

States government, the recruitment of settlers to him was of secondary importance. His immigration efforts, sporadic and disorderly, often irritated Miró, and relations between the two men were frequently strained. For example, Gardoqui on occasion indiscreetly allowed self-proclaimed immigration agents to journey to New Orleans, where their inadmissible proposals clashed with Miró's immigration policy. On other occasions, the chargé sent destitute colonists who needed assistance to settle on the land, whereas Miró steadfastly insisted that it was neither necessary nor desirable to introduce destitute people into Louisiana. As a result, Gardoqui was not influential in developing immigration policy, nor did he send many settlers to Louisiana.

In 1787 the first foreign immigration agents presented their projects to Spanish authorities. These early proposals requested the introduction of either Irish or American Catholics into Spanish territory. One immigration plan was devised by Agustín Macarty, an Irishman who had served as an officer in the French army in the American War for Independence. He petitioned Governor Miró for permission to bring from two to three thousand of his countrymen from the United States. He was motivated by the abject conditions under which they lived as indentured servants. He requested for them land, implements, food rations, and medical care, benefits which several years earlier had been afforded the Acadian and Canary Islander families who settled in Louisiana. Miró, aware that these prospective settlers were Catholics, endorsed the project when he forwarded it to Spain despite its obvious costliness. The Spanish Court, however, waited nearly two years before finally rejecting the proposal.[5] By then the Spanish government was

---

5. "Memorial of Agustín Macarty," New Orleans, August 14, 1787, and Esteban Miró's marginal notation on the document, New Orleans, August 16, 1787; royal order to the governor of Louisiana, Aranjuez, May 14, 1789; both in Archivo Histórico Nacional, Estado, legajo (hereafter cited as AHN, Est., leg.), 3888bis. On immigration proposals, see Lawrence Kinnaird, "American Penetration into Spanish Louisiana," in *New Spain and the Anglo-American West*, 2 vols. (Los Angeles: privately published, 1932), 1: 211-27, and Kinnaird, ed., *Spain in the Mississippi Valley, 1765-1795*, 3 Parts (Washington, DC: GPO, 1946-1949), 2: xxiii-xxvi; Mattie Austin Hatcher, "The Louisiana Background of the Colonization of Texas," *Southwestern Historical Quarterly* 24 (January 1921): 172-83; and Caroline Maude Burson, *The Stewardship of Don Esteban Miro, 1782-1792* (New Orleans: American Printing Company, 1940), 124-43.

permitting both Catholic and Protestant Americans to settle in Louisiana at their own expense. It concluded that there was no need to underwrite expensive enterprises when Americans would soon fill Louisiana at little or no cost.

Meanwhile in 1787, Diego de Gardoqui received a memorial presented by William Fitzgerald, who represented thirty dissatisfied Catholic families numbering about eight hundred persons, both free and slave, of St. Mary's County, Maryland. They wished to settle in Spanish territory rather than in Kentucky because of disagreeable religious conditions in Maryland and because their farms suffered from soil depletion. The prospect of recruiting these settlers delighted Gardoqui, and he immediately visualized a massive exodus to Louisiana, even though he had had no prior success in gaining emigrants for that colony. Lacking instructions under which the settlers might be admitted, he gave Fitzgerald a passport and letter of introduction to Governor Miró. Early in July 1787, Fitzgerald sailed aboard the Spanish mail packet *Ynfante* bound for New Orleans. Even before he arrived there, the Spanish Court, acting on Gardoqui's letter of May 12, had already issued its approval of Fitzgerald's request.[6] In Louisiana, Miró readily acquiesced to the American's petition and informed him that land would be given to the families. Before departing from New Orleans to return for the immigrants, Fitzgerald borrowed 1,000 pesos from Miró for travel expenses. In Maryland, Fitzgerald learned that only six families were ready for immediate departure, and leaving instructions for others to follow, he sailed with his group for New Orleans aboard a small vessel of thirty-six tons. Storms and contrary winds tossed the tiny craft about for twenty-six days until it reached Puerto Rico, where the Spanish authorities refused the passengers permission to disembark. After moving on to Santo Domingo, Fitzgerald wrote to Gardoqui informing him that their vessel was no longer seaworthy and, in any event, no one wished to continue the perilous voyage. The weary travelers begged authorization to remain where they were. It appears that they never arrived in New Orleans. As

---

6. Diego de Gardoqui to the Conde de Floridablanca, no. 180, New York, May 12, 1787, AHN, Est., leg. 3893bis; "Memorial of William Fitzgerald," New York, May 12, 1987; royal order to the governor of Louisiana, San Ildefonso, August 23, 1787; both in AHN, Est., leg. 3889, exped. 6.

late as 1791, the loan made to Fitzgerald remained unpaid.[7]

Another petitioner was Mauricio Nowland, who appeared in Havana in 1787 to inform Capt. Gen. José de Ezpeleta of a rumored invasion of Louisiana by American frontiersmen and proposed a plan for immigration to the colony. Nowland, an Irish Catholic, had fought in the British army during the American Revolution. Having retired from service, he first approached the Spanish ambassador in London about his project. From there he was directed to New York to see Gardoqui, who in turn sent him to Cuba. Nowland came on behalf of English royalists in the United States who wished to settle in Spanish territory. They were willing to take oaths of loyalty to the Spanish government, but they considered religion an obstacle since most of them were Protestants. Unable to give him satisfaction, Ezpeleta sent him to New Orleans to consult Governor Miró. In Louisiana, Nowland proposed bringing in wealthy families at no cost if he could import duty free goods for one year in the form of slaves, tools, clothing, and food rations, which would not be traded or sold. Furthermore, he offered to transport destitute Catholic families to Louisiana if they received the same assistance rendered earlier to the Acadians. In yet another proposal, Nowland requested to introduce merchandise into the colony up to the value of ten thousand pounds sterling for the length of time the king granted.[8]

Miró declined Nowland's offer to bring indigent families because Americans would soon populate the province at no expense to the Crown. But not wishing to spurn his services, Miró informed him that if he brought thirty families who needed no assistance, the governor would consider him worthy of a reward. Miró added that he could import a cargo of goods valued at £10,000 and more if he brought additional families. The Spaniards did not reach a decision on the Nowland project until May 14, 1789, at which time the government granted him permission to proceed as Miró had instructed him, but not to repeat the

7. Fitzgerald to Gardoqui, Santo Domingo, July 18, 1788, AHN, Est., leg. 3894; Josef de Orue to Miró, New Orleans, November 19, 1791, Miró to Orue, New Orleans, November 25, 1791, both in Archivo General de Indias, Papeles Procedentes de Cuba (hereafter cited as AGI, PC), leg. 601.

8. "Memorial of Mauricio Nowland," Havana, December 11, 1787, AGI, PC, leg. 115A; "Nowland Memorial," New Orleans, February 29, 1788, AGI, PC, leg. 119.

introduction of goods without securing authorization in advance. There was, however, no reason for concern because there is no indication that Nowland returned to Louisiana.⁹

James Kennedy, an Irish merchant and two-year resident in New Orleans, also presented a project for the introduction of Irish families. In March 1788, he proposed to Miró a plan in two parts. He offered to conduct to Louisiana Irish Catholic families who needed only land and who would bring with them all the prerequisites for settlement, on which he requested that no duties be levied. Secondly, he petitioned for permission to take to Louisiana any number, or a fixed number, of families who would receive benefits identical to those given to the Acadians who came in 1785. Only the first part of the plan interested Miró because he believed that the better class of immigrants was more effective in stimulating the development of agriculture and industry. Despite the fact that the settlers in the second part were European Catholics and thus preferred colonists, Miró opposed the project. Nevertheless, the decision rested in Spain, not America. Kennedy soon left for Bordeaux, France, where he intended to wait for the royal determination. In August the Court suspended judgment for the present, and finally on May 14, 1789, it disapproved Kennedy's proposals because other plans had been adopted and Spain did not wish to anger England by enticing away some of its Irish subjects.¹⁰

A proposal that bore some result was that of Bryan Bruin, who offered to bring Irish Catholic families from Virginia to settle in Louisiana. In March 1787, he requested authorization to import goods for their establishment in the form of slaves, animals, tools, seeds, and other items, all of which were permitted entry except sugar and *aguardiente*. Miró agreed to allow the families to settle where they desired and specified that the land grants they received would be twenty arpents of river- or bayou-

---

9. Miró's marginal notation on the Nowland Memorial, New Orleans, March 8, 1788, ibid.; royal order to the governor of Louisiana, Aranjuez, May 14, 1789, AGI, PC, leg. 176B.

10. "Memorial of James Kennedy," New Orleans, March 1, 1788; Miró to Antonio de Valdés, New Orleans, March 8, 1788; royal order to Ygnacio de Asso, San Ildefonso, August 13, 1788; Valdés to the governor of Louisiana, Aranjuez, May 14, 1789; all in AHN, Est., leg. 3888bis.

front by forty deep, and with the privilege of receiving additional land when the first grants had been placed under cultivation. The governor declined to impose the 6 percent duty normally exacted on goods entering the province since the settlers' property was meant only for their use and not for sale, a practice he subsequently adopted.[11] Bruin waited until his proposal was accepted by the Spanish government, and then he sailed from New Orleans to bring the twelve families authorized by the royal order of July 14, 1787.[12]

Although Miró endorsed Bruin's project and allowed American Catholics in general to settle in Spanish territory, royal approbation was required before it became established policy. This was received almost immediately, and soon afterwards, on August 23, 1787, Spain extended permission to allow American Protestants to settle in Louisiana and West Florida.[13] By the middle of 1787, Spain recognized that its previous policy of excluding Americans from settlement in Louisiana and denying them use of the Mississippi River as an exit for their produce might result in invasion of the colony. The Spanish government now desired to reduce the mounting hostility of the western American settlements and, at the same time, to employ their frontiersmen in its counter-colonization efforts in Louisiana and West Florida.[14]

While Bruin waited in New Orleans for a reply to his petition, his son in Virginia, Peter Bryan Bruin, encouraged by the description of the Spanish province that his father had sent him, wrote to Gardoqui

11. Bryan Bruin to Miró, New Orleans, March 31, 1787; Miró to Bruin, New Orleans, April 20, 1787; Miró to the Marqués de Sonora, New Orleans, May 1, 1787; all in ibid.

12. Royal order to the intendant of Louisiana, Madrid, July 14, 1787, AGI, PC, leg. 2317B. See also William S. Coker, "The Bruins and the Formulation of Spanish Immigration Policy in the Old Southwest, 1787-88," in *The Spanish in the Mississippi Valley, 1762-1804*, edited by John Francis McDermott (Urbana: University of Illinois Press, 1974), 61-71.

13. Royal order to the governor of Louisiana, San Ildefonso, August 23, 1787, AHN, Est., leg. 3889, exped. 6.

14. Arthur Preston Whitaker, *The Spanish American Frontier: 1783-1795: The Westward Movement and the Spanish Retreat in the Mississippi Valley* (1927; repr., Gloucester, Mass: Peter Smith, 1962), 79-82, 103-107; Din, "Immigration Policy," 161-63.

soliciting permission to settle in Louisiana. In January 1788, the chargé offered to give Bruin a passport, and two months later, former brigadier general James Wilkinson, on his return from New Orleans by ship to the eastern seaboard, notified Bruin that his father had secured permission to conduct families to Louisiana via the Ohio and Mississippi rivers.[15] By June 10, 1788, Commandant Carlos de Grand-Pré, in Natchez, had informed Miró of Peter Bryan Bruin's arrival with two barges bringing a total of sixty-six persons, thirty-one of whom were African slaves. His uncle also arrived before the end of the year conducting more settlers, and still another barge soon brought an additional forty-two persons.[16] The significance of Bruin's arrival in Natchez was that it seemingly confirmed the governor's belief that a deluge of immigrants, hungry for land and seeking a market for their goods, would soon descend upon the province. The trickle of settlers that continued through 1789, however, never reached the proportions that the governor anticipated.

In March 1789, William Butler, another Irishman, presented Gardoqui in New York with an offer to take forty-five families consisting of 174 persons to Louisiana. The Spanish chargé, however, preferred to give Butler a passport to New Orleans and let him present his proposition to the governor in person. His commission came from several residents in the United States who desired to emigrate. In New Orleans Miró rejected Butler's request for transportation to bring in the families. The agent then counter-proposed to transport them at his own expense if he was authorized to import flour, salted meat, tools, and other equipment for construction and agriculture up to the value of 100,000 pesos, which would repay his expenditures. When Miró refused to approve

15. Peter Bryan Bruin to Gardoqui, Bath, Virginia, July 15, 1787, and March 1, 1788; AHN, Est. leg. 3893bis, and leg. 3888bis, respectively. For a biographical sketch of Peter Bryan Bruin, see Jack D. L. Holmes, "Some Irish Officers in Spanish Louisiana," *The Irish Sword* 6 (Winter 1964): 245-46; and Coker, "Bruins and the Formulation of Spanish Immigration Policy," 61-71.

16. Miró to Valdés, New Orleans, June 18, 1788, AHN, Est., leg. 3888bis. Peter Bryan Bruin received 1,450 arpents of land when he settled at Bayou Pierre in 1788. Later, he obtained an additional 2,300 arpents for his services to the Spanish government. Jack D. L. Holmes, *Gayoso: The Life of a Spanish Governor in the Mississippi Valley, 1789-1799* (Baton Rouge: Louisiana State University Press for the Louisiana Historical Association, 1965), 37.

his plan, Butler offered to introduce settlers at no cost to the Spanish government if he was allowed to import a thousand barrels of flour, a needed commodity in Lower Louisiana, and Miró accepted it. In January 1790, the Court ratified the governor's actions. But it does not appear that Butler returned with the families and merchandise.[17]

When a fire destroyed much of New Orleans in 1788, a severe food shortage resulted. In response to Miró's appeal for help, Gardoqui dispatched two ships to carry flour to New Orleans, and he used this opportunity to send colonists aboard them. The chargé's immigration effort, however, only antagonized the governor because Gardoqui sent the wrong kind of settlers. The *Lydia* that arrived in New Orleans in September 1788 brought 130 persons, 79 of whom required assistance to settle. The immigrants claimed that in Philadelphia, Gardoqui, through his assistant John Leamy, had promised them rations, livestock, tools, and other items useful in their settlement. Miró protested to the chargé against sending colonists who required help because it was contrary to his plan of not spending money to promote immigration. But before his letter arrived in New York, the *Concepción* sailed for Louisiana bearing an additional 173 colonists, 130 of whom needed aid. When the settlers arrived, much against his will the governor sent them to the Feliciana District, fifty leagues above New Orleans, giving them almost everything they allegedly had been promised. Gardoqui, in answer to Miró's protests that alleged thousands of destitute inhabitants of Kentucky would descend on Louisiana seeking identical favors, denied that the immigrants had been assured of assistance other than lands. He privately lamented to Captain General Ezpeleta in Cuba the impossibility of maintaining harmonious relations with the governor.[18]

Miró's anxiety about being inundated by immigrants lacking

---

17. Gardoqui to Miró, New York, March 20, 1789, AGI, PC, leg. 104A; "Memorial of William Butler," New Orleans, July 28, 1789; Miró to Valdés, New Orleans, July 31, 1789; royal order to the governor of Louisiana, Madrid, January 24, 1790; the last three documents are in AGI, PC, leg. 202.

18. Miró to Valdés, no. 125, New Orleans, October 20, 1788; Miró to Gardoqui, New Orleans, September 30, 1788; Miró to Valdés, no. 166, New Orleans, March 15, 1789; Gardoqui to Miró, New York, November 8, 1789; all in AHN, Est., leg. 3888bis; Gardoqui to Ezpeleta, New York, July 19, 1789, AGI, PC, leg. 1425.

the essentials for settlement increased when Peter Paulus appeared in the colony and presented his exorbitant demands. Arriving in New Orleans early in March 1789, after having conducted thirty-four persons to Natchez, Paulus claimed to be a Dutch captain of militia from Pennsylvania, and he offered to bring in up to three thousand families if certain conditions were met. He wanted their transportation paid, six hundred arpents of land for each family, freedom of religion, and a number of other special considerations, all of which clearly exceeded Spanish regulations.[19] Questioned by Miró, Paulus confessed that he had been influenced by the news of George Morgan's proposed settlement at New Madrid, as well as by the assistance Gardoqui and Leamy had promised the families who went by ship to New Orleans. The governor rejected Paulus's proposal, but he reimbursed the captain for the 350 pesos that he had allegedly spent to convey the thirty-four settlers to Natchez. Miró then gave Paulus a copy that outlined the conditions for the admittance of immigrants in the colony. The governor offered Paulus the rank of captain and a position as a commander of a settlement if he brought one thousand families who required no help in their establishment. Paulus replied that he thought he might be able to bring nine hundred families under those conditions.[20]

The probability that Paulus ever returned to Louisiana, much less brought families, remains remote. On his arrival in the United States, he boasted that the governor had given him fourteen square leagues of land and that he had hoodwinked Miró out of 350 pesos; instead of his paying the expenses of the thirty-four persons he took to Natchez, Paulus hooted that they had maintained him on their journey.[21]

The most celebrated of all the immigration agents of this period was Col. George Morgan, who, after the United States government had denied his claims to western lands, approached Gardoqui in an effort

19. Miró to Valdés, no. 133 reserved, New Orleans, March 15, 1789; "Memorial of Peter Paulus," New York, March 6, 1789; both in AHN, Est., leg. 3888bis.

20. Miró's marginal notation on the "Paulus Memorial," March 7, 1789; Miró to Valdés, New Orleans, March 15, 1789; both in ibid.

21. "A Literal Copy of a paragraph of the Letter of Dn. Juan de Leamy of July 15, 1789," attached to Gardoqui's letter to Ezpeleta, New York, July 19, 1789, both in AGI, PC, leg. 1425.

to recoup his losses with a Spanish land grant.[22] In late August 1788, Morgan inquired about the possibility of establishing a settlement on the Mississippi composed of several thousand industrious persons. In his response, Gardoqui stated that he considered the plan feasible. The next month Morgan wrote out his scheme that outlined the autonomy and government for the colony, the formation of militia companies for defense, the creation of schools, and the development of produce he intended to distribute in many parts of the Spanish Empire. Morgan's proposed compensation for himself included the rank of colonel with its corresponding salary, an extensive land grant, and the right to export his produce duty-free. He also offered to conduct indigent persons to the settlement at the fixed rate of twenty pesos per person. Displaying cavalier disregard for Louisiana's immigration policy, Gardoqui voiced no objection to Morgan's plan and considered his suggested remuneration as reasonable.[23]

In October the chargé gave Morgan a passport, letters of introduction to Spanish authorities in Louisiana, and 600 dollars for travel expenses. Officially, Morgan received only permission to reconnoiter the banks of the Mississippi River for a site for his proposed settlement. By February Morgan had reached the Mississippi, and for the next two months he explored possible sites before selecting l'Ance à la Graisse, located a few leagues below the mouth of the Ohio River but on the opposite bank. Morgan renamed the site New Madrid and began marking off 320-acre

---

22. Much has been written about George Morgan. See Max Savelle, "The Founding of New Madrid, Missouri," *Mississippi Valley Historical Review* 19 (June 1932): 30-56; and *George Morgan, Colony Builder* (New York: Columbia University Press, 1932); Fernando Solana Costa, "La Fundación de Nuevo Madrid," *Cuadernos de Historia de Jerónimo Zurita* 4-5 (1956): 91-108; and Louis Houck, *A History of Missouri from the Earliest Explorations and Settlements Until the Admission of the State into the Union*, 3 vols. (New York: Arno Press and the New York Times, 1972), 2: 108-29. For published documents relating to Morgan and his project, see Louis Houck, ed., *The Spanish Régime in Missouri*, 2 vols. (1909; repr., New York: Arno Press and the New York Times, 1972), 1: 275-309.

23. Morgan to Gardoqui, New York, August 30, 1788; Gardoqui to Morgan, New York, September 2, 1788; Gardoqui to Valdés, New York, October 4, 1788; "George Morgan's Plan for Settlement, Prospect, New Jersey, September 1788 (which is also in Houck, *Spanish Régime*, 1: 299-306); all in AHN, Est., leg. 3895.

parcels of land that he intended to sell to immigrants. In April, when Morgan wrote to Governor Miró in New Orleans to explain his activities in New Madrid, the colonel had already exceeded the authorization that Gardoqui had given him.[24] It is probable that Morgan hoped to induce Miró to surrender to his *fait accompli* at New Madrid. Morgan, however, did not reckon on the tenacity with which Miró would adhere to his own plans and to the immigration laws of the colony.

The governor had firm ground for opposing Morgan's grandiose scheme. Miró refused to allow the colonel to sell land the Crown granted freely since purchased soil would not secure for Spain the loyalty it sought from foreign settlers. Miró regarded self-governing settlements within Louisiana dangerous because the colonists would regard the Spanish government as an alien power, and any attempt by Spanish officials to exercise authority over the settlers might provoke them into rebellion. Freedom of religion, another of Morgan's conditions, was likewise counter to the interest of the Spanish government since the settlers would never become Catholic. Because these points were inadmissible, Miró rejected all of the colonel's propositions when he arrived in New Orleans in May. The governor, however, attempted to elicit some advantage from this episode, for he approved the 320-acre grants that Morgan had made to the settlers who followed him to New Madrid. At the same time, Miró offered the colonel employment as an agent to bring in families and to establish them at New Madrid, or at any other location where they might prefer to settle. The governor further informed Morgan that the Spanish Crown would reward him in proportion to the number of families he brought. Miró also assured him that he would receive at least a thousand acres for himself and for each of his children.[25] Morgan accepted the offer and initially seemed willing to fulfill his new assignment. When he returned to the United States, however, he bitterly assailed the governor, blaming the failure of his project on the animosity that Miró harbored

---

24. Gardoqui to Floridablanca, New York, October 24, 1788, AHN, Est., leg. 3895; Morgan to Miró, New Madrid, April 14, 1789, AHN, Est., leg. 3888bis.

25. Miró to Valdés, no. 39 and no. 41 both reserved, New Orleans, May 20 and June 12, 1789, both in AHN, Est., leg. 3888bis. Miró declared in hyperbole that so extensive were Morgan's demands that if granted, in less than ten years, Louisiana would gain the majority of the inhabitants of the United States and, perhaps, even Congress itself.

for Gardoqui. Although Morgan published a brochure in Philadelphia designed to attract settlers to New Madrid, he soon gave up his post as immigration agent in order to attend to family matters.[26]

Another proposal made to Gardoqui came from Baron William Frederick von Steuben, who had recently served in the Continental Army. As early as 1786, Steuben first contacted the Spanish chargé and expressed an interest in Louisiana. In March 1788, he finally submitted a plan for a military settlement on the Mississippi River. His proposal called for a colony of 4,200 farmers and artisans and a land grant of 200,000 acres, which he and his associates would distribute in blocks of 230 acres to colonists at no cost. The settlers were to come from the United States or other foreign lands; colonists from Germany would have their transportation paid for them. Steuben asked for religious freedom as well as the practice of some laws found in the United States, but in other respects the colonists were to be entirely under the Spanish judicial system. All the settlers would be required to render military service, with Steuben in charge of eight hundred soldiers under his personal command. The baron estimated the cost of the settlement to be 100,000 pesos annually. The Spanish Court, however, never considered the project because of the features that made it objectionable. In any case, Steuben soon gave up the idea to devote more time to his own lands in Oneida County in New York state.[27]

Besides the proposals mentioned here, a number of minor plans were presented to Spanish officials, all of which kept Governor Miró optimistic for several years about a rapid influx of people to Louisiana. From 1787 on, Miró had as his preferred immigration agent James Wilkinson, who was to send American settlers from Kentucky. In September of that year, Wilkinson presented his well-known plan calling for the separation of the American West and the formation of an alliance with Spain. In

26. "Letter of Col. George Morgan to Don Diego de Gardoqui—1789," Prospect, New Jersey, August 20, 1789, in Houck, *Spanish Régime*, 1: 286-99. A pamphlet on New Madrid is in AGI, PC, leg. 2361.

27. Gardoqui to Floridablanca, no. 13 reserved, New York, October 18, 1788, AHN, Est., leg. 3893bis; Friedrich Kapp, *Life of William Frederick von Steuben, Major-General in the Revolutionary War* (New York: Mason Brothers, 1859), 586-89; Hatcher, "Louisiana Background," 181-83.

addition, he presented a second proposal to allow American colonists to settle in Spanish territory. The second plan, which was really the work of Miró and not Wilkinson, was adopted by the Spanish Court on December 1, 1788. However, American settlement in Louisiana and West Florida had been authorized earlier by the royal order of August 23, 1787, and when Miró learned of it, he urged Wilkinson to send colonists immediately. But over the next few years, Wilkinson revealed himself to be unenthusiastic about promoting immigration because he regarded it as contrary to his principal objective of detaching Kentucky from the United States. Wilkinson instead complained about the liberal Spanish commercial laws that made the prospective settlers prefer to remain in Kentucky rather than emigrate. By 1790 Miró had become thoroughly disillusioned with Wilkinson's behavior as an immigration agent and the relationship between the two men cooled considerably. The governor at last began to realize that the flood of American immigrants to Louisiana that had been expected for several years would not occur.[28]

Although some settlers made their way to Louisiana and West Florida, their numbers were small in comparison with those anticipated.[29] Many of the American colonists who entered Spanish territory during this period settled in the Natchez District of West Florida, which the Spanish government had designated as Lower Louisiana's first line of defense. About 1784 the district's inhabitants were estimated to number around 1,600. It required four years for the population to increase to 2,679. By 1792 the Natchez District's population had risen to 4,691, and in 1796, a census revealed 5,318 inhabitants. Thus, in the twelve-year period from 1784 to 1796, the district's residents rose by about 3,700, an average of 300 persons annually.[30] However, not all the growth in population was

---

28. Din, "Immigration Policy," 164-68, 171-74.

29. As examples of settlers who arrived in Spanish territory, from January to July 5, 1788, 128 whites and 36 blacks reached Natchez from the United States; from October 2 to December 29, 1788, only 35 whites and 7 blacks arrived at Natchez from the United States; and in Upper Louisiana, from December 1, 1787, to December 31, 1789, a total of 293 persons from the United States settled there; however, the overwhelming majority of the last group were French. Kinnaird, *Spain in the Mississippi Valley*, 2: 257-58, 264-65, 290.

30. Charles Gayarré, *History of Louisiana*, 4 vols. (New Orleans: Armand Hawkins,

due to immigration since natural increase undoubtedly accounted for a part of it.

In 1792, when Miró was in Spain after having retired as governor, he wrote a report in which he stated that Louisiana's population had not grown in the manner anticipated, although it did rise by 25,000 during his ten-year term. In 1782 Louisiana had about 20,000 inhabitants, and by 1792, the number of residents exceeded 45,000. But the average annual addition of 2,500 for the vastness of Louisiana can hardly be considered spectacular when compared to the growth of Kentucky and Tennessee. In 1790 Kentucky's population was placed at 73,677, whereas Tennessee possessed 35,691 inhabitants. Ten years later residents of Kentucky and Tennessee numbered 220,955 and 105,602, respectively, while Louisiana's population had grown to only about 50,000.[31]

A number of reasons can be advanced to explain why the Spanish scheme to counter-colonize Louisiana and West Florida with American settlers resulted largely in failure. Many Americans unfamiliar with Spanish laws initially considered the Spanish government to be totalitarian and unsympathetic toward self-government. Although Protestants were allowed to enter Louisiana, they were not permitted public worship, and the imagined threat of forced conversion to Catholicism frightened away many of them. A major inducement for establishment in Louisiana in the late 1780s was the presence of a market where they could sell their produce. With the change in Spanish laws in December 1788, however, Americans learned that they could trade without leaving their homes by paying a 15 percent tariff, and many seemed to prefer this to emigrating. Furthermore, in 1790 the Spanish government, overstocked with tobacco, sharply curtailed further purchases of this commodity and, at the same time, the West began to experience prosperity which made emigration even less appealing. Finally, the absence of land speculation possibly deterred some persons from going to Louisiana, although Spanish

---

1885), 3: 215; Holmes, *Gayoso*, 116.

31. Esteban Miró to the Conde de Alange, Madrid, August 11, 1792, in Jack D. L. Holmes, *Documentos inéditos para la historia de la Luisiana, 1792-1810* (Madrid: Ediciones José Porrua Turanzas, 1963), 24; *World Almanac* (New York: American Heritage Press, 1962), 157-62.

officials freely granted land to genuine colonists.[32]

By the royal orders of August 23, 1787, and December 1, 1788, Spain opened the doors of Louisiana and West Florida to American settlers. Spanish authorities realized that the best security for their North American possessions was a large population. Unable to recruit colonists elsewhere who did not require transportation and assistance in settlement, Spain decided to allow Americans to enter. Rather than continue to exclude them and risk invasion, the Spanish government permitted them to come in and establish themselves in supervised settlements with Irish priests and small detachments of Spanish soldiers to preserve order. For several years, Governor Miró anticipated that many Americans would come to take advantage of free land and other inducements in Louisiana, and the many colonization schemes that were presented supported his belief. Yet not one immigration agent was able to stimulate a massive movement of people to Louisiana. In spite of the open door to Americans, relatively few took advantage of it.

---

32. Whitaker, *Spanish American Frontier*, 157-62.

CHAPTER 5

Pierre Wouves d'Argès in North America: Spanish Immigration Commissioner, Adventurer, or French Spy?

In the 1780s, Pierre Wouves d'Argès, chevalier of the Order of St. Louis and recently captain of grenadiers in the American War for Independence, emerged from the North American wilderness and appeared before Spanish officials in New Orleans, Paris, and Madrid.[1] He bore news from the Ohio River Valley and stated that he had a petition from hundreds of Kentucky families who desired to emigrate to Spanish Louisiana. Despite his status as an unknown individual when he was summoned to Madrid, his information about families willing to emigrate so excited Spanish Court authorities that he was promptly made a commissioner to direct them to Louisiana. Amazed by the ease with which the Spanish government adopted his proposals, the Frenchman's ambitions widened to demand a larger role in Spain's affairs in North America, thus raising questions by cautious Court officials about his true intentions. In New York and New Orleans d'Argès clashed with Spanish officials who hinted enigmatically that he was either an adventurer or a French spy. They refused to permit him to continue his commission. Blocked in his effort to reach Kentucky and bring in immigrants—and perhaps do more, d'Argès dejectedly returned to France. Nevertheless, the mystery surrounding him has lingered on, and historians after his time have perpetuated the uncertainty about him and his pursuits in North America.[2]

    1. This article first appeared in *Louisiana Studies* 12 (Spring 1973): 354-75.

    2. The literature on Pierre Wouves d'Argès appears substantial, but it is mainly cursory. The two better works are Samuel Flagg Bemis, *Pinckney's Treaty: America's Advantage from Europe's Distress, 1783-1800*, rev. ed. (New Haven: Yale University Press, 1960), 127-30; and, despite a number of errors, Arthur Preston Whitaker, *The*

The first mention that d'Argès was in Louisiana occurred in August 1786. Two and a half years before, Captain d'Argès, then about forty-six years of age and from a middle class French background, journeyed to the vicinity of Louisville, Kentucky, to lands he had received like many other discharged veterans of the recent war. However, the frontier conflict raging between the Americans and Indians induced him to abandon his homestead and return to the family estate on the island of Martinique. Several weeks before leaving Kentucky on June 4, 1786, d'Argès stated that 1,582 families requested that he seek permission from Spanish authorities in New Orleans for them to settle in Louisiana, if they received three hundred acres of land per family and freedom of religion. In return the families promised to live on Spanish soil as good and loyal vassals. D'Argès allegedly presented the petition to the governor of Louisiana, Esteban Miró, and to the intendant, Martín Navarro, in New Orleans in August. The two officials informed him that they lacked authority to accept the petition inasmuch as freedom of religion and the settlement of Americans in Louisiana were prohibited at that time. Nevertheless, aware that change was in the air, Miró and Navarro encouraged d'Argès to submit the petition to the Spanish ambassador in Paris since he was now going there. With this advice, the former soldier departed New Orleans.[3]

Spanish American Frontier, 1783-1795: The Westward Movement and the Spanish Retreat in the Mississippi Valley (1927; repr., Glouster, Mass.: Peter Smith, 1962), 78-89. See also Caroline Maud Burson, *The Stewardship of Don Esteban Miró, 1782-1792* (New Orleans: American Printing Company, 1940), 136-42; Charles Gayarré, *History of Louisiana*, 4 vols. (New Orleans: Armand Hawkins, 1885), 3: 197-201, 217-18; Alcée Fortier, *A History of Louisiana*, 4 vols. (New York: Goupil and Company, 1904), 2: 131-37; José Navarro Latorre and Fernando Solano Costa, *¿Conspiración española? 1787-1789: Contribución al estudio de las primeras relaciones históricas entre España y los Estados Unidos de Norteamérica* (Zaragoza: Talleres Editorial Librería General, 1949), 45-50; Lawrence Kinnaird, "American Penetration into Spanish Louisiana," in *New Spain and the Anglo-American West*, 2 vols. (Los Angeles; privately printed, 1932), 1: 216; and Mattie Austin Hatcher, "The Louisiana Background to the Colonization of Texas," *Southwestern Historical Quarterly* 24 (January 1921): 175-76. D'Argès received the patent of chevalier of St. Louis on December 15, 1779. Conde de Aranda to Conde de Floridablanca, Paris, April 2, 1787, Archivo Histórico Nacional (Madrid), Estado, legajo (hereafter cited as AHN, Est., leg.) 3888bis.

3. Pedro Rezard Wouves d'Argès to Aranda, Paris, February 18, 1787, AHN, Est.,

By February 1787, d'Argès was in Paris where he wrote the Spanish ambassador, the Conde de Aranda, informing him about the petition he carried. Eager to hear news from the Mississippi Valley, Aranda interviewed the chevalier several times and urged him to write down his impressions, which d'Argès did in two memorials. In them he commented at length on how Spanish closure of the Mississippi River to the Americans and Spanish confiscation of American goods found on the river in Spanish-claimed lands affected them. He further stressed the development of Louisiana's potential wealth if colonization were encouraged. D'Argès commented on the mounting strength of American settlements upstream and on the weaknesses of Louisiana's military defenses, but he believed that Americans could defend the colony if they were permitted to settle in the Natchez District. Furthermore, he asserted that Protestant Anglo-Americans could be converted to Catholicism and culturally assimilated through the employment of English-speaking Irish missionaries.[4]

Most of these suggestions, however, did not originate with the chevalier since he had absorbed virtually all the information he possessed about Louisiana from Miró and Navarro in New Orleans.[5] In Paris d'Argès foisted these ideas as his own, and he completely deceived Aranda in the

---

leg. 3889, expediente 6, in French. D'Argès used acres in his memorial. However, the Spaniards subsequently translated it as fanegas (1.59 acres). The petitioners were mostly Germans or of German descent. D'Argès suggested that the settlers have an English-speaking commandant. D'Argès to Aranda, Paris, March 18, 1787, ibid. Miró reported neither d'Argès nor his petition to the Spanish government, which in May 1787, searched his letters to see if he had. Floridablanca to the Marqués de Sonora (José de Gálvez), San Ildefonso, May 10, 1787; Sonora to Floridablanca, Aranjuez, June 2, 1787; both in ibid. Whitaker, in *Spanish American Frontier*, 79, erroneously states that d'Argès's petition was from 5,000 families. D'Argès did not suggest in his two Paris memorials, as Whitaker declares, that he wished to return to the United States.

4. D'Argès to Aranda, Paris, February 18 and March 18, 1787, AHN, Est., leg. 3889, exped. 6.

5. Gilbert C. Din, "The Immigration Policy of Governor Esteban Miró in Spanish Louisiana," *Southwestern Historical Quarterly* 73 (October 1969): 155-75. Compare d'Argès's memorials to Miró's suggestions for the Anglo-American Protestants of West Florida in Miró to Bernardo de Gálvez, New Orleans, September 5, 1785; and Conde de Gálvez (Bernardo de Gálvez) to José de Gálvez, Mexico City, October 27, 1785; both in AHN, Est., leg. 3888bis.

process. D'Argès's knowledge about Louisiana's defenses, commerce, and population thoroughly captivated the ambassador. In forwarding the chevalier's memorials to the Spanish Court, Aranda added his own lengthy endorsement of the immigration project. He described the Frenchman as an educated man conversant in both English and Spanish, of sound judgment, and well informed. At this time, the chevalier had not yet committed himself to becoming an immigration agent, and he believed his contribution consisted only of passing along the petition and his information. But Aranda insisted that d'Argès travel to Spain and personally present his suggestions there. The ambassador informed the Spanish Court that he regarded it as vital that the Natchez District acquire the 1,582 Kentucky families, who would contribute enormously in developing Louisiana's commerce and in defending the province against all invaders. The Protestant faiths of the immigrants constituted no hindrance since, as Aranda insisted, in time they could be converted to Catholicism by persuasive Irish, German, and French missionaries; by prohibiting them from having Protestant ministers; and by excluding non-Catholic immigrants from civil and military employment.[6] Aranda's arguments exerted considerable influence at the Spanish Court.

In Spain the ambassador's suggestion that d'Argès be interviewed received the attention of the first minister of state, the Conde de Floridablanca, and the minister of the Indies, José de Gálvez. By June 2, the Crown agreed to interview the Frenchman in Madrid.[7] The Spanish government was then in the midst of altering its practice of excluding American Protestants as settlers in Louisiana. Only the year before the Crown first deviated from this policy when it permitted the Anglo-Saxon residents of West Florida to remain permanently on their lands after the province had been conquered by the Spaniards in 1779 and ceded to Spain in the peace treaty of 1783. Governor Miró convinced the Court to allow the West Florida settlers to stay under pledges of fidelity, but with the denial of Protestant ministers and the public worship of

6. Aranda to Floridablanca, Paris, April 2, 1787, AHN, Est., leg. 3888bis. Aranda expressed great confidence in d'Argès and did not suspect him of being an adventurer.

7. Aranda's letter arrived at Court by May 10, 1787. Floridablanca to Sonora, Aranjuez, May 10, 1787, AHN, Est., leg. 3885, exped. 13; (Sonora) to Floridablanca, Aranjuez, June 2, 1787, AHN, Est., leg. 3889, exped. 6.

their religion.⁸ Four English-speaking Irish priests had recently been sent to West Florida to begin the conversion of the British inhabitants to Catholicism.⁹ Miró further believed that American immigrants could be established under similar conditions on supervised settlements with additional priests. Although the proposal was potentially hazardous, the governor considered it preferable to risking invasion by excluding Americans. The project that d'Argès presented in 1787 employed Miró's thinking on immigration.¹⁰ Ironically, the Spanish Crown adopted it before the Louisiana governor approached the Court with his own proposal.

Along with a change in immigration policy, the Spanish government in the summer of 1787 was revising its attitude toward the western American settlements. Because of the boundary dispute that emerged between Spain and the United States in 1783, Spain closed the Mississippi to Americans and hoped that it would stunt the growth of their frontier settlements.¹¹ However, by mid-1787 Spain's policy was increasing the likelihood of a western invasion of Louisiana in order to open the river. A cold war that sometimes flared up went on in the Mississippi Valley

---

8. Royal order to Conde de Gálvez, El Pardo, April 5, 1786, AHN, Est., leg. 3888bis. In 1787 the Spanish government began to accept American Catholics as immigrants in Louisiana and exempted them from the 6 percent duty imposed on goods introduced for their own consumption. Royal order to the governor of Louisiana, Madrid, July 14, 1787, ibid., which answered Miró's letter to José de Gálvez, New Orleans, May 1, 1787, ibid.

9. Gilbert C. Din, "The Irish Mission to West Florida," *Louisiana History* 12 (Fall 1971): 315-34. See also Michael Curley, *Church and State in the Spanish Floridas (1782-1822)* (Washington, DC: Catholic University Press, 1940).

10. Din, "Immigration Policy of Miró," 159.

11. For Spanish policy during the American War for Independence and at the subsequent peace conference, see Samuel Flagg Bemis, *The Diplomacy of the American Revolution* (1957; repr., Bloomington: University of Indiana Press, 1965); and J. F. Yela Utrilla, *España ante la independencia de los Estados Unidos*, 2nd ed., 2 vols. (Lérida, Spain: Gráficos Academia Mariana, 1925). On boundary problems, see Bemis, *Pinckney's Treaty*, 25-45; José de Gálvez to the governor of Louisiana, Aranjuez, June 26, 1784, in Louis Houck, ed., *The Spanish Régime in Missouri*, 2 vols. (1909; repr., New York: Arno Press and New York Times, 1972), 1: 237. Governor Miró proclaimed the Mississippi River closed on September 7, 1784. Miró to the Conde de Gálvez, New Orleans, June 14, 1785, AHN, Est., leg. 3885bis, exped. 11.

with the reciprocal confiscation of American and Spanish property.[12] An atmosphere of rumor and tension permeated the American settlements. Besides feeling anger at their own government for failing to defend their interests, some westerners actively discussed the possibility of secession from the United States. They considered either joining Spain or seeking an alliance, either of which would permit westerners use of the Mississippi. Alerted to these developments, the Spanish government watched events in the American West closely. When the d'Argès petition came, the Spanish Court seized it as the opportune moment to adopt a new relationship toward the frontiersmen.

On June 28, the Court sent a royal order to Aranda in Paris approving the chevalier's journey to Spain. By July 11, the Frenchman was on his way.[13] Before the end of the month, he was at the Spanish Court in San Ildefonso, where he soon met Floridablanca. Apparently encouraged by his talks with the minister, d'Argès began to envision a larger role for himself than merely that of a bearer of a petition. Unfortunately, his conversations with the minister were not committed to writing to divulge what they discussed.

On August 1, and again on August 4, d'Argès wrote two new documents on his views of conditions in the Mississippi Valley. The most important new item he advocated was a "commissioner of boundaries," who would travel to Kentucky, keep his eyes open, and attempt to dissipate the anger of the local populace toward Spain. The Frenchman asked for the rank of lieutenant colonel should he be selected the commissioner. It is possible that by this time Floridablanca had discussed the separatist movement on the American frontier to a greater or lesser degree with d'Argès.[14]

By early August the Spanish government was debating on how to employ d'Argès. On August 3, Floridablanca mentioned sending a

12. Navarro Latorre and Solano Costa, *¿Conspiración española?*, 17-24; Lawrence Kinnaird, ed., *Spain in the Mississippi Valley, 1765-1794*, 3 Parts (Washington, DC: GPO, 1946-1949), 2: xvii-xix.

13. Royal order to Aranda, Aranjuez, June 28, 1787; Aranda to Floridablanca, Paris, July 9 and 11, 1787; all in AHN, Est., leg. ?°89, exped. 6.

14. D'Argès to Floridablanca, (San Ildefonso), August 1, 1787; d'Argès memorial to Floridablanca, San Ildefonso, August 1, 1787; d'Argès to Floridablanca, San Ildefonso, August 4, 1787; all in AHN, Est., leg. 3884, exped. 13.

commissioner to Kentucky to the new minister of the Indies, Antonio Valdés, who had replaced the recently deceased José de Gálvez. The confidential commissioner's announced duty was to gather information prior to the fixation of boundaries between Spanish and American territory, but his actual purpose was to recruit colonists for Louisiana.[15]

The Supreme Council of State took the most important action, however, by reviewing Spanish policy in the Mississippi Valley and rendering a number of decisions on August 9. First of all, it declared that two points were not negotiable: the Natchez District was to remain in Spanish hands regardless of where the boundary line was fixed, and the navigation of the Mississippi River was prohibited to other nations where both banks belonged to Spain. Beyond these two points, the Supreme Council accepted the petition of the 1,582 families, who were artisans or laborers, to come to the Natchez District, provided they swore loyalty and obedience to the Spanish government. In return their religion was to be tolerated, but only Catholics among them would enjoy public worship and receive civil and military employment. This decision opened up Louisiana and West Florida to all Americans who wished to emigrate there. The immigrants would be established on supervised settlements under the guidance of Irish priests who were to guide the conversion and assimilation of the Protestants. Spain also permitted Kentucky residents to trade with Louisiana under a 25 percent tariff in the hope of reducing tension in the Mississippi basin. Finally, the commissioner that Floridablanca had proposed earlier was to be sent to Kentucky.[16]

---

15. Ibid.; Floridablanca to Antonio Valdés, San Ildefonso, August 3, 1787, AHN, Est., leg. 3889, exped. 6.

16. (Valdés) to Floridablanca, San Ildefonso, August 9, 1787, ibid. The Court again approved the entry of American Catholic families in Louisiana and exempted them from paying the 6 percent duty on goods brought for their own consumption. Royal order to the governor of Louisiana, Madrid, July 14, 1787, ibid. For the post of commandant of the Natchez District, the Court considered the Irishman Henry White, sergeant major of the Fixed Infantry Regiment of Louisiana, who was then on a year's leave. However, the Court determined the post to be below his merit, and it later selected Lt. Col. Manuel Gayoso de Lemos. Royal order to the governor of Louisiana, San Lorenzo, November 3, 1787, AHN, Est., leg. 3899, exped. 5. Gayoso arrived in New Orleans on April 12, 1789. Miró to Valdés, New Orleans, May 20, 1789, AHN, Est., leg. 3901, exped. 3; Whitaker, *Spanish American Frontier*, 82. For a biography of

Doubtlessly, the actions of the Spanish Court pleased d'Argès. Since he viewed his role in Kentucky as that of a secret agent, he proposed establishing a code for private communication with the Court, using for this purpose the 1786 two-volume edition of *Novelas de Miguel Cervantes*. The Court demurred.[17] On August 19, Floridablanca officially informed the chevalier of the Supreme Council's decisions and that he had been selected as the commissioner to go to Kentucky. He was to leave from La Coruña, in northwestern Spain, for New York, where the Spanish *chargé d'affaires*, Diego de Gardoqui, would bring d'Argès up-to-date on recent developments on the frontier. The Frenchman was to collaborate with Gardoqui and follow his advice, as well as that of the Louisiana governor, in carrying out his commission. Floridablanca gave the chevalier 600 doubloons for expenses and informed him that he would receive more as the need arose. The title d'Argès bore was that of "chargé to reconnoiter the lands for the fixation of boundaries," which was purely honorific and carried no power. The Spanish government issued him no documents out of fear that his real mission to gather settlers might be compromised.[18]

Denying d'Argès documents was only one way the Court displayed its uncertainty about him. It also sent both Gardoqui and Miró lengthy instructions about the chevalier's duties and charged both of them to watch over his conduct. Floridablanca confided to Gardoqui that d'Argès was "a person who still is not well known." As a final measure of precaution, Gardoqui was free to send an associate with d'Argès to

---

Gayoso, see Jack D. L. Holmes, *Gayoso, The Life of a Spanish Governor in the Mississippi Valley, 1789-1799* (Baton Rouge: Louisiana State University Press for the Louisiana Historical Association, 1965).

17. D'Argès to Floridablanca, (San Ildefonso), August 16, 1787, AHN, Est., leg. 3889, exped. 6; *minuta*, with a marginal notation, ibid.

18. Floridablanca to d'Argès, San Ildefonso, August 19, 1787; Floridablanca to Valdés, San Ildefonso, August 20, 1787; both in ibid. Whitaker, in *Spanish American Frontier*, 83, believed that the d'Argès commission was designed to "encourage the secession of the American West." However, the documentation does not confirm this. While Floridablanca probably briefly mentioned conditions on the western frontier, intrigue was not a part of d'Argès's assignment.

Kentucky.[19] This last restraint on the chevalier provoked a bitter protest when he learned about it. However, his protest increased the Court's suspicions about him, and it insisted that an associate accompany him on his journey to the West.

One of the Supreme Council's decisions of August 9 had been the opening of the Mississippi River to Americans under a 25 percent tariff. However, Floridablanca subsequently felt that Spain should derive some advantage from it. Therefore, he informed Gardoqui that this privilege should be used as a bargaining point in his negotiations with the United States government. For d'Argès it meant that the river was to remain closed to the Americans until Gardoqui declared otherwise.[20] Floridablanca's decision deprived the chevalier of the dramatic announcement he had planned to make on the American frontier. In New York he would soon employ his complete resolve to obtain Gardoqui's consent to open the river.

Once Spanish policy had been agreed upon, final preparations were made for d'Argès's journey. He traveled to La Coruña in northwestern Spain on the post road, taking with him a servant and a third horse bearing his luggage.[21] On September 12, he sailed aboard the mail packet *Galveztown*. But after it departed, the vessel encountered storms that eventually forced its return to port fifteen days after weighing anchor. The tempests severely battered the brigantine and broke its main mast. Undaunted, the chevalier valiantly requested another ship. However, the delay in sailing meant that he could not reach Kentucky before winter set in; therefore, he asked the Court that Gardoqui furnish him with financial aid in New York.[22] In informing d'Argès that the Court

---

19. Royal order to Diego de Gardoqui, San Ildefonso, September 5, 1787; Valdés to the governor of Louisiana, San Ildefonso, August 23, 1787; d'Argès to Miguel Ottamendi, Madrid, August 22, 1787; (Ottamendi) to d'Argès, (n.p., n.d.); all in AHN, Est., leg. 3889, exped. 6.

20. Floridablanca to Gardoqui, no. 5, San Ildefonso, September 5, 1787, ibid. For Gardoqui's negotiations with the United States, see Bemis, *Pinckney's Treaty*, 60-108.

21. Royal order to the Director General de Correos, San Ildefonso, August 25, 1787; (royal order) to Pedro Lerena, August 25, 1787; (royal order) to Josef de la Quadra, (San Ildefonso), (n.d.); all in AHN, Est., leg. 3889, exped. 6.

22. D'Argès to Floridablanca, La Coruña, September 29, 1787; d'Argès to Ottamendi,

would do this, it reiterated that he follow instructions and not promise use of the Mississippi to westerners until Gardoqui informed him. Very carefully the Court repeated that the commissioner should proceed in agreement with the *chargé d'affaires* in New York.[23] As a precaution, the Spanish government alerted Gardoqui that d'Argès was impatient about proclaiming the Mississippi River open to commerce.[24]

Although the Court agreed that d'Argès should continue his journey on another ship, the *Galveztown* was quickly repaired. He sailed aboard it with the promise that he would obey his instructions with "scrupulous exactitude."[25] The Court denied his request for the military rank of lieutenant colonel, but it encouraged him to retain hope. His final instructions before leaving Spain informed him not to send all the families simultaneously. Once his work in Kentucky had been completed, he was to journey to New Orleans to consult with the governor on the way the families were to be established.[26]

The *Galveztown* sailed again in October and required nearly twelve weeks to cross the tempestuous Atlantic Ocean. However, the unpleasant voyage seemed not to have dampened the chevalier's spirits and aspirations. He had been fairly successful in getting his plans adopted at the Spanish Court. Now he must have believed that in the United States he would be freed from the intolerable restrictions placed on him. But unforeseen by d'Argès was the uncompromising obstinacy in New York displayed by Gardoqui who sought to further his own plans instead.

Two days after reaching the city, the chevalier sent Gardoqui a note requesting a meeting. In it d'Argès explained the nature of his commission and his intention to report to Spain on the formulation of a political and commercial policy for the American frontier. He made two proposals to Gardoqui. First, he asked that the chargé name him a confidential agent

---

La Coruña, September 29, 1787; both in ibid.

23. Royal order to d'Argès, San Ildefonso, October 6, 1787, ibid.

24. Royal order to Gardoqui, San Ildefonso, October 6, 1787, ibid.; Whitaker, *Spanish American Frontier*, 82.

25. D'Argès to Floridablanca, La Coruña, October 13, 1787, AHN, Est., leg. 3889, exped. 6.

26. *Minuta*, ibid.

sent from the Spanish Court to inspect frontier lands prior to a fixation of boundaries and to listen to complaints. Second, as an alternative to the first point, he believed it convenient to declare the Mississippi River open to commerce immediately as a favor to the western Americans.[27] D'Argès must have hoped that Gardoqui would accept one of his two proposals, but the chargé d'affaires was not caught unprepared.

Warned by the Court instructions that arrived with d'Argès, Gardoqui naturally refused to accede to the commissioner's demands. But the Spaniard dissembled his feelings so as not to alienate the chevalier. It must have given d'Argès encouragement because a week later he returned with new propositions to obtain his goals. The Frenchman's intention now was to journey to Fort Pitt, where he would work to calm the westerners angry about the Mississippi River's closure. He asked Gardoqui for 600 doubloons to cover his travel expenses. D'Argès believed it necessary to open the river to commerce to promote immigration and stimulate trade, but the Spanish official disagreed emphatically. As far as security was concerned, d'Argès regarded the Texas plains, which he had never seen, as an adequate barrier against further American expansion.[28]

Gardoqui, however, again rejected the new proposals. He reminded the chevalier that his obligation in Kentucky was to obtain immigrants and to disseminate news of the free Spanish lands downriver. For the Kentucky residents who preferred not to emigrate, the commissioner could insinuate that in the future the Mississippi might be opened to trade. As for the 600 doubloons d'Argès wanted, Gardoqui told him to expect only a monthly salary.[29]

---

27. D'Argès to Gardoqui, New York, January 19, 1788; Gardoqui to Floridablanca, New York, February 16, 1788; both in ibid. Gardoqui had already heard of d'Argès before his arrival in New York. The chargé had written earlier, "There is a person of the same [French] nation in Danville [Kentucky], Chevalier of St. Louis who lives in splendor and spends much so that common opinion states he is subsidized by his Government. He tried to go down the Mississippi to New Orleans but I denied him [permission], and I am following his movements though it is almost impossible at so great a distance & without communication or mail." Gardoqui to Floridablanca, New York, July 6, 1787, AHN, Est., leg. 3893.

28. D'Argès to Gardoqui, New York, January 27, 1788, AHN, Est., leg. 3889, exped. 6.

29. Gardoqui to d'Argès, New York, January 30, 1788, ibid.

Despite being rebuffed twice in his debates with Gardoqui, on January 30, the indefatigable d'Argès again put forth new proposals. He wanted to take his own route to the American frontier, one better and shorter, he contended, than the path Gardoqui had shown him on a map. D'Argès insisted on a salary advance of 600 doubloons. He also rebuked the chargé by declaring that in Spain he had been treated with more consideration and, as Gardoqui's associate, he was entitled to more respect. The chevalier wanted to select his own companion on his western journey and issue licenses to persons he deemed useful, if Gardoqui permitted him, so they might send their goods to New Orleans. Anticipating the chargé's rejection, d'Argès declared his intention to return to the Spanish Court, after receiving 200 doubloons, to explain why his commission had failed. If, however, Gardoqui wanted him to wait for further instructions in New York, he would accept a monthly stipend of 150 pesos.[30]

After several conferences with d'Argès, Gardoqui was exasperated and replied curtly to the latest impossible demands. He reiterated bluntly how inadmissible they were. He was willing to let d'Argès choose his own route as long as it was the shortest and cheapest way to the frontier. Gardoqui admitted his own financial problems inasmuch as he had not received funds since José de Gálvez died in the summer of 1787. Nevertheless, Gardoqui refused to countenance d'Argès's selection of his own traveling companion since it exceeded Court instructions.[31]

Finding the chargé intractable, the commissioner resorted to reasoning with him. Despite d'Argès realizing that his immediate task was to send settlers to Louisiana, he regarded as more important "tranquilizing" the Americans where they lived. For this purpose he wanted to open the Mississippi to commerce under a 25 percent duty. He further believed that the success of his commission hinged on choosing his own associate, and he needed at least 300 pesos to cover his expenses. He again insisted on opening the Mississippi River, which he declared had to be done soon. If it was not, he wanted permission to allow certain persons to use the river in order to achieve "the other ends mentioned." D'Argès did not clarify the meaning of this statement, but no doubt it was

30. Gardoqui to d'Argès, New York, February 1, 1788, ibid.

31. Ibid.

a veiled reference to securing the confidence of Americans with separatist views. Sensing that Gardoqui would again decline his proposals, d'Argès once more offered to wait in New York for new instructions from Spain with a monthly salary of 150 pesos.[32]

When he wrote again on February 4, Gardoqui amenably made concessions to d'Argès. The chevalier could choose his own route to the west, and Gardoqui reluctantly permitted him to choose his own traveling companion. The chargé also agreed to a 300-peso salary advance, but he went no farther. He refused to give d'Argès the powers he wanted, and he reminded the Frenchman of his instructions. Then Gardoqui added that, inasmuch as the western rivers were then frozen, it was preferable that d'Argès journey on the *Galveztown* to New Orleans, where he could present his proposals to Miró in person. The chargé's suggestion carried the weight of an order.[33]

D'Argès must now have sensed a complete failure in his discussions with Gardoqui, and he meekly expressed his desire to obey the advice. Although he initially declined the Spaniard's offer of money, on February 23, shortly before leaving New York, he asked for and received 150 pesos. D'Argès stated that when he arrived in New Orleans, he would request permission to retire from Spanish service; he no longer considered himself useful.[34] While his discussions with Gardoqui frustrated d'Argès deeply, nevertheless a spark of hope still lingered deep within him that he could reach Kentucky by ascending the Mississippi River and commence his commission as outlined by the Court.

The voyage from New York to Cuba gave d'Argès time to regret his lack of discretion and some of the discord he engendered in talking with Gardoqui. In writing to Floridablanca from Havana, d'Argès regarded Gardoqui uninformed about the west; the Frenchman's attempt to discuss conditions on the frontier with the chargé had met with frigid

32. D'Argès to Gardoqui, New York, February 3, 1788, ibid.

33. Gardoqui to d'Argès, New York, February 4, 1788, ibid. D'Argès later declared that from his third day in New York, Gardoqui suggested to him orally to journey to Louisiana. D'Argès to Floridablanca, Havana, March 27, 1788, ibid.

34. D'Argès to Gardoqui, New York, February 5, 1788; Gardoqui to d'Argès, New York, February 6 and 20, 1788; Gardoqui to Floridablanca, New York, April 18, 1788; all in ibid.

silence. D'Argès felt that Gardoqui's inflexible position prevented him from fulfilling his commission according to his own ideas. He complained about his lack of documents and Gardoqui's unreasonable attempt to impose an outsider on him as an associate. Nevertheless, the chevalier carefully omitted reference to his desire to proclaim the Mississippi River open to trade immediately. Although he consented to go to New Orleans because he found agreement with Gardoqui impossible, d'Argès nurtured the hope of procuring the immigrant families. Before leaving New York, he sent word to Kentucky that the Spanish government was prepared to accept settlers. He again repeated his intention to retire from Spanish service once he completed his commission.[35]

Gardoqui also justified his position in dispatches written to Floridablanca and Miró. In opposing the commissioner, the chargé adhered to Court instructions, which suited his plans fully. Besides his frustrated negotiations with the United States government to obtain a fair treaty and boundary settlement, Gardoqui was aware of the separatist sentiment in American frontier regions. From 1786 he had conversed with James White about secessionist fervor in the Cumberland District of North Carolina. Gardoqui refused to sacrifice any of his spade work in this area to the ambitions of an obscure Frenchman whose motives were unknown.[36] The chargé regarded the d'Argès commission to obtain settlers as easy to accomplish; in his opinion, it sufficed to grant the Americans religious freedom. Numerous individuals had already approached him with offers to conduct immigrants to Louisiana. He probably rightly concluded that if the Mississippi River were opened, as d'Argès wanted, numerous Kentuckians would not immigrate to Spanish territory.[37]

D'Argès's behavior in New York also made Gardoqui thoroughly suspicious, especially the commissioner's insistence on powers that

35. D'Argès to Floridablanca, Havana, March 27, 1788; ibid.

36. Gardoqui to Floridablanca, New York, October 28, 1786, AHN, Est., leg. 3893, exped. 2.

37. Gardoqui to Floridablanca, New York, February 16, 1788, AHN, Est., leg. 3889, exped. 6. For immigration proposals that Gardoqui was receiving at this time, see Gilbert C. Din, "Proposals and Plans for Colonization in Spanish Louisiana, 1787-1790," *Louisiana History* 11 (Summer 1970): 197-213; and Gardoqui to Floridablanca, New York, April 18, 1788, AHN, Est., leg. 3889, exped. 6.

exceeded his instructions. The chargé described the Frenchman as egotistical, impertinent, contradictory, and inarticulate when confronted with probing questions. Gardoqui learned from private sources that several years before d'Argès had lived extravagantly in Kentucky, and he insinuated that an influential person had confided that many westerners considered d'Argès to be a French agent. Gardoqui purposely declined to talk to the chevalier about conditions in the American West, nor did he want d'Argès to learn anything about the fluid situation there. The chargé dismissed the commissioner's knowledge of the frontier as superficial and obtained from old newspapers.[38] To Miró, Gardoqui confided that the chevalier was a landowner in Kentucky, and his desire to open the Mississippi was merely to increase the value of his land, an objective other speculators sought.[39] However, the chargé's last accusation was unsubstantiated, and d'Argès's real motive remains unclear.

While the Frenchman journeyed by sea to Louisiana, Governor Miró in New Orleans learned from the Court about d'Argès's commission. He found the news distressing because it conflicted with his own plans, which he had laid out the year before.[40] In the summer of 1787, the former brigadier general James Wilkinson of Kentucky arrived in New Orleans with his separatist proposal that was written into his memorial

---

38. Gardoqui to Floridablanca, New York, February 16 and April 18, 1788, ibid. Whitaker, *Spanish American Frontier*, 86-88, states that Gardoqui was envious of d'Argès and sabotaged his commission to continue his intrigues with James White. The Court informed Gardoqui that the Spanish government's aim was to obtain immigrants and encourage the American creation of an independent state in the west that was friendly toward Spain and function as a barrier between Spanish and English possessions. Or it could later join Spain in an alliance or enter the Spanish Empire. Floridablanca to Gardoqui, Aranjuez, May 24, 1788, AHN, Est., leg. 3889, exped. 6. This statement from the Court appears to indicate that it had received James Wilkinson's proposal of September 1787, with Miró's endorsement. Gardoqui informed the Court that d'Argès was not personally suited to deal with western intrigue. Gardoqui to Floridablanca, New York, July 25, 1788, AHN, Est., leg. 3893, exped. 3.

39. Gardoqui to Miró, New York, February 21, 1788, AHN, Est., leg. 3889, exped. 6. Whitaker, in *Spanish American Frontier*, 87, states that Gardoqui's dispatch was designed to delay d'Argès in New Orleans. Actually, it was Miró's plans that stopped d'Argès.

40. Miró to Valdés, New Orleans, January 8, 1788, AHN, Est., leg. 3888bis.

in September.[41] A second project by Wilkinson, that was really Miró's, called for allowing American immigration to Spanish lands.[42] After the brigadier's proposals were sent to Spain, Miró spent many anxious months waiting for a favorable reply from the Court. Instead, in January 1788, came the royal order about d'Argès. Miró immediately opposed it for fear it might jeopardize Wilkinson's main objective—the separation of the American West, which the governor regarded as fundamental to the defense of Louisiana and Mexico. He similarly regretted the Court's decision to open the Mississippi River to trade subject to a 25 percent tariff, and he informed Madrid that Wilkinson had been emphatic about keeping the river closed if his separatist plot was to succeed. Moreover immigration, too, would suffer. Miró endorsed Wilkinson's plan to grant commercial privileges to only a few influential individuals in Kentucky. As for conceding religious freedom to immigrants, the governor regarded it as unnecessary and on his own authority disallowed it. Miró declared it possible to populate the province merely by promising the Americans that they would not be required to become Catholic. He preferred to give American immigrants the same conditions that prevailed for the Anglo-Americans of West Florida. Finally, he rejected the Court notion that trade with Kentucky would create prosperity in Louisiana and that many merchants would soon flock there. Instead, Miró asserted that Louisiana's produce reached only a small market, and that an increase in exports from New Orleans would be detrimental to the markets of other Spanish provinces. These contentions demonstrated Miró's inadequate understanding of the dynamics of economics. If given a choice, the governor would suspend the d'Argès project until the Court decided

---

41. Of the extensive literature on James Wilkinson, see William R. Shepherd, "Wilkinson and the Beginnings of the Spanish Conspiracy," *American Historical Review* 11 (April 1904): 490-506; Bemis, *Pinckney's Treaty*, 121-24; Whitaker, *Spanish American Frontier*, 96-119; James Ripley Jacobs, *Tarnished Warrior, Major-General James Wilkinson* (Freeport, N.Y.: Books for Libraries Press, 1972 rpt.), and Andro Linklater, *An Artist in Treason: The Extraordinary Double Life of General James Wilkinson* (New York: Walker Publishing Company, 2009). Wilkinson's original memorial, New Orleans, September 3, 1787, is in Archivo General de Indias (Seville), Papeles procedentes de Cuba (hereafter cited as AGI, PC), leg. 2373.

42. Din, "Immigration Policy of Miró," 165. Compare Wilkinson's views on immigration to those of Miró and d'Argès mentioned in n.4.

on Wilkinson. However, because Miró believed the Frenchman was in Kentucky, he promised to work with him.[43] Therefore, Miró alerted Commandant Carlos de Grand-Pré at Fort Panmure in Natchez of the impending deluge of immigrants.[44]

But as the weeks progressed, no word of d'Argès came down the Mississippi. Not even Wilkinson, Miró's eyes and ears in Kentucky, mentioned the chevalier in his letters.[45] On April 20, however, much to Miró's amazement, the commissioner disembarked in New Orleans after a thirteen-day crossing from Havana. With him came all of Gardoqui's correspondence. It gave the governor the upper hand in dealing with the Frenchman, who now seemed to want no more than to fulfill his commission. D'Argès's opportune arrival by sea permitted Miró to stop him until the Court rendered a verdict on the Wilkinson proposal.[46]

43. Miró to Valdés, New Orleans, January 8, 1788, AHN, Est., leg. 3888bis. Miró declared that if Kentucky became a part of the Spanish Empire, then religious freedom should remain because it already existed there; but there was no need to grant it in Louisiana. Miró also claimed that d'Argès never mentioned his petition from the 1,582 families in 1786; but Intendant Martín Navarro, in his report affirmed that d'Argès had mentioned it. Navarro, Madrid, November 11, 1788, ibid.

44. Miró to Carlos de Grand-Pré, New Orleans, February 2, 1788; March 21, 1788, AGI, PC, leg. 6. Miró's proclamation in English inviting immigrants to Louisiana is in AGI, PC, leg. 2373. Land which the settlers would receive varied from 240 to 800 arpents, depending on how many workers or slaves the recipients had. Immigrants were not to be forced to become Catholics, but only Catholicism would have public worship. Miró to Grand-Pré, New Orleans, February 20, 1788, ibid. In the oath that immigrants were required to take, they had to promise vassalage, obey Spanish laws, give immediate warning of invasion, and take up arms at the first call from the authorities. Miró to Valdés, New Orleans, March 21, 1788, ibid. Miró opened up Louisiana and West Florida to immigration, but prohibited Kentucky residents from trading with the Spanish provinces. (Miró) to Manuel Pérez, New Orleans, May 12, 1788, AGI, PC, leg. 120.

45. Miró to Gardoqui, New Orleans, March 24, 1788, AGI, PC, leg. 104A; Miró and Navarro to Valdés, New Orleans, April 11, 1788, AHN, Est., leg. 3888bis. On learning about the clash between Gardoqui and d'Argès in New York, the Court ordered the latter to adhere to his instructions. The Louisiana governor was informed about the change in d'Argès's itinerary. Royal order to the governor of Louisiana, Aranjuez, May 28, 1788; Floridablanca to Valdés, Aranjuez, May 27, 1788; both in AHN, Est., leg. 3888bis.

46. Miró to Valdés, New Orleans, May 15, 1788, AHN, Est., leg. 3888bis. Whitaker,

To detain the commissioner, the governor used the pretext of the duty the immigrants were to pay on goods they intended to sell in Louisiana. The only merchandise allowed free entry at that time were work tools and goods settlers brought for their own use; but merchandise they obtained from selling their homes and lands had to be taxed at 25 percent. Miró regarded the tariff as detrimental to immigration since it favored the entrance of propertyless individuals. Therefore, he had requested the Court to lower the duty to 6 percent, and he convinced the Frenchman that he expected supplemental royal instructions momentarily. Once they arrived, d'Argès could proceed and offer prospective immigrants a greater inducement for relocating.[47]

D'Argès found Miró's explanation reasonable and New Orleans congenial, and he soon behaved like a new man. The governor's gentle demeanor helped him to recover much of his former zeal and enthusiasm, and Miró never mentioned the unpleasantness that had occurred in New York. The commissioner appeared to accept his role as an immigration agent, and he no longer unleashed the feisty demands that had alienated Gardoqui. Miró consulted d'Argès periodically and made him feel useful. In fact, so able was the governor that the chevalier did not suspect he was being purposely detained. However, after talking with several persons in New Orleans, d'Argès discovered that Wilkinson's visit had been for reasons other than trade, as Miró had informed him. The commissioner ascertained more about the controversy raging in Kentucky over separation from the United States. He now deduced that this was the reason behind Gardoqui's refusal to declare him a person of confidence. D'Argès shrewdly grasped that the dissention in Kentucky afforded the Spaniards with an opportunity that should not be dissipated.[48]

---

in *Spanish American Frontier*, 88, states that Miró's reason for stopping d'Argès was to promote the governor's intrigue "from which he hoped to win promotion and perhaps undying fame." Whitaker exaggerates the venality of Spanish officials, and he erroneously declared that d'Argès arrived in New Orleans in May.

47. Miró to Valdés, New Orleans, May 15, 1788, AHN, Est., leg. 3888bis; d'Argès to Floridablanca, New Orleans, May 22, 1788, ibid. On trade in Louisiana, see Arthur P. Whitaker, "The Commerce of Louisiana and the Floridas at the End of the Eighteenth Century," *Hispanic American Historical Review* 8 (May 1928): 190-203.

48. D'Argès to Floridablanca, New Orleans, May 22, 1788, AHN, Est., leg. 3889,

He initially waited patiently and tried to be useful. In June he sent a letter to Col. Richard Anderson in Kentucky to inform the families that the Spanish government had agreed to grant them lands near Natchez.[49] But by August, d'Argès had tired of waiting and asked permission to begin his commission. Although Miró did not have authorization to detain him, he refused to permit him to leave.[50] He dismissed the chevalier as having only questionable value since his plans called for Wilkinson to send immigrants. Despite Miró's belief that Floridablanca had spoken confidentially to d'Argès about conditions in Kentucky, he tenaciously refused to divulge anything about Wilkinson's designs. Notwithstanding the commissioner's sincerity, Miró assumed that no harm would come from detaining him.[51]

Prevented from proceeding with his commission, on August 12, d'Argès requested the governor's consent to journey during the winter to Martinique. Four mail packets had arrived without bearing new orders, and it was now too late in the season to commence the trip upstream.

---

exped. 6. Miró did not treat d'Argès well in the payment of his salary. In June the chevalier asked for 300 pesos, which Miró refused to supply immediately. Although the Spanish government authorized d'Argès a salary of 100 pesos monthly from January 1, 1788, and assumed costs for his travel expenses while in government service, Miró frugally paid him only from February 1, 1788, and deducted the 100 pesos for the cost of his voyage from Havana to New Orleans. Miró to Valdés, New Orleans, June 15, 1788; royal order to the governor of Louisiana, Aranjuez, May 28, 1788; Miró to Valdés, New Orleans, August 7, 1788; all in AHN, Est., leg. 3888bis. The Crown approved Miró's actions. Royal order to the governor-intendant of Louisiana, August 10, 1789, ibid.

49. D'Argès to (Floridablanca), New Orleans, June 17, 1788; d'Argès to Col. Richard Anderson, New Orleans, June 15, 1788; both in AHN, Est., leg. 3889, exped. 6. D'Argès's letter was entrusted to Maj. Isaac Dunn, a confident of Wilkinson, and that makes it doubtful that the letter ever reached Anderson.

50. Miró to Floridablanca, New Orleans, August 17, 1788, ibid. Floridablanca, in his letter to d'Argès on May 25, 1788, confirmed the chevalier's commission and authorized him to proceed. This was done several months after the Wilkinson proposal had been received in Spain. Royal order to d'Argès, Aranjuez, May 28, 1788, AHN, Est., leg. 3889, exped. 6. In ibid., see Miró to Valdés, New Orleans, August 7, 1788.

51. Miró to Valdés, New Orleans, June 18, 1788, AHN, Est., leg. 3888bis. Miró stated that immigrants then arriving at Natchez knew nothing about d'Argès, and the governor added, "so that still no word has come from don Pedro Wouves d'Argès to promote immigration."

The chevalier requested a monthly salary of 250 pesos while traveling and waiting.⁵²

The prolonged delay in getting new instructions from the Court irritated Miró considerably. Seemingly d'Argès had not given cause for offense, but Miró lost his earlier composure and now reminded the Frenchman of his deplorable behavior in New York that had forced him to come to New Orleans. The governor repeated the desirability to wait for new orders. Since he had informed the Court that d'Argès was currently detained in New Orleans, Miró felt that he could not permit him to go up river. Nevertheless, the governor consented to the chevalier's absence until February if d'Argès waited for one more mail shipment before departing. Thus if orders came, he still had time to leave for Upper Louisiana and begin his commission from there in the spring. As for salary, Miró declared that he could only provide the commissioner with the Court-authorized one hundred pesos per month.⁵³

D'Argès agreed to wait for the additional mail boat. But if instructions did not arrive, he intended to take the first ship headed for Martinique and return in March.⁵⁴ To Floridablanca in Spain, the chevalier complained of the meagerness of his allowance, and he requested the rank of army colonel for himself.⁵⁵ Since the September mail packet failed to bring the desired orders, d'Argès informed Miró on September 30, that he was ready to depart for Martinique.⁵⁶ Nonetheless, deprived of the proper transportation his sojourn in New Orleans continued. In January he decided to leave for Guarico (Cap Français, Saint-Domingue). The same month, he wrote to Floridablanca that the immigrant families had come as far as Louisville, but they refused to go farther for fear the conditions

---

52. D'Argès to Miró, New Orleans, August 12, 1788, AHN, Est., leg. 3889, exped. 6.

53. Miró to d'Argès, New Orleans, August 13, 1788, AHN, Est., leg. 3888bis.

54. D'Argès to Miró, New Orleans, August 21, 1788, AHN, Est., leg. 3889, exped. 6.

55. Miró to Valdés, New Orleans, August 28, 1788, AHN, Est., leg. 3888bis; d'Argès to Floridablanca, New Orleans, August 27, 1788, AHN, Est., leg. 3889, exped. 6. D'Argès explained in his request for promotion that he had been a captain since July 30, 1758, which made him the oldest captain in that part of the world.

56. D'Argès to Miró, New Orleans, September 30, 1788, AHN, Est., leg. 3889, exped. 6.

they had sought earlier had not been granted. Repeated messages from Miró and himself had failed to convince them.[57] The commissioner's last statement was highly suspicious. Miró never mentioned any exchange of messages with d'Argès's immigrants in Kentucky, which he surely would have done had it taken place.

By February, the chevalier's presence in New Orleans had become an embarrassment to Miró who now wanted him gone. Gardoqui had informed him that James White of Cumberland would arrive shortly. White was attempting to induce the Cumberland residents to join Spain. Miró disbelieved it prudent for d'Argès to remain in New Orleans when White was there. In fact, the governor never wanted to see the Frenchman again and informed him that if instructions came while he was in Guarico, he could proceed directly to Philadelphia, and from there journey to Kentucky. In February, after ten fruitless months in New Orleans, the commissioner sailed for Guarico with his commission not only unfulfilled but uncommenced.[58] He would not again step foot in Louisiana.

Soon after d'Argès departed, the instructions Miró had long awaited reached New Orleans on February 25, 1789. The royal order of December 1, 1788, suspended the d'Argès commission and permitted Miró to continue with the Wilkinson project. However, the Court wanted d'Argès to be employed in some useful way.[59] Accordingly, a week later Miró wrote to the chevalier to inform him in part of the new orders. Kentucky residents could trade with Louisiana, paying only a 15 percent duty, and immigrants were exempted from taxes on the goods

57. D'Argès to Floridablanca, New Orleans, January 2 and 20, 1789, ibid.

58. Miró to Valdés, New Orleans, February 12, 1789, AHN, Est., leg. 3888bis.

59. Royal order to the governor of Louisiana, Madrid, December 1, 1788, ibid. Eugenio de Laguna, in a *minuta* of December 1, 1788, stated that d'Argès was not to be abandoned, and suitable employment for him was to be found elsewhere. Ibid. After debating immigration policy all through 1788 and hearing ex-intendant Navarro (Navarro to Valdés, Madrid, November 11, 1788, ibid.), the Supreme Council of State made its determination on policy for the Mississippi Valley on November 20, 1788. Ibid. It did not accept Wilkinson's first proposal for the separation of Kentucky from the United States; instead, Spain would delay acting until Kentucky had freed itself from the United States.

they brought with them. Settlers would receive free lands and not be molested in their private religious beliefs. The governor anticipated that vast numbers of immigrants would soon descend on Lower Louisiana and populate both banks of the Mississippi River. He assured d'Argès that he could be of valuable assistance in their settlement. Miró offered him the position of commandant of the new post to be created at l'Ance à la Graisse (today's New Madrid), located below the mouth of the Ohio River and on the opposite bank. He would have the rank of lieutenant colonel and salary of one hundred pesos monthly. From this post, d'Argès was to promote immigration in Illinois and guard against an American invasion of Louisiana. If the Court approved Miró's plan, d'Argès was to return to Louisiana by August.[60] At the same time, the governor wrote to Wilkinson in Kentucky to direct some families to settle at l'Ance à la Graisse.[61] However, Miró's efforts regarding d'Argès were in vain.

When the Frenchman received the governor's offer, he was neither pleased by the news nor enticed by the terms of employment. On June 17, d'Argès answered Miró's letter of March 4. He stated that his fifty-years of age prohibited him from accepting command of such a secluded corner as l'Ance à la Graisse, where no house existed for forty leagues around. The rigors and inconveniences of life there were excessive for him. D'Argès was amenable, nevertheless, from his residence in New Orleans to visit the families who settled on the Mississippi periodically, provided he received the rank of colonel. But for the present, d'Argès haughtily declared that he had business and family matters to attend to in Paris.[62] From the French capital on August 21, he directed a final message to Floridablanca, with news that when his affairs concluded in two and a half months, he was prepared to return to New Orleans to begin work.[63] Perhaps unknown to him, it was d'Argès's last letter on

60. Miró to d'Argès, New Orleans, March 4, 1789, AHN, Est., leg. 3889, exped. 6; Miró to Floridablanca, New Orleans, March 15, 1789, AHN, Est., leg. 3888bis.

61. Miró to Wilkinson, New Orleans, March 1, 1789, AGI, PC, leg. 174A.

62. D'Argès to (Miró), Guarico, Saint Domingue, March 26, 1789, AGI, PC, leg. 120; d'Argès to Miró, Guarico, Saint Domingue, June 17, 1789, AHN, Est., leg. 3889, exped. 6. In the June letter, d'Argès mentioned a message from Miró dated May 6, 1789, which the author failed to find in the Spanish archives.

63. D'Argès to Floridablanca, Paris, August 21, 1789, AHN, Est., leg. 3889, exped. 6.

immigrants. Possibly the French Revolution that erupted that summer redirected his attention to matters closer to home. In any case, no more was heard from him.

Although d'Argès's services for the Spanish government came to naught, uncertainty remains among historians and others as to who the eccentric Frenchman was and what his true intentions were. It does not appear likely that he was a French spy, as Gardoqui stated in 1787 and as Wilkinson hinted in 1789, when he wrote to Miró attempting to discredit d'Argès.[64] On several occasions, the former general's insane jealousy compelled him to attempt to destroy anyone who might interfere with his plans.[65] The accusations by Gardoqui and Wilkinson, however, cannot be taken seriously since both of them did not want d'Argès to interfere with their intrigues. Had the chevalier been a French agent, he would doubtlessly have deported himself with greater circumspection and not been so quarrelsome; certainly he would have avoided the clash with Gardoqui that prevented the commissioner from reaching Kentucky.

While he cannot be branded a French spy, it seems very likely that d'Argès was an opportunist and an adventurer. It was extremely unlikely that he possessed a petition from 1,582 families as he alleged.[66] Nor was

---

D'Argès informed Floridablanca that he was writing a new memorial which he would present to him upon its conclusion. It, however, does not appear to be in the Spanish archives.

64. Wilkinson to Miró, Lexington, Kentucky, February 12, 1789, AHN, Est., leg. 3888bis. Wilkinson declared about d'Argès, "I am well informed that for years the Court of Versailles has been collecting information on this Country, and that it would pay a high price to recover its first possessions on the Mississippi. About the year 1785 a Knight of St. Louis called D'Arges came to the Falls of the Ohio, he called himself a Naturalist, and that his occupation was to inquire about the curious productions of this Country, but his style of living contradicted his story; he had few friends, he stayed apart, and in a year that he was here he never went more than two leagues from the town of Louisville where he lived." Wilkinson also pointed out that d'Argès has close connections with French officials in the United States.

65. Wilkinson's attempt to demolish George Morgan's colonization scheme is in Wilkinson to Miró, Lexington, Kentucky, February 14, 1789, AHN, Est., leg. 3888bis; and Wilkinson's effort to do the same to his former confederate Benjamin Sebastian is in Wilkinson to Miró, Louisville, February 6, 1791, AGI, PC, leg. 2374.

66. During this period several persons promoting immigration projects stated

his information about the Mississippi Valley original. In New York he relied upon old newspapers to provide some knowledge, as Gardoqui had contended; in New Orleans, Miró and Navarro served as his sources and inspirations for the memorials he subsequently presented in France and Spain. Only in Europe was d'Argès's intelligence deemed valuable while in North America it was dismissed as common knowledge. It was a small wonder that both Gardoqui and Miró did not regard stopping him as detrimental to Spain's interests. Furthermore, in North America d'Argès showed that his temperament was ill-suited to act as a confidential agent in Kentucky.

Despite the commissioner's failure to reach the American West, the real importance of his role should not be overlooked. From the conclusion of the war against Great Britain in North America in 1783, Spain sought a policy for the Mississippi Valley that would allow it to retain the advantages it had won in the war. Louisiana, however, was a vast ground practically devoid of European settlers. On the other hand, the western American settlements were growing rapidly and refusing to accept Spain's monopoly of the Mississippi River. Instead, they angrily demanded that the river be opened to them and growingly threatened to invade Louisiana if it was not done. Against this menace, Spain's effort to build up Louisiana's defenses failed to achieve satisfactory results. When d'Argès came along in 1787 with his petition, he provided the Spanish Court with a new option—American immigration for the defense of Louisiana. Floridablanca, Valdés, and Aranda recognized the opportunity and immediately seized it. Not to accept American immigration might well result in the loss of the province to the same people in a war. That d'Argès did not fulfill his commission to acquire the Kentucky families did not really matter; with the change in immigration policy and a new relationship toward the western Americans, his work was done. Lastly,

---

grandiosely that they each could introduce thousands of settlers. Among them were George Morgan who claimed he could bring several thousand industrious persons (George Morgan to Gardoqui, Prospect, New Jersey, August 30, 1788, AHN, Est., leg. 3894); Peter Paulus who asserted he would bring 3,000 families ("Memorial of Peter Paulus," New Orleans, March 6, 1789, AHN, Est., leg. 3888bis); and Baron Frederick von Steuben envisioned a settlement of 4,200 persons (Gardoqui to Floridablanca, New York, October 18, 1788, AHN, Est., leg. 3893bis).

it must be acknowledged that had d'Argès not come along the Spanish government probably would soon have adopted the same position as a consequence of the Wilkinson memorial and Miró's influence in it promoting American immigration. However, with the information that d'Argès acquired from the governor and intendant in New Orleans, he became the catalyst that produced a new policy a year earlier than would otherwise have happened.

Chapter 6
Spain's Immigration Policy in Louisiana and the American Penetration, 1792-1803

"I wish a hundred thousand of our inhabitants would accept the invitation. It may be the means of delivering to us peaceably what may otherwise cost a war."[1] With these words, Thomas Jefferson, writing to President George Washington, greeted the Spanish invitation of 1788 to Anglo-Americans to settle in Louisiana. This change in Spanish policy signaled the beginning of Anglo-American penetration of Louisiana. Because settlement with Spaniards and European Catholics had proved too costly, Spain resorted to Anglo-American colonization. The government planned to Hispanize these settlers who entered the province, convert them to Catholicism, and instill in them loyalty so that they would defend the colony against all invaders—even those from the United States.[2] However, the implementation of this new and potentially dangerous policy required an era of peace, and peace did not exist in that region during the 1790s. Instead, Louisiana experienced numerous crises as the French, British, and Anglo-Americans menaced the province. Concurrently, the rapid growth of the western settlements of the United States brought their inhabitants closer to Louisiana. As some of them entered the colony and many others left behind threatened to inundate it, apprehensive Spanish officials began to doubt whether Anglo-Americans

---

1. This article first appeared in the *Southwestern Historical Quarterly* 76 (January 1973): 255-76. The quotation is from Isaac Joslin Cox, "The New Invasion of the Goths and Vandals," *Proceedings of the Mississippi Valley Historical Association* 8 (1914-1915), 183.

2. On Spanish immigration policy in Louisiana before 1792, see Gilbert C. Din, "The Immigration Policy of Governor Esteban Miró in Spanish Louisiana," *Southwestern Historical Quarterly* 73 (October 1969): 155-75; and Mattie Austin Hatcher, "The Louisiana Background of the Colonization of Texas, 1763-1803," *Southwestern Historical Quarterly* 24 (January 1921): 169-94.

in Louisiana and West Florida would protect the provinces against attack from the United States. As early as 1792, Louisiana governors, who also governed West Florida, sought ways to augment the colonies' non-American population. For a decade local authorities struggled with the question of Anglo-American immigration and promoted colonization schemes to increase loyal inhabitants in the province. In the end, Spain averted the war Jefferson thought might come when it retroceded Louisiana to France, which in turn soon sold it to the United States.[3]

The changed and defensive attitude toward Anglo-American colonization in Louisiana and West Florida began immediately after Francisco Luis Héctor, Baron de Carondelet, became governor of these provinces on December 30, 1791, replacing Esteban Miró.[4] Only two weeks after assuming the governorship, he recommended to Madrid encouraging Europeans to come to Louisiana and, contrary to earlier Spanish policy against making expenditures to introduce immigrants, he urged their assistance in settlement beyond being given free lands, a liberal commercial policy, and religious tolerance. While the Baron did not suggest stopping Anglo-American immigration—believing it impossible to do—he and subsequent governors were concerned about being outnumbered by what they increasingly regarded as a subversive element.[5] Thus with Carondelet, immigration policy emphasized securing

---

3. Spain retroceded to France only that territory it had received from France in 1763. Officials in the United States, particularly Thomas Jefferson tried to buy West Florida, which Spain refused to sell, and later he insisted that West Florida constituted a part of the Louisiana Purchase, a contention Spain rejected. American historians of the Borderlands have generally accepted the Spanish point of view, but United States historians have taken diverse views, often accepting Jefferson's and James Madison's tenuous arguments.

4. Arthur Preston Whitaker, *The Spanish American Frontier, 1783-1795: The Westward Movement and the Spanish Retreat in the Mississippi Valley* (1927; repr., Gloucester, Mass: Peter Smith, 1962), 162, states that Spanish policy against permitting Anglo-Americans to enter Louisiana changed as a result of the French terror and a reactionary government in Spain. On the contrary, archival documentation clearly indicates that Governor Carondelet initiated it. See also Lawrence Kinnaird, "American Penetration into Spanish Louisiana," in *New Spain and the Anglo-American West*, 2 vols. (Los Angeles: privately printed, 1932), 1: 220.

5. Baron de Carondelet to the Conde de Floridablanca, New Orleans, January 13,

a loyal European Catholic population, one that was more compatible with Spanish rule and monarchical government.

Through the spring of 1792, Governor Carondelet continued to promote the immigration policy he believed was best suited to the colonies in his charge. He issued announcements that favored the admittance of *émigrés* fleeing the French Revolution, and Irish, Flemish, and German immigrants. When he learned that large numbers of these people were arriving in the United States, he exhorted the Court to bring them to Louisiana and advised making "small expenditures," such as furnishing their transportation from New Madrid in Upper Louisiana to their new homes down river, and supplying them with food and seed. He believed that once the first settlers were established, the malicious falsehoods about the tyranny of the Spanish government would dissipate. The governor feared that Anglo-Americans would swarm into Louisiana and seize it without "unsheathing the sword." He scoffed at the oaths of allegiance they took upon settling in the province, stating that despite the oaths they could easily turn against Spain. Because of their unreliability, Carondelet began to exert every effort to impede their settlement on the west bank of the Mississippi and admit them with moderation on the east bank only.[6] In accordance with this aim, he stopped the projected settlement of Alexander Fowler on the Maramec River in Upper Louisiana, but he still allowed Anglo-Americans to settle on the Amite River in Lower Louisiana.[7]

1792, Archivo Histórico Nacional (Madrid), Estado, legajo (hereafter abbreviated as AHN, Est., leg.), 3898, no. 1 reserved; Carondelet to Floridablanca, no. 9 reserved, New Orleans, February 25, 1792, Biblioteca Nacional (Madrid), Sección de Manuscritos, "Documentos de la Luisiana," 3 vols. Gov. Manuel Gayoso de Lemos of the Natchez District advised Floridablanca that it was impossible to prevent Americans from entering Louisiana. Gayoso to Floridablanca, no. 4 reserved, New Orleans, January 26, 1792, AHN, Est., leg. 3902. On Carondelet's character, see Whitaker, *Spanish American Frontier*, 153-56; and Gilbert C. Din, "Francisco Luis Hector, Baron de Carondelet," in *American National Biography*, 24 vols. (New York: Oxford University Press:1999), 4: 423-25.

6. Carondelet to Floridablanca, no. 9 reserved, New Orleans, February 25, 1792; Carondelet to the Conde de Aranda, no. 1 reserved, June 10, 1792; both in AHN, Est., leg. 3898.

7. Lawrence Kinnaird, ed., *Spain in the Mississippi Valley, 1765-1794*, 3 Parts

In order to attract European immigrants in the United States to Louisiana, the governor dispatched two agents there. The first to leave was Capt. Henri Peyroux de la Coudrenière, who in 1785 had arrived with the Acadian families from France. On April 6, 1792, Peyroux received a copy of the conditions under which French, German, Irish, and Flemish immigrants would be admitted in the province. Soon he departed for Philadelphia aboard the *Amable María* with the promise of promotion to lieutenant colonel and an increase in salary if he was successful in his commission.[8]

Meanwhile in Philadelphia, the Spanish ministers to the United States, José de Jáudenes and José Ignacio de Viar, were discreetly attempting to direct French royalists and German and Dutch Catholics to Louisiana. They purposely avoided advertising in the city's newspapers for fear of offending the United States government. With the arrival of Peyroux, they believed that a general exodus of persons bound for Louisiana would begin if the Crown provided their transportation and if Anglo-American merchants were permitted to send merchandise to Louisiana.[9]

Once in Philadelphia, Captain Peyroux went to work. He hired a brigantine to take colonists to New Orleans. But when Jáudenes and Viar learned that the ship carried only twenty-five immigrants while taking

---

(Washington, DC: GPO, 1946-1949), 3: xxv-xxvi. Fowler's project is described in "A Royal Invitation to the Industrious," ibid., 46-51. For Carondelet's instructions to stop the settlement, see Carondelet to Lt. Gov. Zenon Trudeau of Upper Louisiana, New Orleans, June 8, 1792, ibid., 51-52. See also "Carondelet: Instructions to Trudeau, New Orleans, March 28, 1792," in Abraham P. Nasatir, ed., *Before Lewis and Clark: Documents Illustrating the History of the Missouri, 1785-1804*, 2 vols. (St. Louis: St. Louis Historical Society, 1952), 1: 152.

8. "Notes sur l'arrive et le séjour en Louisiane de M. Henri Peyroux de la Coudreniere," September 27, 1800, Archivo General de Indias (Seville), Papeles procedentes de Cuba (hereafter abbreviated as AGI, PC), leg. 217; (Carondelet) to Josef de Jáudenes and Josef de Viar, New Orleans, April 17, 1792, ibid., leg. 104A, Paquete A. Earlier Jáudenes and Viar had informed the Spanish Court of the large numbers of immigrants who were arriving in the United States. Jáudenes and Viar to the (Court), Philadelphia, September 21, 1791, AHN, Est., leg. 3894bis.

9. Jáudenes and Viar to Floridablanca, nos. 98 and 110, Philadelphia, June 5 and 14, 1792, both in AHN, Est., leg. 3894bis.

1,040 barrels of flour, they sternly warned him against allowing this to happen again. By letter Peyroux protested and informed the ministers they had misinterpreted his actions. He assured them he would soon go to Philadelphia and personally explain what had happened. However, the Frenchman departed for Delaware instead, neither justifying his behavior nor attempting to acquire more immigrants.[10]

Carondelet's second agent was Thomas Wooster. Two years earlier, Wooster had attempted to secure permission to take colonists to St. Augustine in East Florida. Although the proposal was rejected, he settled in Louisiana where he became a militia captain. In June 1792, he left for the United States to attend to private matters and agreed at the same time to send colonists back to Louisiana.[11] In Philadelphia Jáudenes and Viar at first considered him better equipped than Peyroux to the task inasmuch as he spoke English. But Captain Wooster's peculiar behavior soon disappointed the Spanish officials. Instead of openly soliciting colonists, he posted a notice on a café wall announcing that anyone wishing a passport to New Orleans or desiring to become a Spanish citizen could obtain information from him. Appalled by this news, the ministers denied in the local newspapers that they had a connection with Wooster and declared definitively that only they were authorized to grant Spanish passports. Thus ended Wooster's role as an immigration agent, and, in any case, he was soon jailed for debts.[12]

---

10. Jáudenes and Viar to Henri Peyroux, Philadelphia, June 6, 1792; Jáudenes and Viar to Floridablanca, no. 110, Philadelphia, July 31, 1792, ibid. Peyroux eventually returned to New Madrid, his misconduct apparently forgiven. Jack D. L. Holmes, ed., *Documentos inéditos para la historia de la Luisiana, 1792-1810* (Madrid: Editoriales J. Porrúa Turanzas, 1963), 279.

11. Carondelet to Jáudenes and Viar, New Orleans, May 31 and June 20, 1792, AGI, PC, leg. 104A.

12. Jáudenes and Viar to Floridablanca, no. 113, Philadelphia, July 31, 1792; Jáudenes and Viar to Floridablanca, no. 119, and 3 enclosures, Philadelphia, October 29, 1792; all in AHN, Est., leg. 3894bis. Wooster gave out circulars listing the advantages of settling in Louisiana to interested persons. One such individual, Midad Mitchel, traveled to Gallipolis, where some residents joined him on his journey to Louisiana. Although arrested on his arrival, Governor Gayoso subsequently employed him at Natchez. "The Arrest of Mitchel—1793," in Louis Houck, ed., *The Spanish Régime in Missouri*, 2 vols. (1909; repr., New York: Arno Press and New York Times, 1971 rpt.), 2: 4-8.

With the failure of these two agents, Carondelet abandoned this method of recruiting colonists from the United States. It probably would have been necessary to furnish them transportation, and the Spanish government several years earlier had determined not to spend money on the acquisition of settlers. Furthermore, since it did not want to be accused by the United States of stealing its population, Spanish officials moved cautiously. Consequently, the Crown issued a royal order that ended commissions to acquire destitute settlers in the United States.[13] However, Governor Carondelet did not abandon his labors to increase Louisiana's population and continued to listen to proposals he received in New Orleans.

In the summer of 1792, he learned from several sources that a substantial number of French *émigrés* resided in the western United States settlement of Gallipolis. Established under the auspices of the Scioto Company, which had foundered, it left the royalists in considerable hardship and exposed to Indian raids. Since the settlement was dying, Friar Josef Didier, a Benedictine monk, and twenty others departed Gallipolis to seek settlement in Spanish territory. In New Madrid, Spanish authorities received the Frenchmen enthusiastically. Encouraged by the friendly reception, Didier wrote to the governor in New Orleans in June and applied for permission for other Gallipolis *émigrés* to enter Louisiana. Carondelet readily acceded to his request. Over the next several years a small but steady stream of Frenchmen arrived in Upper Louisiana.[14]

A month after Didier penned his letter to Carondelet, another Frenchman, Barthélemi Tardiveau, a merchant of fifteen years' residence in the United States, also wrote to the governor about securing the colonists of Gallilpolis for Louisiana. From Kaskaskia, Tardiveau warned Carondelet against allowing Anglo-Americans to settle on Spanish lands and urged fortifying the west bank of the Mississippi with loyal settlers. Besides offering to bring the Gallipolis *émigrés*, he proposed to travel to Europe and recruit colonists among the French refugees residing in

---

13. Minuta, royal palace, October 26, 1792, AHN, Est., leg. 3895bis.

14. Benedictine Monk of the Congregation of St. Mauro to Carondelet, New Madrid, June 22, 1792, Biblioteca Nacional, Madrid, 2 vols., "Documentos de la Florida," 2: 191-95. Friar Josef de Didier served as a priest at St. Louis from 1793 to 1799. He died in New Orleans on September 2, 1799. Holmes, *Documentos inéditos*, 273n.

several nations. He asserted that merely through the nominal cost of his commission, Louisiana could gain 300,000 French immigrants. Despite his exaggerated claim, the governor approved his suggestion and invited him to New Orleans. Carondelet authorized him to bring merchandise to defray the cost of his journey. The Baron also promised Tardiveau 2,000 pesos if he presented his project personally at Court.[15]

Carondelet was then enthusiastic about some German families that had recently arrived from Philadelphia and whom he had settled at Galveztown, giving them houses and rations for a year. He informed the Conde de Aranda, the minister of state, that he would continue to establish German and Flemish families at Galveztown until they numbered a hundred. The governor intended to distribute colonists along the length of Lower Louisiana, on both banks of the Mississippi, from the river's mouth to Nogales (Vicksburg today), over three hundred miles upstream.[16]

Although Tardiveau did not make the trip to Europe because of the revolution in France, he appeared in New Orleans the following spring. He presented the governor with a memorial requesting a loan for the construction of a wheat mill in New Madrid. Carlos DeHault DeLassus and Pedro Audrain were to be his partners in this venture. Besides their proposal for the mill, the partners volunteered to conduct the Gallipolis families to Louisiana, if the government paid the immigrants' transportation costs and rations until their first crop was harvested. The petitioners asked that the new settlement be named New Bourbon. Governor Carondelet made a contract with the three men, in which he loaned them 9,000 pesos with which to build two mills on condition that they supply the province with 6,000 barrels of flour for ten years at

15. Barthélemi Tardiveau to Carondelet, Kaskaskia, July 17, 1792; Carondelet to Aranda, no. 15, reserved, New Orleans, October 1, 1792; both in AHN, Est., leg. 3898. Tardiveau's letter is translated in Kinnaird, *Spain in the Mississippi Valley*, 3: 60-66. A biography of Tardiveau is in Howard C. Rice, *Barthélemi Tardiveau: A French Trader in the West* (Baltimore: Johns Hopkins University Press, 1938).

16. Carondelet to Aranda, no. 15 reserved, New Orleans, October 1, 1792, AHN, Est. leg. 3898. The Galveztown settlement in Louisiana began during the American War for Independence, when Gov. Bernardo de Gálvez allowed Americans to settle there. Bernardo de Gálvez to José de Gálvez, no. 233, New Orleans, January 15, 1779, in Kinnaird, *Spain in the Mississippi Valley*, 1: 326-27.

a fair price. The Frenchmen also accepted responsibility for bringing a hundred families from Gallipolis, for which they received an additional loan of 2,500 pesos, plus the cost of transporting the families to their new homes.[17]

Soon the partners left New Orleans to fulfill their contract. Charged with bringing the Gallipolis colonists, Audrain traveled by sea to Philadelphia and then journeyed overland to the American West while his two associates ascended the Mississippi to Upper Louisiana. DeHault DeLassus received the civil and military command of New Bourbon, which was soon founded. Carondelet expressed much faith in this project and glowingly termed it "an epoch in the annals of this Province, and perhaps in Septentrional America." He hailed it as the start of halting the Anglo-American and English advance and the preservation of Louisiana intact.[18]

About the same time that Tardiveau made his proposal, Jacques Clamorgan of St. Louis also offered to increase Upper Louisiana's population. His project, however, was the type that the Spanish Crown could not accept because it entailed heavy expenditures. Clamorgan wanted to charter ships to bring German colonists from Europe to Philadelphia and then to Spanish territory. The immigrants would receive land, poultry, oxen, cows, farm tools, and rations for ten months, which the settlers technically purchased on credit and were obliged to repay. Clamorgan presumed that his enterprise could bring a thousand families

---

17. "Memorial of DeHault DeLassus, Barthélemi Tardiveau, and Pedro Audrain," n.p., April 17, 1793, AGI, PC, leg. 2363; Carondelet to the Duque de la Alcudia (Manuel Godoy), no. 6 reserved, New Orleans, April 26, 1793, AHN, Est., leg. 3898. The partners never used the 9,000 pesos and returned the money to the Spanish treasury. They invested their own money and lost it in the venture. In 1796 they renewed their request for the loan. Their mill was then two-thirds completed. Carondelet to the Prince of the Peace (Manuel Godoy), no. 74 reserved, New Orleans, March 1, 1796, AHN, Est., leg. 3900; Hatcher, "Louisiana Background," 183-85. The population of New Bourbon in 1795 was not over 153; in 1796 it was 383; and the next year it was 461. Holmes, *Documentos inéditos*, 267n.

18. Carondelet to Alcudia, no. 6 reserved, New Orleans, April 26, 1795, AHN, Est., leg. 3898; Louis Houck, *A History of Missouri from the Earliest Explorations and Settlements Until the Admission of the State into the Union*, 3 vols. in 1 (New York: Arno Press and New York Times, 1971 rpt.), 1: 365. The quotation is in Carondelet's letter.

to Upper Louisiana.[19] However, this proposal, like so many others of its kind, was not accepted.

From 1793 on, Louisiana's problems began to increase noticeably. Spain warred on revolutionary France (1793-95), along with several other conservative monarchies, upon the republicans' execution of Louis XVI. A lull in the presentation of immigration proposals coincided with the threat of a French invasion. The danger stemmed from the activities of Citizen Edmond Genet, the revolutionary French government's minister to the United States, who was scheming with American frontiersmen to attack Louisiana and Florida. Moreover, Governor Carondelet faced internal turmoil as French Jacobins began cropping up in Louisiana. Despite his expulsion of a number of these overly zealous republicans and his restriction placed on their entry into the province, he found tranquility difficult to maintain. On one occasion Carondelet summoned the Anglo-American militia from Natchez and the French and Spanish militias of other settlements to preserve order in New Orleans.[20] Aside from the problem of unrest among some of the New Orleans French Creoles, tension existed within the ranks of the slaves, who were as numerous as the whites. The abortive slave insurrection of 1795 at Pointe Coupée led to the governor's ban on the importation of slaves. In the midst of all this disorder, Carondelet tried to promote a freer trade policy to reduce dissatisfaction among the established residents and to encourage new immigrants. However, since loyalty of the new settlers to the Spanish government was an imperative, European colonization received greater

---

19. "Plan of Population for [Spanish] Illinois," in Kinnaird, *Spain in the Mississippi Valley*, 3: 208-15. For information on Clamorgan's activities in Louisiana, see A. P. Nasatir, "Jacques Clamorgan: Colonial Promoter of the Northern Border of New Spain," *New Mexico Historical Review* 17 (April 1942): 101-12.

20. Carondelet to the Prince of the Peace, no. 77, New Orleans, April 1, 1796, AHN, Est., leg. 3900; Whitaker, *Spanish American Frontier*, 171-73, 187-92; Jack D. L. Holmes, *Gayoso: The Life of a Spanish Governor in the Mississippi Valley, 1789-1799* (Baton Rouge: Louisiana State University Press for the Louisiana Historical Association, 1965), 170-73; Ernest R. Liljegren, "Jacobinism in Spanish Louisiana, 1792-1797," *Louisiana Historical Quarterly* 22 (January 1939): 47-97; Frederick Jackson Turner, "The Origin of Genêt's Projected Attack on Louisiana and the Floridas," *American Historical Review* 3 (July 1898): 650-71; F. R. Hall, "Genêt's Western Intrigue, 1793-1794," *Journal of the Illinois State Historical Society* 21 (October 1928): 359-81.

encouragement than in the past.[21]

In June 1794, the Baron emphasized the urgency of populating Louisiana and stressed the need to retain the colony to safeguard Mexico. He suggested that each ship bound for New Orleans transport from six to eight German or Flemish settlers. He also advised opening the Mississippi to trade and obtain in this way the defection of the American West. Several months later, in November, he dispatched a lengthy communication to the Court in which he reiterated the necessity to stimulate trade and increase the colony's population.[22] Soon the governor received an immigration proposal that he actively promoted.

It came from a refugee Frenchman, the Marquis de Maison Rouge. Only shortly before, Maison Rouge had arrived in Louisiana, claiming to represent other *émigrés* in the United States. He brought with him several settlers, agricultural tools, and materials to build a sawmill. In a proposal the Marquis soon presented to the governor, he stated that his plan was to begin a wheat-growing settlement in Ouachita, which would also be useful in the defense of Louisiana.[23] Carondelet quickly endorsed the project, and he agreed to pay the transportation costs of Maison Rouge's settlers from New Madrid to Ouachita and for their rations as well. The governor also proposed to do this for all new settlers coming to Louisiana. Moreover, he reprimanded Commandant Thomas Portell of New Madrid for temporarily detaining the Marquis's party, and instructed him to permit all French royalists and Dutch, Flemish,

---

21. Carondelet to Alcudia, no. 30 and no. 34 reserved, New Orleans, March 27 and May 1, 1794, in AHN, Est., legs. 3900 and 3899, respectively; Jack D. L. Holmes, "The Abortive Slave Revolt at Pointe Coupée, Louisiana, 1795," *Louisiana History* 11 (Fall 1970): 341-62; Gilbert C. Din, *Spaniards, Planters, and Slaves: The Spanish Regulation of Slavery in Louisiana* (College Station: Texas A&M University Press, 1999), 154-76.

22. Carondelet to Alcudia, nos. 36 reserved and 128, New Orleans, June 3 and November 24, 1794, both in AHN, Est., leg. 3899. The November letter is published in "Carondelet on the Defense of Louisiana, 1794," translated by W. F. Giese, *American Historical Review* 2 (April 1897): 474-505.

23. "Memorial of the Marquis de Maison Rouge," n.p., n.d., AGI, PC, leg. 2364. For a detailed study of Maison Rouge in Louisiana, see Jennie O'Kelly Mitchell and Robert Dabney Calhoun, "The Marquis de Maison Rouge, the Baron de Bastrop, and Colonel Abraham Morhouse—Three Ouachita Valley Soldiers of Fortune," *Louisiana Historical Quarterly* 20 (April 1937): 289-368.

Irish, German, or any other European immigrants to enter and settle in Louisiana, including Anglo-American farmers and artisans. However, French republicans and Jacobins were denied entry or to be expelled if they were already in the colony.[24]

Maison Rouge's contract obligated him to bring in only thirty agricultural families, each of which would receive a cash bonus of a hundred pesos once they had settled down in Louisiana. The Crown agreed to pay the transportation costs for 3,000 pounds of baggage per family that came by sea to New Orleans and then was sent up to Ouachita. Thirty square leagues of land were set aside for Maison Rouge's colonists.[25] Although Carondelet believed the contract would bring in many of the right kind of settlers, the result proved disappointing. Despite the governor's order excluding Anglo-Americans and Irishmen, some came in nonetheless.[26] After the Court approved the contract, the Marquis introduced fewer colonists than the governor had expected: thirty-one brought by Augustus de Breard in 1796, and twenty-two more came the following year. Moreover, not all of them were agricultural workers; some were Anglo-Americans, and slaves accounted for about twenty of the total number.[27] Maison Rouge's failure to live up to the terms of the contract raised suspicion about his real purpose for being in the colony; Commandant Carlos de Grand-Pré at Avoyelles believed that the Marquis would soon leave.[28] Although he stayed in Louisiana until his death in 1799, Maison Rouge did little to justify the great enthusiasm with which Governor Carondelet had initially greeted his proposal.

---

24. (Carondelet) to Gayoso, no. 79, New Orleans, January 20, 1795; Carondelet to Thomas Portell, New Orleans, January 30, 1795; both in AGI, PC, leg. 22.

25. "Maison Rouge Contract," (New Orleans), March 18, 1795, AGI, PC, leg. 22. The contract was approved by the royal order mentioned in Diego de Gardoqui to the Intendant of Louisiana, Madrid, July 14, 1795, AGI, PC, leg. 560.

26. Carondelet to Juan Filhio, no. 898, New Orleans, November 20, 1795, AGI, PC, leg. 22.

27. Carondelet to Juan Ventura Morales, New Orleans, June 5, 7, and 27, 1796, AGI, PC, leg. 89; Morales to Carondelet, New Orleans, August 11, 1796, ibid.; (?) Filhio to (Carondelet), n.p., May 7, 1797, AGI, PC, leg. 214; Mitchell and Calhoun, "Marquis de Maison Rouge, the Baron de Bastrop, and Colonel Abraham Morhouse," 325-26.

28. Carlos de Grand-Pré to Carondelet, Avoyelles, July 30, 1796, AGI, PC, leg. 2354.

About the same time that Maison Rouge's settlement at Ouachita was beginning, several other proposals to bring colonists reached the governor. In April 1795, Joseph Piernas, a former officer in the Louisiana regiment and son of deceased Col. Pedro Piernas who once headed the Louisiana infantry regiment, offered to establish at his own expense five hundred loyal Irish and German agricultural families on the Calcasieu River near the Gulf of Mexico and about thirty-six miles east of the Sabine River. Piernas pledged to construct within eight years a village of three hundred persons, which would have a church with a priest, a surgeon, and a schoolmaster. Besides this he would also maintain a guard at the mouth of the Calcasieu River. In return Piernas requested the duty-free entry of 30,000 pesos worth of merchandise for each fifty families he introduced, land for the settlement, and all the privileges entitled to him as founder of the colony.[29] Although Carondelet endorsed the plan and the Court approved it in 1798, no settlement resulted. In 1799 Piernas again attempted to promote his project. On this occasion, he authorized Calvin Adams to bring in two hundred Dutch and Irish Catholic families. Once more, however, his scheme failed and no settlement blossomed up.[30]

In July 1795, Capt. Luis de Vilemont, a French Creole and Louisianan in Spain's service, also presented a plan to introduce colonists. Vilemont had arrived in Philadelphia the previous year purportedly to study natural history. In Louisiana he talked with the governor, and doubtlessly Carondelet influenced him inasmuch as Vilemont's proposal called for bringing in French, Dutch, German, and Flemish refugees. The Baron gave the project his hearty endorsement. In his memorial, Vilemont pointed out the emptiness of Louisiana and the rapid increase in population of the United States' western settlements. He warned against letting in Anglo-Americans and non-Catholics, terming such action as settling the Goths at the gates of Rome and predicting they would

---

29. "Memorial of Joseph Piernas," New Orleans, April 24, 1795, ibid.; Jack D. L. Holmes, "Joseph Piernas and a Proposed Settlement on the Calcasieu River, 1795," *McNeese Review* 13 (1962): 59-80, contains a translation of the Piernas proposal. The Spanish text is in Holmes, *Documentos inéditos*, 148-69.

30. Jack D. L. Holmes, ed., "The Calcasieu Promoter: Joseph Piernas and His 1799 Proposal," *Louisiana History* 9 (Spring 1968): 163-67.

usurp the colony. Instead, he preferred bringing Europeans to Louisiana aboard Spanish naval vessels and creating a settlement similar to that at Natchez where Anglo-Americans resided. The Europeans could establish villages similar to those in their native lands and retain their customs and languages. Vilemont predicted that the increase in population would stimulate commerce enormously and convert Louisiana into the granary of the Spanish colonies.[31]

In Spain the Vilemont project was not considered until after the signing of the 1795 Treaty of San Lorenzo between Spain and the United States. The treaty marked the start of Spain's retreat in the Mississippi Valley and the diminished importance of Louisiana at Court. It was not surprising, therefore, that the Council of State on November 13, deemed the proposal impractical because of the great cost it entailed; the impossibility of allowing religious tolerance (which Vilemont asked for); and the discontent it would engender in France, England, and Holland, lands where the colonists would be recruited. Finally it alleged that Vilemont had incorrectly assumed that Louisiana's defense was vital for the retention of Mexico. The rejection, especially the fourth point, clearly reflected Louisiana's decreased significance in Spanish diplomatic thinking, in particular by the inexperienced Minister of State Godoy, the queen's favorite.[32]

The last proposal of 1795 came in December, presented by a Mr. Butler who was a friend of José de Jáudenes, the co-Spanish chargé in Philadelphia. Butler wished to become an immigration impresario and desired Spanish approval of his ownership of land he sought to buy from the heirs of recently deceased Jonathan Bryan. He had allegedly obtained it from the Creek Indians. Butler was also prepared to journey with maps to Flanders, where he would sell tracts of Florida land. He proposed that the Spanish government obtain the Creeks' consent to the

31. (Luis de Vilemont) to Carondelet, New Orleans, October 31, 1794, AHN, Est., leg. 3895bis; Vilemont to (Carondelet), New Orleans, July 10, 1795; "Petition of Luis de Vilemont," attached to Carondelet to Alcudia, New Orleans, July 30, 1795; *minuta*, palace, November 12, 1795, last three documents are in AHN, Est., leg. 3890, exped. 34.

32. Conde de Montarco to Alcudia, San Lorenzo, November 14, 1795, AHN, Est., leg. 3890.

land exchange by providing them with gifts. The Crown was to pay for Butler's trip to Europe, gifts to the Indians, maps, surveying expenses, all of which he calculated would cost a modest 40,000 pesos.[33] The lack of further information about this project seems to indicate that the Spanish government declined to take an interest in it.

However, a possible result of Butler's plan was one made by José de Jáudenes that was very similar. Jáudenes also proffered a land-selling scheme to attract European immigrants to Louisiana, but one that entailed no cost to the Crown. Land agents were to be placed in the principal European cities and advertisements in newspapers were to induce the public to buy the land. Spanish consuls would issue titles to the purchasers. Once in Louisiana the settlers would take oaths of loyalty and vassalage to Spain. While Jáudenes stated that the United States government engaged in such practices without engendering complaints from foreign nations, the Spanish government, nevertheless, refrained from entering into land promotion schemes to gain settlers for the North American colony.[34]

Spain acted cautiously in the mid-1790s because Great Britain declared war in 1796 upon Spain becoming a French ally. Even in the far-off Mississippi Valley, Spaniards feared invasion from the United States or from the British in Canada. In order to gain an ally and settle disagreements, Manuel Godoy, the Spanish first minister of state, decided to reach an accord with the United States. By the Treaty of San Lorenzo of October 1795, Spain accepted the thirty-first parallel as the boundary line that extended from the Mississippi River's left bank eastward between the southern United States and the Spanish Floridas, gave Americans use of the Mississippi, and granted them the right of deposit at New Orleans for the duty-free export of their goods passing through Spanish territory. The treaty gave away the principal Spanish defenses in West Florida and on the east bank of the Mississippi, which really mattered little to Godoy as he was now guided only by the wish to obtain the best possible terms in disposing of Louisiana. Inasmuch as Godoy's government in

---

33. Jáudenes to Alcudia, no. 320, Philadelphia, December 1, 1795; "Butler Memorial," Philadelphia, November 30, 1795, AHN, Est., leg. 3896.

34. Jáudenes to Alcudia, no. 299, Philadelphia, July 29, 1796, ibid.

Spain chose not to defend the colony, local officials tried to protect it as best they could. Upon learning of the treaty, Governor Carondelet held back surrendering the military posts, an act that Madrid belatedly and temporarily sustained. But Spanish procrastination in giving up the posts combined with Anglo-American impatience produced the Natchez revolt of 1797, which increased tension in Louisiana. The next year Spain relinquished control of the lands stipulated in the 1795 treaty.[35]

Besides surrendering the Spanish forts, the Treaty of San Lorenzo decreased Lower Louisiana's security because the Natchez District of West Florida, filled with the largest concentration of Anglo-American inhabitants, passed to the United States. The large population in Natchez partially explains Carondelet's attempt to build up Ouachita, not far away on the Mississippi's west bank, with a European population loyal to Spain. However, at about this time the governor temporarily shifted ground on Anglo-American immigration to Louisiana. After Spain negotiated peace with France and joined it in an alliance in 1796, Great Britain became the immediate enemy. Consequently, the governor encouraged United States frontiersmen to come to Louisiana to build up the colony's defenses against a possible invasion from British-held Canada. He issued advertisements to Anglo-Americans to settle in the province; and when William Murray presented his proposal in New Orleans in 1796, Carondelet endorsed it.[36]

Murray represented a group of Kentucky speculators, who included Harry Innes, Benjamin Sebastian, and others involved in

---

35. Samuel Flagg Bemis, *Pinckney's Treaty: America's Advantage from Europe's Distress, 1783-1800*, rev. ed. (New Haven: Yale University Press, 1960), 245-93; Arthur Preston Whitaker, *The Mississippi Question, 1795-1803: A Study in Trade, Politics, and Diplomacy* (1934; repr., Gloucester, Mass.: Peter Smith, 1962), 51-67.

36. Carondelet to Morales, New Orleans, June 11, 1797, enclosed in Ramón López y Ángulo to Miguel Cayetano Soler, New Orleans, July 13, 1801, AGI, Santo Domingo, leg. 2617. Carondelet still tried to exclude Anglo-Americans from Lower Louisiana and West Florida, where he favored European settlement. DeHault DeLassus issued a pamphlet inviting immigrants, "A Sketch of the Advantages that are made, and Quantities of land that are granted to farmers by the Spanish Government, in the District of New Madrid...." (n.p., April 8, 1796), Louisiana Collection, Bancroft Library, University of California, Berkeley. See also Kinnaird, "American Penetration into Spanish Louisiana," 221-22; and Houck, *History of Missouri*, 2: 183-84.

James Wilkinson's plot to separate Kentucky from the United States. While the real intent of Murray's group was to acquire a ten-million-acre land grant for speculation, they claimed discontent with the United States government as the reason for inquiring about the formation of a settlement with four thousand families. The group believed that with a liberal trade policy the project could be realized within six years. Murray asked that the settlers be permitted to regulate their community and select their own officials. The governor rejected this provision, but in all other respects he approved the project.[37] His endorsement of this proposal, however, raises a question about his motives inasmuch as the plan was obviously designed to acquire a huge land grant for speculation. Possibly his true reason for accepting it was his wish to keep alive the Wilkinson conspiracy. However, since Murray's plan was so much at variance with Spanish immigration and land policy, there should not have been much expectation that Madrid would approve it.[38]

The immigration proposals Governor Carondelet most favored were those made by European noblemen, such as that of the Baron de Bastrop, Philip Hendrik Nering Bögel. The governor, however, little suspected that Bastrop's credentials as a Dutch aristocrat were spurious. In his first communication to Carondelet, brought to Louisiana by Maison Rouge, Bastrop proposed bringing directly from Europe three hundred Dutch families. He wanted a compensation of fifty pesos for each white working person he brought.[39] His proposal delighted the governor who quickly obtained Intendant Francisco Rendón's approval. Carondelet authorized Bastrop to bring in the families immediately without waiting for a time-delaying Court approval. In 1795 the bogus Baron came to Louisiana

---

37. "Petition of Benjamin Sebastian, John Hollingsworth, Harry Innes et al.," (Louisville?), July 5, 1796; Carondelet to William Murray, New Orleans, November 24, 1796; "Contract of William Murray," all in AGI, PC, leg. 674.

38. Whitaker, *Mississippi Question*, 156.

39. "Memorial of Baron de Bastrop," place, August 25, 1794, AGI, PC, leg. 2364. A survey of Bastrop's activities is in Charles A. Bacarisse, "Baron de Bastrop," *Southwestern Historical Quarterly* 58 (January 1955): 319-30. Benjamin Fooy, one-time commandant of the Spanish post of Campo de Esperanza, opposite present-day Memphis, proposed forming a Dutch or German settlement. He received royal approval in 1798, but nothing came of it. Houck, *Spanish Régime in Missouri*, 2: 114.

with the settlers that Augustus de Breard brought to Ouachita for Maison Rouge.[40] The following year he requested from the governor a land grant of twelve square leagues on which to establish the families he proposed to bring, granting each one a maximum of 400 arpents (336 acres) of land for the cultivation of wheat. Inasmuch as his settlers in this proposal were to come from the United States, he wanted the Crown to pay for their transportation and rations from New Madrid as well as rations for several additional months. Carondelet accepted these terms in a contract made on June 21, 1796, reserving the right to reclaim lands that had not been ceded after three years.[41] Soon Bastrop left Louisiana for Kentucky where he had business interests.

Over the next several years Bastrop's immigration efforts and business ventures achieved only modest success. In the spring of 1797, the Baron descended the Mississippi River with ninety-nine persons. By April 19, he was in Ouachita, where he spent a few days settling the colonists before he continued to New Orleans to lay new projects before the governor. Carondelet approved Bastrop's plan to build up Ouachita with European settlers as a barrier against the Americans of Natchez, and he was willing to spend money to do so. However, he was dependent on the intendancy to grant the needed funds. In June the governor made a lengthy exposition to the intendant of the advantages to be gained in supporting Bastrop's proposal. Carondelet also requested money to support the Baron's settlers with rations for six months and to reimburse him for his expenses in bringing them from New Madrid. The message was the first inkling the interim intendant Juan Ventura Morales had of Bastrop's second project.[42]

---

40. Carondelet to Grand-Pré, no. 712, New Orleans, September 16, 1795; AGI, PC, leg. 22; (Carondelet) to Francisco Rendón, New Orleans, March 9, 1795; Rendón to Carondelet, New Orleans, March 17, 1795; both in AGI, PC, leg. 2364.

41. Bastrop to Carondelet, New Orleans, June 20, 1796; "Bastrop Contract," New Orleans, June 21, 1796; both in AGI, Santo Domingo, leg. 2580.

42. Bastrop to Morales, New Orleans, June 20, 1797, AGI, PC, leg. 601; Carondelet to the Prince of the Peace, New Orleans, June 16, 1797; Carondelet to Morales, New Orleans, June 11, 1797, the last two documents in AHN, Est., leg. 3900. Bastrop sought to build wheat mills in Ouachita and requested lands on both banks of Bayou Barthélemy and Bayou Siard on which to establish them. Carondelet approved the

Morales soon disapproved of Carondelet's plans for Bastrop. He informed the governor that the war in Europe had eradicated funds for the project. Furthermore, Morales called a meeting of the Council of the Royal Treasury, and it also opposed acting on Bastrop's project until officials in Spain could either approve or reject it. Although Morales's decision disappointed the governor, he nonetheless urged the Spanish government to accept Bastrop's proposal, describing the cost as modest and the plan necessary to increase the production of flour and prevent a slave insurrection or an Anglo-American revolt. The intendant allowed the governor to pay for the colonists already in Ouachita and for their rations. Nevertheless, the Bastrop commission was suspended. Morales warned that Bastrop would only bring in Anglo-American Protestants, not Europeans or Catholics. Moreover, he cautioned correctly that Ouachita was not suited to the cultivation of wheat.[43]

After his initial effort to bring colonists failed to receive the proper authorization, Bastrop made two additional proposals. In October 1797, he requested permission to bring in five hundred families aboard five or six ships. While the new governor, Manuel Gayoso de Lemos, approved the project, Intendant Morales did not, and the Baron soon abandoned it. Bastrop next tried to sell his "rights" to the land grant, which had been set aside for the colonists he had enlisted, to Col. Abraham Morhouse. However, the Spanish government rejected his claim to ownership, and the Dutchman drew up a new offer to introduce colonists. By this proposal of 1800, he would introduce five hundred families and pay all their travel expenses, rations, and settlement costs. He pledged to accomplish the project in five years. Bastrop also requested the land he had previously solicited from Carondelet. This time the Baron intended to bring in slaves

---

request and granted the land. Bastrop to Carondelet, New Orleans, June 12, 1797, AGI, Santo Domingo, leg. 2580. Bastrop brought no more than ninety-nine persons to Ouachita: sixty-four on May 8, 1797, and thirty-five more on May 10, 1797. L. M. Perez, "French Immigrants to Louisiana, 1796-1800," *Publications of the Southern History Association* 11 (1907): 106-12.

43. Morales to Carondelet, New Orleans, June 13, 1797; "Decision of the Junta," Carondelet to the Prince of the Peace, New Orleans, June 16, 1797; all in AHN, Est., leg. 3900; Morales to Carondelet, no. 129, New Orleans, June 30, 1797, AGI, Santo Domingo, leg. 2580.

to raise cotton and work in cotton gins. The Marqués de Casa-Calvo, who arrived as interim governor in September 1799 after Gayoso's death that July, approved the plan.[44] Bastrop at this time proposed to sell part of his land grant to Morhouse, but the new intendant, Ramón López y Ángulo, suspecting that Bastrop wanted to leave the colony after making the sale, refused to permit it. Furthermore, López y Ángulo halted the sale of all land grants. He also blocked Bastrop's purchase of a cypress forest from Juan Filhio; the Baron had intended to build a sawmill and supply the province with lumber.[45] Stymied in his efforts, Bastrop returned to Ouachita to construct a forge for the manufacture of iron. The next year he obtained an exclusive license for trade with the Indians and a partnership in the New Orleans trading firm of Lille Sarpy Colsson and Company. Although filled with entrepreneurial spirit, Bastrop was plagued by business reversals. This was especially true after the United States took control of Louisiana in December 1803. Less than two years later the Baron de Bastrop departed for Texas, following the retreating Spanish flag.[46]

In August 1797, Carondelet's term as governor of Louisiana ended, and he left for his new post as president of the Audiencia of Quito. For five and a half years he had attempted to build up the colony's population, particularly through the acquisition of European settlers. While he received a number of proposals to bring in Europeans, they usually required spending government money that was neither available nor permitted by the Crown. Toward the end of his governorship, Anglo-American immigration to Louisiana increased considerably, and it was stimulated in part by the governor's own efforts. But Spanish officials

44. Gayoso to Morales, New Orleans, October 5, 1797, AGI, PC, leg. 44; Francisco de Saavedra to the Prince of the Peace, Aranjuez, Febrary 23, 1798; Bastrop to the Marqués de Casa-Calvo, New Orleans, June 18, 1800; Casa-Calvo to López y Ángulo, New Orleans, July 10, 1800; the last three documents are all in AHN, Est., leg. 3901.

45. Casa-Calvo to Luis de Urquijo, New Orleans, August 8, 1800, AHN, Est., leg. 3901; López y Ángulo, nos. 94 and 95, both reserved, New Orleans, August 12 and September 25, 1800, respectively, both in AHN, Est., leg. 3888. The Crown rejected Bastrop's commission in 1802. Soler to Pedro Cevallo, Madrid, July 13, 1802, AHN, Est., leg. 3901.

46. François-Xavier Martin, *The History of Louisiana, from the Earliest Period* (1827-29; repr., New Orleans: James A. Gresham, 1882), 2: 180; Bacarisse, "Baron de Bastrop," 327-30.

after Carondelet worried more than he had about the Anglo-American influx and feared that the province would be overwhelmed. Therefore, and not surprisingly, in the last years of Spanish rule local officials tried to discourage such settlements. Desperately but in vain, they also sought to acquire the kind of colonists that would preserve the province for Spain.

Carondelet's successor, Manuel Gayoso de Lemos, who assumed office in August 1797, was confronted by more problems with fewer resources than his predecessor had faced on becoming governor. A sizeable colony of Anglo-Americans inhabited Natchez, which was across the river from Lower Louisiana. Spanish fortifications were virtually nonexistent and military strength was barely sufficient to maintain internal order. Moreover, in Spain there was little support for safeguarding Louisiana. By 1796 Minister of State Godoy was prepared to sell the province at the first opportune moment. The next year when the Spanish minister in Philadelphia, Carlos Martínez de Irujo, informed Godoy about William Blount's threat to invade Louisiana, he dismissively wrote on Irujo's dispatch, "You can't lock up the countryside."[47] Years earlier Spain had stopped spending money to foster immigration to the colony; now there was not even money to spend on defense.

During his administration, Governor Gayoso was even more adamant in his opposition to American immigration than Carondelet had been. Undoubtedly the Natchez rebellion in 1797, where he had been governor of the district, convinced him that most Anglo-Americans could not be trusted to become loyal Spaniards. The oath of allegiance they took on entering Louisiana meant nothing to them. For that reason during his two years as governor, Gayoso attempted to acquire only select American immigrants.

From September 1797, Gayoso began issuing instructions to post commandants on the admittance of immigrants and on land grants. Unmarried and destitute settlers could not receive land immediately; they first had to demonstrate their willingness to work for several years. Gayoso also abrogated the previous policy of religious tolerance and stated that henceforth tolerance would be granted only for the present generation; their children would be required to become Catholic.

---

47. Martínez de Irujo to the Prince of the Peace, no. 73, Philadelphia, August 5, 1798, AHN, Est., leg. 3891, exped. 23, with Godoy's marginal notation of October 20, 1797; Holmes, *Gayoso*, 196.

Individuals unwilling to accept these conditions were required to leave Louisiana immediately. Furthermore, anyone who was not a Catholic farmer, artisan, or a person of importance who had held a public office in the United States, would no longer be admitted in the province.[48]

Until his death in July 1799, Governor Gayoso remained preoccupied with the Anglo-American penetration of Louisiana. Using the "Natchez example," he pointed out to the commandant of New Madrid that an indiscriminate admittance of Anglo-American settlers would inundate the "old and good inhabitants of this country." He advised allowing only useful and trustworthy persons in the province. He realized how difficult the task would be inasmuch as the paucity of Spaniards in the colony, but he hoped that future generations would become Hispanized. In numbers Spaniards ranked after the French, Americans, English, and possibly the Germans. Because Louisiana's defenses were weak, he considered it imperative that an untrustworthy element not arise in the colony.[49] Upper Louisiana's small population was particularly susceptible to being overrun by the Anglo-Americans. Lt. Gov. Zenon Trudeau of Upper Louisiana believed it desirable to acquire colonists from any available source, which for him was the Ohio Valley where Germans, Irishmen, and French *émigrés* resided as well as United States citizens disillusioned with their own government. Similar to Commandant James Mackay of St. Andrew on the Missouri River, Trudeau recommended restoring religious tolerance. In mid-1798, he blamed Gayoso's new regulation on religion for the virtual halt of immigration to Louisiana.[50]

Trudeau's exhortation, however, failed to convince the governor, who believed that the danger extended beyond Louisiana to Mexico as

---

48. Gayoso issued two sets of immigration instructions in New Orleans, on September 3, 1797, and February 20, 1798, AGI, PC, leg. 220, and leg. 2365, respectively. See also Martin, *History of Louisiana*, 2: 153; and Holmes, *Gayoso*, 227-28. Gayoso permitted some Americans to settle in New Feliciana, Concordia, and Bayou Boeuf, but he exercised caution in doing so.

49. Gayoso to DeHault DeLassus, New Orleans, September 9, 1797, AGI, PC, leg. 44.

50. Trudeau to Gayoso, St. Louis, January 15, 1798, AGI, PC, leg. 214; Santiago Mackay to Gayoso, St. Andrew, November 28, 1798, AGI, PC, leg. 215B; Houck, *History of Missouri*, 1: 332.

well. He counseled caution in building up the colony's population and felt it preferable to wait for the right kind of settlers rather than court disaster with the admittance of potential enemies. He also remained intransigent that new immigrants be Catholic. Even if no colonists arrived, he considered it imperative that the king's orders be obeyed. Nonetheless, he advised Trudeau to preserve the friendship of persons already settled and remove pretexts they might have for complaint.[51]

Because he desired to obtain colonists from a new source, Gayoso suggested that Trudeau contact persons who traded in Canada and induce them to bring families to settle in Upper Louisiana. Any agent bringing in French Canadian families would receive ten arpents (8.4 acres) for each one hundred arpents granted to new families. The agents could dispose of their earned lands in any way they wished, except by selling them to persons residing outside the province. Gayoso did not expect an immediate influx of French Canadians because Spain was then at war with Great Britain. Nevertheless, he did anticipate their entrance after the war and advised Trudeau to continue his efforts to acquire them.[52]

In July 1799, only days before he died, Governor Gayoso expressed his last thoughts on the matter of immigration. He urged Intendant Morales not to permit any new settlements to be established until peace prevailed again. He rejected the idea of populating Louisiana with Anglo-Americans and even expressed doubt about letting in settlers until the war ended. He was opposed to these immigrants because only those disgruntled with the United States government would come, a group he described as disorderly, vice-ridden, and probable disseminators of new and unwanted ideas. He considered present circumstances as not warranting unsuitable colonists in Louisiana. Gayoso, therefore, recommended to the Court against innovation and the establishment of new settlements. He felt that the Crown could either change Louisiana into a military bastion against Anglo-American immigration or permit United States settlers to come in. However, if such settlers were allowed in Louisiana, he advised that it be done in a manner that would prevent

---

51. Gayoso to Trudeau, New Orleans, July 9, 1798, AGI, PC, leg. 2365.

52. Gayoso to the Prince of the Peace, New Orleans, August 20, and November 22, 1798, AGI, PC, leg. 44, and AHN, Est., leg. 3900, respectively; Gayoso to Trudeau, New Orleans, AGI, PC, leg. 44.

the loss of Louisiana and the downfall of Mexico.[53]

Gayoso's last remarks clearly delineated the hazards Louisiana faced and the vexing problem of Anglo-American immigration. Relying virtually on their own resources, some Louisiana officials attempted to stem the flow of these people into the province, while in Spain Godoy thought only of disposing of the troublesome colony, which he began to do in 1800. Gayoso's death in 1799 also ended the era of strong governors who were dedicated to the preservation of Spanish authority in Louisiana. After his death caretaker administrators followed, and they merely presided over the colony until its transfer to France was completed on November 30, 1803.

As interim governor, the Marqués de Casa-Calvo, who succeeded the deceased Gayoso in September 1799, did very little to establish an immigration policy. He made only a slight effort to halt the Anglo-American advance into Louisiana. Although he advised district commandants to eject from their jurisdictions such immigrants who had settled without proper authority, he appeared reluctant to prevent new settlements on the west bank of the Mississippi as earlier officials had done. The last governor of Louisiana, the mediocre bureaucrat Manuel Juan de Salcedo, replaced Casa-Calvo in July 1801. He too exerted little influence on immigration policy during his two-year governorship.[54]

With governors exercising smaller influence on immigration in the last years of Spanish dominion over Louisiana, the intendancy came to implement greater authority in matters of new settlers and land grants. Morales was the first intendant to assert the prerogatives of his office during the Carondelet administration, and later he also plagued Gayoso with querulous opposition on even the most trivial matters.

53. Gayoso to Morales, New Orleans, July 1, 1799, AGI, Santo Domingo, leg. 2617. Gayoso disapproved a 144-square-league grant to M. Tardiveau near New Madrid and objected to new settlements on the west bank of the Mississippi. Furthermore, he was against developing those already in existence. Gayoso to the Prince of the Peace, New Orleans, July 8, 1799, AHN, Est., leg. 3901. In the fall of 1798, Col. Zacharias Cox arrived in New Orleans and offered to establish six hundred Kentucky families near New Madrid. Gayoso told him to renew his proposal after the war. Gayoso to the Prince of the Peace, New Orleans, AHN, est. leg. 3900.

54. Casa-Calvo to V. Layssard, New Orleans, December 22, 1799, AGI, PC, leg. 3900; Martin, *History of Louisiana*, 2: 172.

Since Carondelet challenged the intendant's sole right to grant lands, the Crown intervened to settle the dispute. In 1798 the king sustained the intendant's competency in this area. Morales celebrated his victory by issuing elaborate instructions on land grants, which were aimed at making it difficult for Anglo-Americans to obtain real estate.[55]

During Casa-Calvo's administration, Intendant Ramón de López y Ángulo was even more militant about preventing Anglo-Americans from entering the province. In July 1801, he asked the Crown to suspend the granting of land. His true purpose, which extended beyond his jurisdiction, was the desire to regulate Anglo-American entry into Louisiana. He declared that these settlers were entering the province at too accelerated a pace. To prove it, he cited the names of persons requesting free lands from the intendancy. He opposed Anglo-Americans because they were establishing themselves everywhere. He recommended that until the Crown determined policy in granting land, it be halted. Echoing Gayoso's advice of two years before, he preferred to wait until more useful and less dangerous immigrants became available. For now, new land grants should be limited to old settlers and used for the promotion of industry. Complaining about a practice that was going on throughout the colony, López y Ángulo pointed out that commandants and district syndics were making interim land grants but were not submitting them to the intendancy for confirmation.[56]

The next year Salcedo took some steps to restrain the flow of Anglo-Americans into Louisiana. In certain districts, he instructed commandants to oust all immigrants who lacked the proper authority to settle while in other districts he ordered them not to let in any Anglo-

---

55. The Gayoso-Morales struggle is discussed in Holmes, *Gayoso*, 217-22; Morales's new regulations are in Charles Gayarré, *History of Louisiana*, 4 vols. (New Orleans: Armand Hawkins, 1885), 3: 632-40. The offices of governor and intendant were united between 1788 and 1793, and then separated when Francisco Rendón became intendant. Governor Carondelet found him congenial and cooperative. After Rendón was appointed to a post in Zacatecas, Mexico, Juan Ventura Morales served as intendant ad interim until 1798. He became a watchdog of expenditures. A royal order of October 22, 1798, confirmed the intendancy's sole right to grant land. Holmes, *Gayoso*, 219.

56. López y Ángulo to Soler, New Orleans, July 13, 1801, AGI, Santo Domingo, leg. 2617. For a study of Louisiana land laws, see Francis P. Burns, "The Spanish Land Laws of Louisiana," *Louisiana Historical Quarterly* 11 (October 1928): 557-81.

American settlers. However, these last minute efforts, doubtlessly futile, were the final ones made in a desperate attempt to prevent the Anglo-Americans from overrunning the province. On January 18, 1803, Spain belatedly dispatched a royal order informing the Louisiana authorities of the colony's retrocession to France. The order was proclaimed in New Orleans in May, and the transfer to French hands was completed on November 30. By then Napoleon Bonaparte had already sold Louisiana to the United States.[57]

When the United States acquired Louisiana from France on December 20, 1803, the colony had not been overwhelmed by the Anglo-Americans, although their numbers were growing steadily.[58] By now they could be found established in virtually every corner of the province, even west of the Mississippi and near the Texas border. In Lower Louisiana, the most densely populated region, where Frenchmen, Acadians, Germans, and Spaniards were present, Americans were not in a position to overwhelm them, and in some respects this would never happen. It was in the thinly inhabited region of Upper Louisiana that Anglo-Americans had recently made their greatest gains. Nonetheless, even here with its scant population, they had not yet succeeded in becoming the dominant element. While the American settlers were primarily located on isolated farms, village life was in the hands of the French, who also controlled industry, commerce, and the majority of the mines in the region. The Americanization of Upper Louisiana, which would come in the near

---

57. Manuel Juan de Salcedo to V. Layssard, New Orleans, October 6, 1802, AGI, PC, leg. 138; Salcedo to Archinard y Poyres, New Orleans, October 6, 1802, ibid.; Martín Duralde to Salcedo, no. 350 reserved, n.p., July 31, 1802; (Salcedo) to Duralde, New Orleans, August 13, 1802, ibid.; Whitaker, *Mississippi Question*, 176-86; Arthur P. Whitaker, "Spain and the Retrocession of Louisiana," *American Historical Review* 39 (April 1934): 454-76; Mildred Stahl Fletcher, "Louisiana as a Factor in French Diplomacy from 1763-1800," *Mississippi Valley Historical Review* 17 (December 1930): 367-76.

58. Louisiana's population has been estimated at over 50,000 in 1803. Four-fifths of it was located in Lower Louisiana. Whitaker, *Mississippi Question*, 276n. While Americans had entered the province in growing numbers before 1803, contrary to the conclusion of Hatcher ("Louisiana Background," 194), they had not yet become the dominant group. Her figure of 27,000 for Louisiana's inhabitants in 1798 is far too low. Ibid.

future, had still not begun in 1803.[59]

Contrary to its earlier efforts, Spain accomplished little in fostering immigration in its final decade of control over Louisiana. When the Crown in 1787 and 1788 permitted Anglo-Americans to settle there, it did so because it could no longer afford to transport Spaniards or loyal Europeans to the colony. The only people obtainable at no cost to Spain came from the United States, but before long Spanish officials came to regard many—albeit not all of them—as unreliable subjects. Nevertheless, Spain did not dare order their total exclusion from Louisiana for fear of invasion. Although Spanish officials in the colony sought to acquire Europeans, only a few, those already in the United States, migrated to the colony after the mid-1780s. Because of Spain's declining power and inability to defend the province, Spain's Minister of State Godoy in 1795 came to terms with the United States and soon took the first step in disposing of the colony to France in 1800.

Spain's removal from the Mississippi Valley, with the temporary exception of West Florida, resolved the dilemma of a military confrontation with the United States over Louisiana. The problem the Iberian nation faced here was, in reality, part of a larger issue. From 1790 on, Spain was in that final phase of its colonial period in the New World which Charles Chapman once called the "defensive defensive."[60] Challenged by more problems than it had solutions for, Spain found itself retreating along the northern periphery of its American Empire. On the surface, the Spanish retrocession of Louisiana to France would have been a brilliant maneuver had France assumed the colony's defense. Instead, Napoleon's sale of Louisiana to the United States surprised Spain; and while the Spanish government protested the sale it did not actively attempt to regain the province. Unable to colonize Louisiana with a loyal population and faced with Anglo-Americans entering it at will, Spain possibly averted a foreign invasion or an internal rebellion by its retrocession to France. Three

---

59. E. M. Vilette, "Early Settlements in Missouri," *Missouri Historical Review* 1 (October 1906): 38-52. In 1803 Upper Louisiana's population was estimated at 10,340; by the next year, it was 25,000. Jonas Viles, "Population and Extent of Settlement in Missouri before 1804," ibid. 5 (July 1911): 189-213.

60. Charles Edward Chapman, *Colonial Hispanic America: A History* (New York: Macmillan, 1933), 184-85.

decades later, Mexico, facing a similar crisis in Texas, lacked a solution to the same dilemma. Consequently, Mexico experienced an insurrection in Texas, led chiefly by Anglo-American immigrants from the United States.

Chapter 7
The Irish Proselytizing Mission to West Florida

The Spanish conquest of British West Florida in the American War for Independence began an unusual episode in Spanish colonial history. With the victory, Spain acquired an Anglo-Saxon Protestant population that Spain attempted to convert and assimilate through the use of English-speaking Irish priests. Three years later in 1787, however, Spain reversed its immigration policy for its colonies of Louisiana and West Florida and permitted Protestants from the United States to settle in them, thus expanding the responsibilities of the Irish priests. They now acquired the task of converting and assimilating the newly arriving Americans as well as the older established Britons. For several years the Spanish government and the Irish priests labored to proselytize these settlers. But for a number of reasons the ultimate result was not favorable.[1]

In 1782 Esteban Miró became the acting governor of Louisiana and West Florida. In this capacity, he inherited the work of fulfilling the terms of the Treaty of Paris with Great Britain that granted the Anglo-Saxon settlers of West Florida eighteen months to evacuate the province. Although some of them departed, a general exodus did not occur.[2] After

---

1. This article first appeared as "The Irish Mission to West Florida," *Louisiana History* 12 (Fall 1971): 315-34. Early Catholic activities on the Mississippi are discussed in Rev. B. J. Bekkers, "The Catholic Church in Mississippi during Colonial Times," *Publications of the Mississippi Historical Society* 6 (1902): 351-57; Patrick W. Browne, "Salamanca and the Beginnings of the Church in Florida," *The Ecclesiastical Review* 84 (1931): 581-87; and V. Alton Moody, "Early Religious Efforts in the Lower Mississippi Valley," *Mississippi Valley Historical Review* 22 (1935): 161-63.

2. Caroline Maude Burson, *The Stewardship of Don Esteban Miró* (New Orleans; American Printing Company, 1940): 24. For accounts of the British in West Florida, see Cecil Johnson, "Expansion in West Florida: 1770-1779," *Mississippi Valley Historical*

the allotted time and a four-month extension expired, twelve Protestant residents, who were representatives of the other settlers, petitioned Miró for permission to remain on their lands under the same conditions that had prevailed from the beginning of Spanish control. They had not been disturbed in their private religious beliefs and understood that only the Roman Catholic faith enjoyed public worship. In addition, the inhabitants were now willing to take oaths of allegiance to the Spanish government. The governor forwarded their petition to Viceroy Bernardo de Gálvez in Mexico City, who still held control over Louisiana and West Florida. Inasmuch as he lacked instructions as to what measures to take regarding the petition, Gálvez ordered Miró to wait until the Crown learned about the matter.[3]

In West Florida these residents were located mainly along the Mississippi River at Baton Rouge, Natchez, Manchac, and at other embryonic settlements. Almost all the families were Protestant, and Governor Miró did not have much hope for their swift conversion to Catholicism. Nevertheless, he advised against their expulsion from the province because nearly all were impoverished. He feared that if ejected they would resettle fifty or a hundred leagues away and from their new settlements threaten the security of Louisiana.[4] But the presence of Protestants inside Spanish domains constituted an anomalous situation and a plan was needed to resolve the curious dilemma. Thereupon Miró proposed sending English-speaking Irish missionaries to work among the Protestants. He believed that the priests could convert the adults to Catholicism through persuasive evangelization and their children should be baptized and instructed in the Catholic faith in a public school.

Review 20 (1934): 481-96; and Wilbur H. Siebert, "The Loyalists in West Florida and the Natchez District," Mississippi Valley Historical Society *Proceedings* 8 (1915): 106-10; and Robin Fabel, *The Economy of British West Florida, 1763-1783* (Tuscaloosa, Ala.: University of Alabama Press, 1988).

3. "Memorial of Harris Alexander *et al.* to the Conde de Gálvez (Bernardo de Gálvez)," New Orleans, March 1, 1785; Bernardo de Gálvez to Esteban Miró, Mexico City, October 20, 1785; both documents in Archivo General de Indias (Seville, Spain), Papeles procedentes de Cuba, legajo (hereafter cited as AGI, PC, leg.), 109.

4. Miró to Bernardo de Gálvez, no. 228, New Orleans, September 5, 1785, Archivo Histórico Nacional (Madrid), Estado, legajo (hereafter cited AHN, Est., leg.) 3888bis.

Settlers who objected to these requirements would be forced to leave West Florida by sea at their expense or, if necessary, at the cost of the Spanish government.[5]

In Spain in April 1786, the Supreme Council discussed the predicament with the West Florida Protestant families. The council soon issued a royal order that essentially incorporated Miró's recommendations which permitted families to remain under pledges of fidelity and obedience to the Spanish Crown. Furthermore, the council directed officials in Louisiana to draw up a scheme for the establishment of parishes and schools at Natchez and other places that would be staffed with Irish priests. It became Miró's duty in New Orleans to devise the plan for West Florida.[6]

Simultaneously in April 1786, the Supreme Council directed Bishop Andrés of Salamanca to select four volunteer priests from the Royal College of Irishmen at the University of Salamanca or elsewhere to serve in the new West Florida mission field. Only two Irishmen at Salamanca qualified to work as missionaries, however. They were Patrick Curtis, rector of the college since 1781, who was needed in Spain; and William Savage, vice-rector and highly recommended by the bishop. Although Savage had pledged to return to Ireland upon completion of his studies, he volunteered to serve in West Florida and was released from his obligation. Bishop Andrés immediately began a search for additional priests in other places in Spain.[7]

By September he had located four more Irishmen and was apprised of the conditions under which they volunteered to serve in West Florida. Michael Lamport in Cádiz requested 9,500 reales (1,187 ½ pesos) for the payment of debts, another 1,000 pesos for clothing, books, and other indispensable items needed in his ministry, and 1,000 pesos for his annual salary. In Seville, Constantine MacKenna and Gregory White, residents of the House of the Venerables, and Bernard Lunney, a Dominican living

---

5. Conde de Gálvez to José de Gálvez, no. 56 preferred, Mexico City, October 27, 1785, ibid.

6. Royal order to the Conde de Gálvez, El Pardo, April 5, 1786, ibid.

7. Royal order to the Bishop of Salamanca, El Pardo, April 5, 1786; Andrés, Bishop of Salamanca, to the Marqués de Sonora (José de Gálvez), Salamanca, May 16, 1786; both in ibid.

in the Convent of St. Peter, sought 1,000 pesos each to equip themselves and a similar sum as their yearly salary. Meanwhile, in Salamanca Savage agreed to the same terms requested by the others. All the priests indicated their wish to remain in the mission field for only ten years and, at the end of that time, return to Spain at government expense with a pension for their services.[8]

The Marqués de Sonora (José de Gálvez), minister of the Indies, regarded their demands as excessive. Sonora reminded Bishop Andrés of two other Irish priests who had been sent earlier to East Florida. They had received 325 pesos to equip themselves, a monthly salary of 30 pesos, and agreed to serve without a fixed time period. Excluding the Dominican monk from consideration, Sonora made a counterproposal to the four priests. He offered them a monthly salary of 40 pesos, 325 pesos for equipment, and the promise of royal compensation in proportion to the length of their service in West Florida. All the priests accepted the terms.[9] Soon MacKenna and White joined Lamport in Cádiz where they were all to sail to their new employment. While Savage delayed in departing from Salamanca, the three priests in Cádiz exhausted their funds, and they petitioned for additional financial assistance which was denied. Later, in April 1787 with Savage now in Cádiz, all four begged for extra compensation, and it was again refused. Instead, they received an advance in their salary. At last, on April 17, an order permitted them to board the frigate *San Juan Nepomuceno*, which transported them to Havana.[10]

Meanwhile, Governor Miró in New Orleans remitted his plan for the establishment of the parishes to Spain. Inasmuch as the Natchez

---

8. Andrés, Bishop of Salamanca, to Sonora, Santa Visita de la Villa de Miranda del Castañar, September 28, 1786, ibid.

9. Sonora to the Bishop of Salamanca, San Lorenzo, October 18, 1786, and Madrid, December 20, 1786; both in ibid. Savage received an additional 250 pesos for transportation expenses from Salamanca to Cádiz. The two Irish priests who went to East Florida were Thomas Hassett and Michael O'Reilly. Browne, "Salamanca and the Beginnings," 583.

10. "Petition of Michael Lamport, Constantine MacKenna, and Gregory White," Cádiz, March 9, 1787; "Petition of William Savage, Michael Lamport, Gregory White, and Constantine MacKenna," Cádiz, April 10, 1787; Ramón Rivera to Sonora, Cádiz, April 17, 1787; all in AHN, Est., leg. 3888bis.

District was the most heavily populated with Anglo-Saxon settlers and they included some recent American arrivals, Miró decided to set up two parishes in the district: one to serve St. Catherine Creek and Second Creek, and another parish to serve Cole's Creek. He also proposed the establishment of a third parish on the Tensas River, some forty-five miles above Mobile where fifty-nine Protestant families resided. The duties of the priests included teaching Catholic doctrine and reading and writing in Spanish. After dispatching his plan to Spain, the governor awaited its approval.[11] But before it arrived he learned that the four Irish priests were on their way to New Orleans from Havana.

The clerics reached New Orleans in August 1787, beset with financial difficulties. In Cádiz they had received a two-month salary advance and in Havana they were given an additional three months' advance. The Crown paid for their transportation but made no similar provision for their lodgings, and delays in obtaining passage had eaten heavily into their funds. In New Orleans they requested that the Crown not charge them for the five months' advancement in salary to enable them to begin their ministry with an income. Governor Miró endorsed their petition when he forwarded it to Spain; he explained that their work among non-Catholics negated the possibility of earning fees for religious services provided. After a lengthy delay, Madrid approved the governor's recommendation in March 1789.[12]

The arrival of the Irish priests forced Miró to take immediate steps to construct the parishes. When two mail boats had arrived without bringing authorization for his plan, Miró decided to proceed in line with his proposal. The governor kept three of the priests—Savage, White, and MacKenna—to serve in the two parishes he intended to establish in the Natchez District, and he dispatched Lamport to serve the settlement on the Tensas River. For the Natchez church, Miró purchased three hundred arpents of land, which included a house suitable as a parochial residence, from Stephen Minor in 1788 for 2,000 pesos. Construction of the church did not begin for another two years. By 1792 the finishing touches were

---

11. Miró to Sonora, New Orleans, February 10 and June 1, 1787, both in ibid.

12. "Petition of William Savage *et al.*," New Orleans, October 15, 1787; royal order to the Governor-Intendant of Louisiana, Madrid, March 23, 1789; both in ibid.

finally put on the church, and William Savage received the office of parish priest. The government bought an additional three hundred arpents of land from James Elliot in 1789 for 2,000 pesos to establish the church at Cole's Creek. Although this church was completed in 1792, it consisted of little more than four bare walls. Gregory White received the assignment to this parish. A third church was built at Tombigbee on the Tensas River, and it too was finished about 1792.[13] The Spanish government paid for the land, construction of the churches and presbyteries, and paraphernalia needed to equip them.

Of the first four Irish missionaries assigned to West Florida, three died in the Spanish province. Only White lived to return to Europe. Lamport's premature death in Mobile on August 2, 1789, came two years after his arrival in the colony. Savage, who served as the first parish priest at Natchez where he gained an excellent reputation as an orator and evangelizer, succumbed at his parish on April 18, 1793. MacKenna initially served as assistant to Savage in Natchez. In February 1792, he was appointed parish priest of the Tombigbee settlement after its church had been built. Over the years, he served at a number of posts before passing away on May 12, 1802, while serving as the parish priest at Bayou Sara. Meanwhile, White became the first priest at the Cole's Creek parish in 1792, a post he retained for a year until he was called to Natchez to replace the deceased Savage. His stay in Natchez was short-lived. Intemperate, irregular in conduct, and alcoholic, White's failure to attract converts resulted in his temporary suspension as priest and his return to Cole's Creek. Here he presided over light duties and served the parish until 1798, when the United States assumed control of the Natchez District. At that time White received the parish of Lafourche, on the west side of the Mississippi in Louisiana, but he requested permission to retire at half

13. Miró to Antonio Valdés, New Orleans, January 8, 1788; royal order to the governor of Louisiana, Aranjuez, May 14, 1789; both in ibid.; Francisco Hector Luis de Carondelet to Theodoro Tirso Henrique Henríquez, New Orleans, March 6, 1792, AGI, PC, leg. 102; Most Rev. Richard O. Gerow, "History of the Catholic Diocese of Natchez," *Catholic Action of the South* (Centennial Edition; New Orleans, October 14, 1937), 5: 6; Jack D. L. Holmes, *Gayoso, The Life of a Spanish Governor in the Mississippi Valley, 1789-1799* (Baton Rouge: Louisiana State University Press for the Louisiana Historical Association, 1965), 73-74; Michael J. Curley, *Church and State in the Spanish Floridas* (Washington, D. C.: Catholic University Press, 1940), 151-54.

pay and return to Europe. In 1800 the Spanish government granted his wish.[14]

About the same time that the first Irish missionaries arrived in Louisiana in 1787, Spain was already taking steps to enlarge their original purpose. The government had found it extremely difficult to induce the settlers it favored to come to Louisiana at their own expense and those who came at government cost imposed an insupportable burden upon the royal treasury. Louisiana and West Florida needed inexpensive colonists to develop and defend the provinces. As Spain witnessed the rapid expansion of the western American settlements after the War for American Independence, it became increasingly sensitive to the defensive needs of Louisiana and West Florida. In 1784 Spain closed the Mississippi River to Americans in an effort to stunt the development of their possessions in the upper Ohio River basin. Nevertheless, they continued to grow, and rumors often filled Louisiana with threats of possible invasion because the river was closed to Americans. Spanish efforts to counter-colonize with their own immigrants against the rising American menace failed. Since the right colonists were not available, Governor Miró helped persuade the Spanish Crown to admit Americans. He did this through the second plan that James Wilkinson presented in New Orleans in September 1787, which was in reality the work of the governor. This proposal allowed American settlers, mainly Protestant in religion, to establish themselves in West Florida and Louisiana, and additional Irish priests would be sent to convert and assimilate them. Ironically, with the royal order of August 23, 1787, the Spanish government had already authorized the entry of Americans into West Florida and Louisiana, with the provision that Irish priests would work among them for their religious conversion. The royal order of August 23 was the action of Pierre Wouves d'Argès, who the year before had journeyed through New Orleans and adopted Governor Miró's plans for his own use. Although the Spanish Court initially appointed d'Argès as an immigration agent to bring families from Kentucky, with the royal order of December 1, 1788, he found himself supplanted by Wilkinson, who Miró and the

---

14. Holmes, *Gayoso*, 71-72; Curley, *Church and State*, 152-54, 241, 245. For personal data concerning the Natchez priests, see Jack D. L. Holmes, "Irish Priests in Spanish Natchez," *Journal of Mississippi History* 29 (August 1967): 169-80.

Spanish government preferred. Wilkinson's greater ambitions included separating Kentucky from the United States and forming a union with Spain. Nevertheless, with the two royal orders of 1787 and 1788, the Irish priests found their tasks immeasurably increased.[15]

Despite the modest movement of Americans into Spanish territory by May 20, 1791, Governor Miró considered the Protestant population sufficiently large in a number of areas to warrant the sending of additional Irish priests and the creation of new parishes. Settlements with significant Americans in the Natchez District included the village of Natchez, Cole's Creek (renamed Villa Gayoso in 1792), Bayou Pierre, and Nogales; in the Mobile District they were Mobile, Tensas, and Tombigbee; and lastly, Arkansas and New Madrid had American inhabitants as well. Miró requested five Irish priests to labor in these settlements and a sixth priest for the Protestants of New Orleans, where a petition had been circulated and signed by thirty-three inhabitants asking for an English-speaking cleric. On October 17, 1791, the Spanish government approved Miró's solicitude and instructed the bishop of Salamanca to locate the six needed priests.[16] Of the six missionaries chosen from volunteers of the Irish College of Salamanca, only one, Patrick Mangan, was an ordained priest. The others—Patrick Walsh, Francis Lennan, James Coleman, George Murphy, and Charles Burke—were still students. A papal dispensation was necessary before they could leave the college; it was granted in February 1792. Their terms of agreement were altered slightly from those obtained by the first four priests to serve in West Florida. Each of the second group

---

15. Gilbert C. Din, "The Immigration Policy of Governor Esteban Miró in Spanish Louisiana," *Southwestern Historical Quarterly* 73 (1969): 159-73; Arthur Preston Whitaker, *The Spanish American Frontier, 1783-1795: The Westward Movement and the Spanish Retreat in the Mississippi Valley* (Glouster, Mass.: Peter Smith, 1962 rpt.), 78-107.

16. Miró to Antonio Portlier, New Orleans, May 20, 1791, AGI, Audiencia de Santo Domingo (hereafter abbreviated as Santo Domingo), leg. 2589; Conde de Floridablanca to the Marqués de Bajamar, San Lorenzo, October 17, 1791, AHN, Est., leg. 3888bis. In 1791 the populations of Pensacola and Mobile stood at 572 and 733, respectively; and in 1792 Tombigbee and Tensas had 348 and 493 inhabitants, respectively. In the last two settlements the population was composed almost entirely of Protestants. Fr. Cirilo de Barcelona to Antonio Portlier, New Orleans, May 18, 1791, AGI, PC, leg. 2351 (information provided to the author by Jack D. L. Holmes).

received a monthly salary of only 30 pesos and 375 pesos with which to equip himself with vestments and other religious paraphernalia essential to his ministry. By May 1792, the priests had sailed from Spain with Mangan in charge of the group. They arrived in Havana on June 26, and the next month, on July 22, they sailed for New Orleans.[17]

When the Irish clerics reached New Orleans, Gov. Francisco Luis Héctor, Baron de Carondelet, who replaced Miró as civil and military governor in Louisiana and West Florida on December 30, 1791, determined their disposition. He sent George Murphy to serve at Attakapas, where he remained for only three years before returning to Europe. Meanwhile, he assigned Francis Lennan to Nogales and Cole's Creek before shifting him to Natchez in 1794. Mangan and Walsh stayed in New Orleans, where Walsh became the chaplain of the Fixed Louisiana Infantry Regiment. He also served at one time as vicar general of the province. Neither Mangan nor Walsh worked among the Protestant settlers. Burke was sent to Baton Rouge, and Coleman was assigned to the Mobile District at Tombigbee and later to Pensacola.[18] These six priests were the last of the clerics to come from the Irish College of the University of Salamanca. After the revolution in France had closed or rendered its seminaries useless, the bishops in Ireland requested that all graduates from Salamanca return home for service there.[19] Even though a few additional Irish priests entered Louisiana and West Florida later, none came from the Irish College.

When Governor Carondelet replied to the royal order of March 13, 1793, which inquired about the state of the parishes and religious conditions in Louisiana and West Florida, he stressed the severe shortage of priests. The Spanish government thereupon made another effort to secure more missionaries. The search quickly produced two Irish priests: Father John Brady, a Carmelite friar who was approved to go to West

---

17. Diego de Gardoqui to the Governor-Intendant of Louisiana, Aranjuez, February 1, 1792; Bajamar to the Governor-Intendant of Louisiana, Aranjuez, March 18, 1792; both in AGI, PC, leg. 2317B; Curley, *Church and State*, 191-94.

18. Curley, *Church and State*, 210, 233, 237-38, 141-44.

19. Ibid., 195-96, 200-204. For a biographical sketch of one priest, see Jack D. L. Holmes, "Father Francis Lennan and his Activities in Spanish Louisiana and West Florida," *Louisiana Studies* 5 (1966): 255-65.

Florida with a monthly salary of 40 pesos, plus 375 more for religious equipment; and James Maxwell, who had served for six years as a chaplain in the French navy and then was expelled by the Republican government for his refusal to take a civil oath. As early as November 1792, Maxwell had applied to serve in West Florida, but the Spanish government delayed his approval until March 30, 1795. The two new missionaries reached New Orleans in September of that year. Since Maxwell was fluent in French, he was sent to Upper Louisiana to serve at St. Genevieve, where he remained for nearly two decades until his death in 1814.[20] Brady meanwhile was assigned to Natchez, where he garnered a reputation as the best shot, rider, and judge of horseflesh in the entire district.[21]

Several other Irish priests and a monk who were not sent from Spain also arrived in West Florida and Louisiana, where they served the Spanish government. In 1789 Thomas Hassett, who five years earlier had landed in East Florida to work among the Protestant settlers there, moved to New Orleans. Until he died in 1804, he resided and worked in the city. At the time of his death, he was vicar general of Louisiana.[22] Around 1797, two other Irish priests, John Maguire and John Bodkin, entered Louisiana following a journey through the United States. Both priests had been educated in France but driven out by the French Revolution. Maguire served at Lafourche and afterwards at Iberville. When Spain lost Louisiana in 1803, he requested a transfer to another Spanish colony and departed. Meanwhile, Bodkin became a military chaplain in New Orleans and later served at Pensacola. Finally, around 1804, Patrick Lonergan, a Franciscan monk, came down the Mississippi River from Pennsylvania to enter service with the Spanish government in West Florida. He was

---

20. Curley, *Church and State*, 204-206; Fermin A. Rozier, "Rev. James Maxwell, Missionary at St. Genevieve," *The United States Catholic Historical Magazine* 1 (1887): 283-86; Louis Houck, *A History of Missouri, from the Earliest Explorations and Settlements until the Admission of the State into the Union*, 3 vols. (Chicago: R. R. Donnelly and Sons, 1909), 2: 298. Maxwell served as vicar general of Upper Louisiana from 1796 until his death in 1814.

21. George Willey, "Natchez in the Olden Times," *Mississippi, as a Province, Territory and State*, by J. F. H. Claiborne (Jackson, Miss.: Power and Barksdale, 1880): 527.

22. Curley, *Church and State*, 116-19, 294.

appointed pastor of the parish at New Feliciana and died there in 1805.[23]

Although great aspirations were held for the conversion of the Anglo-Americans in West Florida to Catholicism, the task proved exceptionally difficult. Catholic religious fervor was almost nonexistent in that province—and in Louisiana—as Bishop Luis Peñalver noted in his report of 1795. He observed the scarcity of conversions to Catholicism among Protestants, the acute shortage of priests (both Spanish and Irish), and the failure to assimilate the alien American population resident on Spanish soil.[24] Besides these problems, the Irish clerics of the Natchez District did not appear to be suited to their spiritual mission. While William Savage lived, his efficacious preaching and earnest dedication produced conversions at Natchez. His early death in 1793, however, robbed Natchez of its most persuasive missionary, and thereafter conversions fell off. Manuel Gayoso de Lemos, Spanish governor of the Natchez District from 1789 to 1797, requested additional priests from Spain but none came. In 1795 he condemned the state of religious affairs within his jurisdiction. Of the three Irish priests in the district, in his opinion not one qualified as fit to work among the American Protestants. White, who briefly held the important Natchez parish after Savage's death, had to be withdrawn because of his intemperateness and fondness for drink; Lennan, who replaced him in 1794, appeared to be more concerned with driving all Protestants from the district, and he condemned the tolerance afforded the Americans; and Brady, while deploring conditions, did nothing to stimulate conversion. Gayoso believed that if the district had but three effective English-speaking priests many conversions would soon occur, and he favored curtailing the entry of Protestants in Spanish territory once the majority of the Protestant residents had converted.[25]

Besides the ineffectiveness of the Natchez missionaries, the attachment of the Protestants to their religion, their objection to Spanish

---

23. Ibid., 207-208, 211; Thomas Hassett to Patrick Mangan, New Orleans, April 18, 1804, AGI, PC, leg. 102.

24. Luis Peñalver y Cárdenas to Eugenio Llaguno, New Orleans, November 1, 1795, Biblioteca Nacional (Madrid), Manuscript Section, vol. 19,248, 2: ff. 24-27; Holmes, *Gayoso*, 225n.

25. Manuel Gayoso de Lemos to the Duque de la Alcudia (Manuel Godoy), Natchez, March 31, 1795, AGI, PC, leg. 2354.

religious laws, and the presence of surreptitious Protestant ministers all combined to impede and demoralize the Irish mission. Much of the success of the missionaries depended on the willingness of the Protestant population to embrace Catholicism. Governor Miró originally believed that by denying the dissenters public worship, ministers of their own faith, and government positions, they would gradually be drawn into the official religion. The Irish priests were asked to convert the adult population through gentle and persuasive preaching while Protestant children were to be baptized as Catholics. Although simple in design the plan proved unworkable. While some persons converted to Catholicism, on the whole, the proselytizing effort met stiffer opposition than Spanish officials had anticipated.[26]

Organized Protestant religious activity in West Florida had begun before the Spaniards took control of the province during the past war, and it continued sub rosa even under Spanish dominion. The first Protestant minister to arrive in the colony was the Rev. Samuel Swayze, who reached the Natchez District in 1772, when it was still a British province. Soon after, a Congregational Church began there with Swayze as its minister, a post he retained until his death in 1784. Earlier, however, the Spanish conquest terminated public worship for all religions except the Roman Catholic, although private services persisted among the more devout. Reportedly, some Protestant groups continued to meet clandestinely in swamps and canebrakes. In spite of not being an ordained minister, Swayze's son attempted to carry on his father's work, but the Congregational Church declined.[27]

The first Protestant church organized in the Natchez District during the Spanish period was Baptist under the fiery leadership of Rev. Richard Curtis Jr. Baptists had been in the district since 1781, but an organized church did not function until 1791. In that year Curtis started his church at Cole's Creek where he served as its pastor. It appears that the congregation did not meet in strict privacy because Governor

---

26. Moody, "Early Religious Efforts," 163.

27. Robert Lowry and William H. McCardle, *A History of Mississippi* (1891; repr., Jackson, Miss.: Power and Barksdale, 1964), 116-18; Rev. Thomas L. Haman, "Beginnings of Presbyterianism in Mississippi," *Publications* of the Mississippi Historical Society 10 (1909): 205-206.

Gayoso of Natchez gained knowledge of its activities. In 1795 Gayoso summoned Curtis and John and Jacob Stampley, his assistants, to appear before him, at which time he warned them to desist from conducting public religious services that violated the law. Curtis then pledged that he would not again preach in public under pain of confiscation of his goods and expulsion from the province. Shortly thereafter, however, during Gayoso's temporary absence from the district, Curtis defied him. The Spaniards soon issued an order for the minister's arrest. Warned by friends, Curtis fled to the safety of South Carolina. His exile did not last long, and he returned to West Florida the following year, where he undoubtedly quickly resumed his evangelical mission. After the Spanish authorities withdrew from Natchez in 1798, the Baptists quickly founded new churches. Furthermore, a Baptist minister is said to have preached in 1799 in Baton Rouge, which was still in Spanish territory and meant that it was done clandestinely.[28]

Besides Curtis, several other Protestant ministers ran afoul of Spanish laws regarding public worship in the Natchez District. While Governor Gayoso made every effort to be as tolerant as he could on the religious issue, the boldness of some Protestant ministers and the protests of the Irish priests at times forced his hand.[29] In 1792 the Rev. Adam Cloud, a clergyman of the Protestant Episcopal Church, settled at St. Catherine Creek, where he became a prominent planter. In time Cloud

---

28. Charles H. Otken, "Richard Curtis in the Country of the Natchez," *Publications of the Mississippi Historical Society* 3 (1900): 147-51; Z. T. Leavell, "Early Beginnings of Baptists in Mississippi," *Publications* of the Mississippi Historical Society 4 (1901): 246-52. Maj. Steve Power, in *The Memento: Old and New Natchez, 1700 to 1897* (Natchez, Miss.: Myrtle Banks Publisher, 1984), 14, declares that a Protestant Episcopal church was built in Natchez in 1791; however, this seems very doubtful.

29. Samuel S. Forman, in *Narrative of a Journey down the Ohio and Mississippi in 1789-90* (Cincinnati: R. Clarke and Company, 1888), 57, states that Gayoso allowed a Protestant sermon to be preached in Natchez in 1791; Holmes, *Gayoso*, 77. While nineteenth-century Mississippi writers have generally praised the Spaniards for being religiously tolerant, tolerance did not reach the level claimed by Lowry and McCardle in their *History of Mississippi*, 131: "The Spaniards were Catholics, of course, but members of the Protestant church were allowed to worship God after their own fashion, with as much freedom as is allowed to any worshiper of Almighty God in any quarter of the United States today."

violated Spanish religious laws, which included preaching a public sermon in Natchez. It was more remarkable because of Gayoso's presence there. He sternly warned Cloud not to repeat his performance, but he ignored the warning. Largely due to Father Lennan's protests, in 1795 Governor Carondelet in New Orleans ordered Cloud's arrest and deportation along with his family after charging him with "preaching, baptizing and marrying people contrary to the laws of the existing government."[30] Another Protestant minister arrested was John Bolls, a ruling elder in the Presbyterian Church. Gayoso ordered his detention on the grounds of having breached the ban on public worship.[31]

Although Spanish authorities expended their resources to curb Protestant activities, it was a strenuous chore. From 1795 religious tensions mounted in the Natchez District. In that year a number of its residents, many of them planters, asked Gayoso for a clarification of the district's religious law. The governor suggested that they all reaffirm their loyalty to the Spanish government and, at the same time, the king would again grant the Protestant community the right of private worship. Gayoso thus hoped to calm the surging restlessness of the Anglo-American dissenters. However, with the signing of the Treaty of San Lorenzo of 1795, in which Spain ceded the Natchez District to the United States, the religious situation gradually heated up.[32] As Spain delayed transfer of this territory to the United States until 1798, anxiety increased among the Protestant inhabitants in anticipation of the lifting of religious restrictions. Already within the Natchez camp of Andrew Ellicott, who was the United States commissioner to determine boundaries, Protestant sermons were delivered from 1797, and several dissident ministers began to challenge Gayoso's ban on the public preaching of any religion other than Catholic. In June 1797, when Gayoso arrested Barton Hannon, an itinerant Baptist shoemaker, for disturbing the peace, it produced a violent reaction among the Americans of Natchez who called the arrest an

30. Haman, "Beginnings of Presbyterianism," 206; Holmes, "Father Francis Lennan," 258-60.

31. Willey, "Natchez in the Olden Times," 528.

32. Whitaker, *Spanish American Frontier*, 201-22; Samuel Flagg Bemis, *Pinckney's Treaty* (New Haven: Yale University Press, 1960 revd. ed.).

example of Spanish religious persecution. Gayoso temporarily withdrew to the safety of Fort Panmure in Natchez, and for several days conditions in the district remained volatile. However, tensions soon eased, and the governor's generous terms to the rebels quieted down the most vehement outburst of Protestant sentiment during the Spanish period. In March 1798, the United States assumed control of the Natchez District, and Protestant religious activities immediately surged upwards. Soon new denominations, such as the Methodist and Presbyterian, began forming religious communities under the direction of their ministers.[33] There can be no doubt that the persistent zeal of the Protestants seriously hindered the work of the Irish missionaries.

In addition to the issue of public worship, the marriage ceremony was another arena of conflict that disrupted relations between Spanish officials and Protestants. According to Spanish law, a Catholic priest and two witnesses were required to attend Protestants' marriages. However, the law was frequently violated. Often Protestant ministers residing illegally in the Natchez District performed the marriage ceremony; or in the absence of any kind of clergyman, the Protestant bride and groom merely solemnized their marriage vows before their neighbors. Still other couples left Spanish territory to be married in the United States. Spanish ecclesiastical authorities took a dim view of these proceedings and attempted to regulate Protestant marriages more closely. By the royal order of November 30, 1792, the Crown issued new instructions for the marriage of dissenters. Protestants could now make their own wedding arrangements, and Catholic priests were forbidden to participate in marriages between Protestants or between a Catholic and a non-Catholic. Though the priest was still required to be present to record the marriage, he was not to offer a nuptial blessing, forbidden to wear a surplice or any other Catholic vestment, and denied use of the Catholic Church to perform the ceremony. Also, Protestants who left Spanish territory to be married were required to regularize their marriages when they returned. If they attempted to circumvent the law governing marriage, their property would be confiscated and they faced expulsion from the province.[34]

---

33. Holmes, *Gayoso*, 189-90.

34. Curley, *Church and State*, 222-30; royal order to the governor of Louisiana, San

The foreign-born population in West Florida regarded Spanish marriage regulations for Protestants both cumbersome and repugnant. It does not appear that the law on this matter was well enforced, and Spanish authorities were frequently lenient. Protestant marriages continued to skirt the law as couples went outside the province to be married while others were married by benevolent military commandants. Furthermore, while some Protestant marriages were performed with the full knowledge that they were circumventing regulations, the shortage of Catholic priests made it difficult for those who sought to conform to the law. Spanish religious conventions created a barrier for Protestants who wanted to embrace Spanish citizenship willingly and wholeheartedly.

The Irish missionaries confronted numerous obstacles to conversion, but the Treaty of San Lorenzo of 1795 between Spain and the United States resulted in an even greater disaster for the West Florida mission. When the treaty was signed Spain surrendered three strategic parishes where considerable energy and funds had been expended in an attempt to convert the Anglo-American inhabitants. The lost parishes were the very ones that Governor Miró had initially established: Natchez, Cole's Creek, and Tombigbee on the Tensas River. Despite the Spanish holdup until 1798 in evacuating the area, demoralization was already evident and little progress toward conversion was made as the Protestant settlers realized that Catholic domination would soon end.

The loss of territory brought about personnel changes as well. Brady, who had been at Natchez, withdrew in 1797 to New Orleans, where he became the chaplain of the Spanish sloop, *La Luisiana*, anchored there. White, pastor of the Cole's Creek church, was reassigned to Lafourche, but instead chose to retire to Spain in 1799. Lennan, who also had been at Natchez, went down to New Feliciana in Spanish territory, and from there he occasionally visited the Natchez church. He was at Pointe Coupée from 1799 to 1800. In the last year, he was reassigned to Baton Rouge and after this time no longer offered services in Natchez. Since priests now neglected that church, decline in Catholic activities set in. Earlier the Tombigbee parish was abandoned in 1794, when Father

---

Lorenzo, November 30, 1792, Biblioteca Nacional, Manuscript Section, vol. 19,248, 3: 233-36.

Coleman went to Pensacola.[35]

Besides the loss of the three parishes, by the late 1790s virtually no effort was being made to implement the original goal of the Irish mission. Spain's agreement in 1800 to retrocede Louisiana to France further hindered the missionaries' efforts. The Irish mission had now reached its final stage. The shortage of priests, which had always been acute, became even more pronounced and a number of parishes were without them. Bishop Luis Peñalver of Louisiana noted the lack of conversions and added that the dissident population had turned a deaf ear to the preaching of the Catholic clergy. He suggested denying Americans entry in Spanish territory. Realizing that it was a matter of time before Spain lost control of Louisiana the bishop requested a new post. His wish was granted and, in November 1801, he departed from New Orleans to become the archbishop of Guatemala. Before leaving, Peñalver appointed Thomas Hassett as acting vicar general for the Louisiana diocese, with Patrick Walsh as his assistant, until a new bishop arrived. Hassett remained as vicar general over Louisiana and the Floridas until his death on April 24, 1804. Although Walsh then temporarily assumed the duties of vicar, he did so without formal authority, thus touching off a storm of controversy initiated by some priests who refused to recognize his power. Eventually, the diocese was placed under the jurisdiction of the archbishop of Baltimore in the United States, who appointed a replacement.[36]

As a result of the Louisiana Purchase, the United States acquired control of Louisiana on December 20, 1803. Now only a strip of territory along the Gulf Coast called West Florida and the larger colony of East Florida remained in Spanish hands. Even here the situation was precarious for the Iberian nation. In less than two decades, the expansionist United States acquired both colonies.[37] As they slipped from Spanish hands, there was little the few remaining Irish priests in West Florida could

35. Curley, *Church and State*, 242, 274, 277-78.

36. Peñalver to José Antonio Caballero, New Orleans, July 30, 1799, AGI, Santo Domingo, leg. 2589; Louis Houck, ed., *The Spanish Régime in Missouri*, 2 vols. (Chicago: R. R. Donnelly and Sons, 1909), 2: 221n.

37. Curley, *Church and State*, 287-99. Walsh died in 1806, ibid., 309. On the gradual loss of Spanish territory, see Issac J. Cox, *West Florida Controversy, 1793-1813* (Baltimore: Johns Hopkins University Press, 1918).

accomplish. In reality the Irish mission was at an end. In the last years of their religious work further personnel changes occurred. Some of the clerics withdrew from West Florida while others elected to remain at their posts and accept the political jurisdiction of the United States.

Among those who departed was Patrick Mangan. His decade of service was spent in New Orleans and its environs. When Louisiana transferred to United States control, he requested and received permission to retire to Mexico. From 1792 Charles Burke labored at Baton Rouge, which included the two nearby areas of Manchac to the south and New Feliciana to the north. Around 1797 Burke became involved in a controversy with the bishop of Louisiana and the governor of the province, which impaired his duties. Two years later, with his health deteriorating, he received permission to undertake an ocean voyage during which time he traveled to Spain without proper authorization. He never returned to West Florida and presumably journeyed home to Ireland. His post at Baton Rouge remained vacant until Lennan moved there from Pointe Coupée. John Maguire was another priest who left when the United States acquired Louisiana; he sought a post as military chaplain with the Spanish government and departed. In 1806 the only remaining parishes in West Florida were Pensacola, Mobile, Baton Rouge, and New Feliciana. Two of the Irish priests still present were Brady at Baton Rouge and Lennan at New Feliciana; within four years these two parishes were also lost to the United States. Brady, who withdrew from Baton Rouge in 1805, later obtained authorization to return to his former parish in 1818. As for Lennan, although he sought permission to leave the colony in 1804, he was in Baton Rouge as late as 1811. Another of the Irish priests was James Coleman, who had served at Pensacola since 1794. He was the last of the Irish missionaries to remain serving the Spanish government. When the United States assumed control of all West Florida and East Florida in 1821, as specified through the Adams-Onis Treaty of 1819, Coleman retired with the last withdrawing Spaniards in 1822 to serve elsewhere in the Spanish Empire.[38]

In looking back to determine the causes for the failure of the Irish

---

38. Curley, *Church and State*, 211, 270-73, 320-21, 333-34; Hassett to Mangan, New Orleans, April 18, 1804, AGI, PC, leg. 102.

mission, several are readily evident. The shortage of Irish priests was but one. Probably more important was the mission's attempt to function in a region whose political fate was fluid, arising from the dispute over boundaries between Spain and the United States, and which Spain lost within a short number of years. Moreover, the effort to convert and assimilate settlers who constituted the dominant element in certain districts and who were still immersed in their own culture was a difficult, if not an impossible, task. Bolstered by the presence of their own ministers, few of the colonists seemed inclined to embrace Catholicism and Spanish culture willingly. While the Spanish government attempted to carry out the mission, it was unable to do so in the most efficacious manner. Spain failed to provide West Florida with the vital ingredients for success: the presence of more effective and greater numbers of priests; the absence of Protestant ministers; the removal of the American colonists from their native environment and their dispersion among a Catholic-Spanish population; and, finally, a prolonged era of peace and the retention of the colony. Conducted without benefit of all or most of these essential factors, the failure of Irish proselytizing mission to West Florida was a foregone conclusion.[39]

---

39. Curley, *Church and State*, 337-41, ascribes the defeat of the Irish mission to Spain's failure to provide adequate cooperation and material aid, and he regards Spanish governmental control of the Catholic Church as pernicious. A closer examination, however, reveals that the mission's failure was due to reasons more transcendental than those described by him.

Chapter 8
The Canary Islander Settlements of Spanish Louisiana: An Overview

Of the settlers who entered Louisiana in the colonial era, perhaps no other people have received less attention than the Canary Islanders.[1] Moreover, until recently the slight output about them was often inaccurate. This is true about the three major "nineteenth-century" histories of Louisiana by François-Xavier Martin, Charles Gayarré, and Alcée Fortier and, of course, all the works based on theirs. Martin erred the least, stating only that in 1778 Louisiana received a large number of Canary Islanders, who settled at Terre-aux-Boeufs, Galveztown, and Valenzuela, and who obtained at royal expense cattle, fowls, housing, farm utensils, and rations for four years. Gayarré repeated as much, and then went on to write that 499 Canary Islanders settled at New Iberia, thus initiating a confusion that lingers on today. Fortier, who wrote after the others, helped to perpetuate earlier mistakes. All three historians, however, failed to mention the fourth settlement of the Isleños ("islanders," a term the Canary Islanders applied to themselves) at Barataria, why the Canary Islanders were sent to Louisiana, and the fate of the settlements after their founding. The absence of studies on Louisiana's Isleños also served to preserve the errors these historians made. In fact, to my knowledge only one study had been done on an Isleño settlement in the Spanish era and its quality left much to be desired.[2]

---

1. This article first appeared in *Louisiana History* 27 (Fall 1986): 353-73. Little of substance had been written about the Canary Islanders to the time this article was published.

2. François-Xavier Martin, *The History of Louisiana, From the Earliest Period*, 3rd. ed. (1827-29; repr., Gretna, 1975), 224; Charles Gayarré, *History of Louisiana*, 3rd ed., 4 vols. (New Orleans: Armand Hawkins, 1885), 3: 116, 119; Alcée Fortier, *A History of Louisiana*, 2nd ed., vol. 2 (Baton Rouge: Claitor's Bookstore, 1972), 60.

The coming of the Canary Islanders to Louisiana can be traced back to the energetic activities of Minister of the Indies José de Gálvez, the Bouligny Memoria that advocated a greater Spanish population for Louisiana, and the need for more soldiers in the colony as Spain and Great Britain moved toward war from 1777 forward. José de Gálvez was committed to building up colonial defenses in recognition that Spain would eventually join the rebelling English colonials of North America against Great Britain. Consequently, the Spanish Crown authorized a new battalion of soldiers for Louisiana on August 15, 1777, and its creation converted the Fixed Louisiana Infantry Battalion into the Fixed Louisiana Infantry Regiment, with now two battalions. The Canary Islands would provide seven hundred recruits, bachelors and married men with their dependents, who were expected to settle down permanently in the colony. Recruitment of the soldiers fell to the king's lieutenant in Tenerife, Matías de Gálvez, brother of José and father of the newly appointed governor of Louisiana, Bernardo de Gálvez. When Matías became the captain general of Central America shortly afterwards, Lt. Col. Andrés Amat de Tortosa completed the task of recruiting soldiers and families between 1778 and 1780.[3]

During those two years, Amat dispatched the recruits on board nine ships, of which only the first five reached Louisiana before war erupted between Spain and Great Britain in June 1779. The five ships and the number of their passengers were: the packetboat *Santísimo Sacramento* (also called *El Jasón*) with 125 recruits (53 had families), and 264 passengers in all; the polacre *La Victoria*, with 88 recruits (63 had

---

On the perpetuation of errors about the Canary Islanders, see for example, John Walton Caughey, *Bernardo de Gálvez in Louisiana, 1776-1783* (Berkeley: University of California Press, 1934), 79-81. The only study of an Isleño community is V. M. Scramuzza, "Galveztown: A Spanish Settlement of Colonial Louisiana," *Louisiana Historical Quarterly* 23 (1930), 553-609, which is based on his 1924 M.A. thesis at Louisiana State University. Scramuzza's main point was to emphasize the inferiority of the Canary Islanders as settlers, ignoring the many hardships they suffered. On the founding of New Iberia, see chapter 2 in this study.

3. Gilbert C. Din, "Protecting the *Barrera*: Spain's Defenses in Louisiana, 1763-1779," *Louisiana History* 19 (Spring 1978): 203-209, explains the military buildup in Louisiana. On the Bouligny Memoir, see Gilbert C. Din, *Louisiana in 1776: A Memoria of Francisco Bouligny* (New Orleans: Louisiana Collection Series, 1977).

families) and 292 passengers, not counting 18 nursing babies; the frigate *San Ignacio de Loyola*, with 115 recruits (95 had families) and 423 total passengers, which omitted 37 nursing infants; the packetboat *San Juan Nepomuceno*, with 53 recruits (48 had families) and 202 total passengers, not counting 19 infants at the breast; and the frigate *Santa Faz*, with 102 recruits (90 had families) and 406 total Isleños, excluding 28 nursing babies. The totals amounted to 483 recruits, 349 families, and 1,587 passengers, both soldiers and dependents, which again omits the 102 nursing infants. Of the five ships, only the *Santísimo Sacramento* stopped in Havana; the other four vessels sailed directly to New Orleans. The five ships arrived in Louisiana between November 1778 and early July 1779. On July 7, 1779, Gov. Bernardo de Gálvez issued a status report on the five ships and their passengers. Up to that date, 1,582 Isleños had come. They consisted of 153 bachelor recruits, 329 married recruits, and 1,100 dependents.[4]

Because of the war, the other four ships Amat de Tortosa sent from Santa Cruz de Tenerife never reached Louisiana. Those ships were the frigate *El Sagrado Corazón de Jesús* (or *Natural*), with 423 passengers of which approximately 117 were recruits who had 95 families; the brig

---

4. On the first five ships that sailed to Louisiana, see Archivo General de Indias, Audiencia de Santo Domingo, legajo (hereafter cited as AGI, SD, with the leg. number) 2661, which contains the documentation on the recruits, their names, and the ships they sailed on; the documentation is too numerous to cite completely. See also Archivo General de Indias, Papeles procedentes de Cuba, legajo (hereafter cited as AGI, PC, with the leg. number) 119, for letters relative to the sailing and arrival of the ships in Louisiana between 1778 and 1782, contracts with ship captains, and expenses. See, in particular, Andrés Amat de Tortosa to Bernardo de Gálvez, Santa Cruz de Tenerife, February 17, and June 5, 1779, AGI, PC, leg. 119; and Bernardo de Gálvez to José de Gálvez, New Orleans, July 7, 1779, AGI, SD, leg. 2662. A list of the passengers that sailed on the first five ships to Louisiana was published in Sidney Louis Villeré, ed., *The Canary Islands Migration to Louisiana 1778-1783: The History and Passenger Lists of the Isleño Volunteer Recruits and Their Families* (Baltimore: Genealogical Publishing Company, 1972). The lists, however, are unsatisfactory because many names were omitted or misread. The accuracy of Gálvez's figures of July 7, 1779, is questionable. It is known that at least six recruits died on the *Santísimo Sacramento* and several more on other ships. Dependents also died on the voyages. Yet Gálvez's figures are almost identical to Amat's in Tenerife. Moreover, Gálvez did not mention the nursing infants and he, too, probably did not count them.

Nuestra Señora de los Dolores, with 17 recruits and 89 passengers in all; the brigantine *San Carlos*, with 47 recruits or 159 passengers; and the brigantine *San Pedro* with 35 recruits and 119 passengers in all. Of those ships, only two put in at Havana, where they were detained because of the war. For unknown reasons, the *San Pedro* arrived in La Guaira, the port for Caracas, Venezuela, and neither the ship nor its passengers went on to Louisiana. The English in the Caribbean, meanwhile, captured the *San Carlos* and took it to the island of Tortosa. The Spaniards on board suffered several deaths and much hardship before they reached Havana via Puerto Rico. In Cuba, Capt. Gen. Diego Joseph Navarro kept the Isleños there, except for the bachelor recruits, because New Orleans had become an active theater of war. While waiting for the conflict to end, the Isleños in Havana experienced births, deaths, marriages, and desertions, most of which diminished the number of settlers who continued to Louisiana once the war ended. Yet others were exempted from traveling to New Orleans because of infirmity, and they received permission to settle in Cuba while still others were assigned to new destinations. Approximately 450 persons from the last four ships never reached Louisiana.[5]

When peace emerged in 1783, the captain general hired two ships to convey the Isleños still in Havana to New Orleans. The ships were the frigate *Margarita*, which had about 40 families on it, and the packetboat *Santísima Trinidad* with 25 families, for a total of 263 persons. Because of desertions and illnesses, a third and final ship, the sloop *Delfín*, left Havana with six Canary Islander families on board. Although additional Isleños went on to New Orleans after this time, their numbers were few,

---

5. On the last four ships to sail from the Canaries, see "Estado," Amat, Santa Cruz de Tenerife, May 31, 1779, AGI, SD, leg. 2661; Amat to Bernardo de Gálvez, Santa Cruz de Tenerife, May 8, 1780, and Bernardo de Gálvez to Amat, Havana, February 23, 1782, AGI, PC, leg. 119; Miró to the Marqués de Sonora (José de Gálvez), New Orleans, no. 155, October 20, 1786, AGI, SD, leg. 2550. In AGI, PC, leg. 689, contains the accounts of the Isleños who were detained in Cuba by the war and a list of the settlers who went to Pensacola in 1782; the latter group consisted of 145 persons from *El Sagrado Corazón de Jesús*. The Pensacola settlement effort failed, and most of the Isleños returned to Havana in 1785. Luis de Unzaga to Arturo O'Neill, Havana, October 24 and 25, November 15, 1785, all in AGI, PC, leg. 85. Possibly a few of these Isleños resettled in East Florida.

they went as individuals, and the documentation on them is unclear.[6]

By the time the *Delfín* arrived in Louisiana in December 1783, approximately two thousand settlers had come from the Canary Islands. They represented the people Gov. Bernardo de Gálvez used to found four settlements. However, not all of them moved onto the land; the bachelor recruits remained in the army, at least during the war, and a number of civilians, probably deemed unfit for the rigors of agricultural work or artisans who possessed skills needed in the city, stayed in New Orleans to earn their livelihood. With their dependents, they constituted a figure possibly as high as four hundred. Over the years, more Isleños would migrate from the rural communities to live and work in the city.

When the first ship, the *Santísimo Sacramento*, arrived with immigrants on November 18, 1778, Governor Gálvez realized immediately the impossibility of the married men serving as both soldiers and providers for their families on the meager wage of twelve reales ($1.50) per day. He, therefore, ordered the married men to become full-time colonists and he created new settlements for them. While the Isleños from the first ship waited in New Orleans, Gálvez searched for sites on which to settle them, and he personally made a reconnaissance journey upriver in November and early December.[7]

On his trip up the Mississippi, Gálvez visited and selected two sites. He stopped first at the junction of Bayou Lafourche and the Mississippi (Lafourche des Chetimachas, where Donaldsonville is today), which had a small Acadian community under Commandant Louis Judice and the Church of the Ascension. Despite its fertile and verdant nature, Bayou Lafourche was then uninhabited. Perhaps Gálvez ventured several miles down the bayou to where Valenzuela would be established in a few months. He then proceeded up the Mississippi to Bayou Manchac on the left bank and followed the bayou to its junction with the Amite River. The two streams also served as the dividing line between British West Florida and Spanish Louisiana. At the junction, on the right bank

---

6. Joseph Petely to Martín Navarro, Baliza, August 17 and 19, 1783, AGI, PC, leg. 608B; Martín Navarro to José de Gálvez, no. 185, New Orleans, September 25, 1783, AGI, SD, leg. 2609.

7. Bernardo de Gálvez to José de Gálvez, no. 229, New Orleans, January 15, 1779, AGI, PC, leg. 2547.

where the lands appeared high, he chose a second site. Several Anglo-American families, refugees from the rebellion in the Atlantic colonies, had recently established themselves there. They gave the settlement its name, Galveztown, in honor of the governor. Gálvez appointed Sub-Lt. Francisco Collell, who perhaps had accompanied him, as the first commandant of the settlement and of the fort he proposed to construct there. The fort would monitor the activities of the English in West Florida on the opposite, or left, bank of the Amite and Manchac. The English employed that waterway to communicate between their posts on the Mississippi and Pensacola. Collell began preparations in December to receive the Isleños.[8]

In selecting sites for the new colonists, Gálvez was motivated by his desire to improve New Orleans's security by safeguarding the water routes that an invading force might use to penetrate Lower Louisiana. Below New Orleans on the Mississippi's left bank, Gálvez accepted the offer from Pierre de Marigny de Mandeville to use lands on Bayou Terre-aux-Boeufs. No information is available on how Barataria on the Mississippi's right bank was selected, but again it seems to have been chosen from the standpoint of defense. Barataria had a waterway that stretched from the gulf to the Mississippi River. Because security alone motivated the selection of the four locations, one of them failed almost immediately while another struggled through the Spanish period and ended once Spain no longer governed the colony.[9]

Little documentation has survived on Barataria and only a sketchy outline describes what happened there. Begun in 1779 with about 150 colonists under Commandant Andrés Jung, it suffered hardship almost immediately. Placed scarcely above sea level on the edge of Lake Barataria, the hurricanes of 1779 and 1780 inundated the area. In addition, periodic crevasses in the Mississippi's banks produced floods. As early as December 1779, a number of colonists rejected living there any longer and left for

---

8. Bernardo de Gálvez to José de Gálvez, no. 233, New Orleans, January 15, 1779, in Lawrence Kinnaird, ed., *Spain in the Mississippi Valley, 1765-1794*, 3 Parts (Washington, DC: GPO, 1946-1949), 1: 326-27; (Bernardo de Gálvez) to Francisco Bouligny, Galveztown, November 22, 1778, AGI, PC, leg. 2358.

9. Pedro Marigny to Manuel Gayoso de Lemos, (n.p.), February 4, 1789, AGI, PC, leg. 1393.

Valenzuela. In August 1782, Intendant Martín Navarro acknowledged that the settlers in Barataria were in the worst condition of all the Canary Islanders. They had made no progress during the three years of their residence. Navarro, consequently, approved the petition submitted by more of the Barataria inhabitants and allowed them to transfer across the river to San Bernardo. They moved in the fall of 1782, with stragglers going later. Only a handful of Isleños remained behind, living on their own and caring for their livestock on the terrain's "trembling prairie."[10]

Probably because of its proximity to New Orleans and its numerous waterways, the Isleño settlement at Terre-aux-Boeufs received more colonists than any other. The community began in 1779, and was augmented by the Baratarians and most of the Canary Islanders who arrived in 1783. Unfortunately, much of the documentation for San Bernardo, which was also called Concepción and Nueva Gálvez, appears to be missing from the Archivo General de Indias. Nevertheless, it is believed that perhaps a total of 160 families settled there, with 42 families numbering 168 persons beginning the settlement. The government built houses for them at three different locations along the bayou, at intervals of about a league; when the colonists from Barataria arrived in late 1782, they established a fourth community farther down on Bayou Terre-aux-Boeufs. Some of the Isleños, however, preferred to live on their lands. Plots that families received were often on both sides of the bayou and consisted of varying depths; they amounted to approximately three arpents of bayou front and forty deep, which was the size of the lands

---

10. Juan Ventura Morales to Martín Navarro, New Orleans, January 12, 1786, AGI, PC, leg. 606. Edna B. Freiberg, *Bayou St. John in Colonial Louisiana, 1699-1803* (New Orleans: published by the author, 1980), 272; Antonio de St. Maxent to the governor, Valenzuela, January 4, 1780, AGI, PC, leg. 192; (Navarro) to Morales, New Orleans, August 6, 1782, AGI, PC, leg. 606, petition of Juan García Raimundo, Antonio Joseph Armas, *et al.*, New Orleans, September 22, 1782, with Navarro's marginal notation; (Morales) to Navarro, New Orleans, November 13, 1782, AGI, PC, leg. 608A; DeMarigny to Morales, (San Bernardo), November 28 and December 16, 1782, AGI, PC, leg. 608A. A list of the Baratarian families who moved to San Bernardo is enclosed in Navarro to Morales, New Orleans, January, 1783, AGI, PC, leg. 689. Governor Gálvez preferred to believe that the four Isleño settlements would soon prosper, even Barataria. See Gálvez to José de Gálvez, no. 461, New Orleans, July 19, 1781, AGI, SD, leg. 2548.

given to settlers at Valenzuela. In the colonial period, the families in San Bernardo never cleared off the trees, palmetto, and brush for more than a few arpents into the interior. Contrary to Martín Navarro's assertion that the colonists would receive rations for four years, the Spanish government wanted them to become self-sufficient in food within a year after arriving. But because of adverse weather conditions and the location of the communities, many Isleños remained needy for years. That was particularly true of widows, orphans, the infirm, and the aged. Rations in San Bernardo finally ended completely in 1787. However, when they first arrived, the government provided these immigrants with clothing, utensils, livestock, money, and much more. San Bernardo appears to have been treated more generously than any other settlement. Each of the three surviving Canary Islander communities had a physician to attend to the sick. And San Bernardo, probably more than the other two, admitted discharged Spanish soldiers and sailors, whom the government encouraged to remain in the colony. The availability of marriageable Spanish women no doubt encouraged some of them to do so.[11]

The government also tried to build a church and assign a resident priest to each community although that was not always possible. Louisiana had a shortage of ministers in the Spanish era. Until 1785 San Bernardo did not have a priest and the settlers had to attend religious services in New Orleans, where marriages and baptisms usually occurred. Occasionally, a priest from the city visited the community to perform religious rites. When a new group of missionaries arrived in Louisiana in 1785, Friar Mariano de Brunete received the parish of San Bernardo, where he remained for two years. In 1787, construction of a church finally started. That year Friar Agustín Lamar arrived and stayed for six years. Father José de Villaprovedo replaced him and served until his death

---

11. "Relación de las Primeras familias Ysleñas del Establecimiento de San Bernardo," AGI, PC, leg. 568; "Yndice de las familias Ysleñas que han de establecer la Nueva Población de Galveztown," no. 1, Libro Maestro, AGI, PC, leg. 568; (Morales) to DeMarigny, nos. 6 and 7, New Orleans, March 18 and 20, 1783, AGI, PC, leg. 83; Navarro to Manuel Ramos, New Orleans, September 12 and 13, 1783, AGI, PC, leg. 689; "Quenta y relación (de las familias) que se han situado en el segundo, tercero, y quarto establecimientos," Pedro Marigny, (n.p.), February 4, 1784, AGI, PC, leg. 689. On the termination of aid, see Navarro to José de Gálvez, nos. 492 and 499, New Orleans, May 4 and June 7, 1787, respectively, both in AGI, SD, 2611.

The Canary Islander Settlements of Spanish Louisiana 161

in 1797. The last priest in the Spanish era was Tirso de Peleagonzalo, who received permission to depart for Cuba in 1803 because his health was broken and he was at "the gates of death." When Gov. Esteban Miró consented in 1791 to the establishment of a tavern in San Bernardo, which was allocated on the basis of the highest annual bid, he stipulated that money from the winning bid be used to support the local church.[12]

Pierre de Marigny, who donated his lands on Bayou Terre-aux-Boeufs to the government, became the first commandant of San Bernardo. Who acted as commandant during the war against Great Britain, while de Marigny was absent, is unknown. De Marigny resumed his duties after peace returned and stayed until April 1788, when he departed with official permission to visit France. In his absence, Sub-Lt. Pierre de la Ronde took over, a task that was prolonged when de Marigny overstayed his visit. On his return, de Marigny became an *alcalde ordinario* (judge) in the New Orleans Cabildo (city government). When at last he was to resume the post of commandant in early 1792, the new governor of Louisiana, Francisco Luis Héctor, Baron de Carondelet, appointed him captain of the Volunteers of the Mississippi (the militia unit located below New Orleans). Consequently, de la Ronde stayed in charge of San Bernardo until the end of the Spanish period.[13]

Little is known about the San Bernardo community in the closing days of Spain's rule in Louisiana. By the early nineteenth century, most of the people still lived in poverty and at the subsistence level, although a few had risen modestly. Several persons even owned slaves. The majority, however, engaged in agriculture, producing corn, kidney beans, "ordinary beans," fowls, eggs, butter, hogs, and assorted vegetables, some of which they sold to the New Orleans market. Several of the Isleños also turned to

---

12. Roger Baudier, *The Catholic Church in Louisiana* (New Orleans: Roger Baudier, 1939), 197, 204, 235; (Miró) to Pierre de la Ronde, New Orleans, January 20, 1791, AGI, PC, leg. 122A; "Asiento" of José de la Villa Proveda and "Asiento" of Agustín Lamar, both in AGI, PC, leg. 538B. Villaprovedo died on September 19, 1797. Villaprovedo worked in New Orleans prior to 1793; the asiento calls him "teniente de Cura" of the New Orleans Parish.

13. Miró to Sonora, no. 283, New Orleans, August 16, 1787, AGI, SD, leg. 2552; (Miró) to De la Ronde, New Orleans, December 20, 1790, and January 1, 1791, both in AGI, PC, leg. 121; Carondelet to DeMarigny, New Orleans, March 13, 1792, AGI, PC, leg. 122B.

the nearby sea for a livelihood and obtained from it fish, shrimp, oysters, and crabs. At the time of the transfer of Louisiana to the United States in late 1803, approximately 800 persons, most of them Canary Islanders, lived in San Bernardo. Despite hardships, San Bernardo became one of the two successful Isleño settlements in Louisiana, and today notwithstanding the ravages inflicted by Hurricane Katrina in 2005, diminished numbers of their descendants continue to inhabit St. Bernard Parish.[14]

Of the four Canary Islander settlements, the documentation on Galveztown is the largest. Galveztown differed from the other Isleño communities in that it alone had a fort because of its strategic location on the Amite-Manchac waterway. The settlement, however, thrust in a remote area and surrounded by lowlands—swamps in reality—suffered all too frequently from inundations and other misfortunes. For twenty years, Spanish authorities insisted that diligent work by the settlers would make the district flourish, although it should have been evident from an early date that the location was a disastrous choice. But influenced by the fact that Governor Gálvez had personally selected the site, the large financial investment in houses and cleared lands, and the usefulness of having a local militia unit to back up the soldiers at the fort, Spanish governors refused to let the settlers leave and relocate to higher and more secure terrain.

Of the misfortunes the Isleños experienced in settling in Louisiana, the deaths they suffered in Galveztown in their first year far surpassed any other tragedy. So many people perished in the settlement that it could have failed soon after its formation. Starting in January and continuing through the summer of 1779, groups of immigrants from New Orleans arrived in the wilderness that was Galveztown to begin the community. White artisans and slaves were then building houses, clearing lands, and attempting to obtain a harvest in the first year of settlement. Initially, five Isleños in the spring came down with fever caused by mange (*sarna*), and

---

14. Amos Stoddard, *Sketches, Historical and Descriptive, of Louisiana* (Philadelphia: Mathew Carey, 1812), 161; William Darby, *The Emigrant's Guide to the Western and Southwestern States and Territories* (New York: Kirk and Mercein, 1818), 8; James Alexander Robertson, ed., *Louisiana Under the Rule of Spain, France, and the United States, 1785-1807*, 2 vols. (New York: Arno Press and New York Times, 1969 rpt.), 1: 97.

it produced the deaths of six children and one woman in April. Gálvez rushed the surgeon Antonio Demar to minister to the afflicted. The uninspiring surgeon employed wine, oil, honey, and aguardiente to cure their ills; not surprisingly, Delmar's patients usually died, and the Isleños quickly lost confidence in his ability. By late spring and early summer, mange, diarrhea, fever, scurvy, and dropsy had attacked the colonists. Bad as they were, those illnesses did not compare to smallpox that struck in mid-summer. By July and August, the entire village appeared afflicted and many homes had been turned into miniature hospitals. To January 17, 1780, when the deaths greatly diminished, approximately 146 persons had died, most of them from smallpox. The deaths totaled more than a third of the settlers in Galveztown. Newborn infants and children perished in unusually large numbers. Most families lost from one to three members, but at times entire households expired. The months from July to October were the deadliest and only as the weather cooled did the epidemic abate. The sorrow the survivors experienced was unbearable. Several persons, crazed with grief at having lost their families, fled the community. A reading of the "Libro Maestro" that recorded the fatalities only suggests the enormity of the calamity that struck Galveztown.[15]

In the midst of the suffering and death, war came to Louisiana, and Galveztown saw the first action in the colony. Governor Gálvez kept secret the news of Spain's declaration of war on Great Britain in an effort to catch the enemy posts upriver in West Florida off guard. He had to notify the nearest commandants, however, to have their men prepared when he marched up the Mississippi to attack the British at Manchac, Baton Rouge, and Natchez. He therefore informed Commandant Collell at Galveztown to put his soldiers and militia in a state of readiness. Gálvez nearly completed his preparations in New Orleans when a great hurricane struck Louisiana on August 18, temporarily delaying him. On August

---

15. "Libro Maestro Para Sentar el Cargo a las Familias de la Nueva Población de la Villa de Galveztown," 1779, AGI, PC, leg. 568. Antonio Acosta Rodríguez, *La población de la Luisiana española (1763-1803)* (Madrid: Ministerio de Asuntos Exteriores, 1979), 141, places the number of victims at 161 in a population of 404, or 40 percent. See Acosta's article, "Overview of the Consumption of Food and Goods by *Isleño* Immigrants to Louisiana," trans. and ed. by Paul E. Hoffman, *Louisiana History* 22 (1981): 299-306.

24, he sent Collell another message, one by which the commandant initiated action against the British six days later. The element of surprise proved fruitful and the Galveztown troops seized seven enemy vessels of different sizes, captured 125 soldiers and sailors, and took Fort Graham (really a warehouse) on the Amite River north of Galveztown. The Isleño settlement and fort had proved to be extremely useful and their importance continued in the following months, standing guard against any attempt the British might take to recover their Mississippi posts. That possibility remained alive until Mobile fell to Gálvez in March 1780.[16] In the postwar years, Spanish authorities kept stressing the fort's and, consequently, the settlement's strategic value. But from the colonists' perspective, the community was inexcusably ill-placed.

Efforts to turn Galveztown into a thriving agricultural settlement had more difficulties than anywhere else except Barataria. In 1779 and 1780, hurricanes destroyed crops in Galveztown and forced the residents to remain dependent on government rations. Then drought dried up their fields in 1781. That year the Galveztown Isleños directed a memorial to Governor Gálvez, who had returned to New Orleans after his victory at Pensacola. Wishing to move to a more encouraging site, they complained of hardship and the less than ideal location of their community. But Gálvez would not hear of it. The government had spent large sums of money constructing seventy-two homes, providing rations, and clearing lands for them to farm. Starting over would entail additional expenditures and, therefore, the settlers stayed. But their situation remained dismal. Commandant Collell remarked in 1781 that the remoteness of Galveztown increased costs of everything there and

---

16. Louisiana historians have overlooked the fact that the first military action between Spain and Great Britain in Louisiana in 1779 occurred on the Amite River. The evidence is clear, however. See Scramuzza, "Galveztown," 583; Collell to Bernardo de Gálvez, Galveztown, August 30, September 3, 7, and 10, 1779, all in AGI, PC, leg. 2351. Miró's statement on the merits of Collell, New Orleans, December 20, 1791, AGI, PC, leg. 122A; Caughey, *Bernardo de Gálvez*, 161; and the documents in "West Florida: The Capture of Baton Rouge by Gálvez, September 21, 1779," *Louisiana Historical Quarterly* 12 (1929): 255-65. See also Gilbert C. Din, "Lieutenant Raimundo DuBreüil, Commandant of San Gabriel de Manchac, and Bernardo de Gálvez's 1779 Campaign on the Mississippi," *Military History of the West* 10 (Spring 1999): 1-30.

that the Isleños were living in poverty.[17]

Instead of permitting the Canary Islanders to abandon Galveztown, Governor Gálvez appointed Lt. Gilbert Antoine de St. Maxent, his brother-in-law who had helped make Valenzuela a fairly successful settlement, as commandant to succeed Collell. But even St. Maxent could not perform a miracle in the three and a half years (1781-1784) he served at Galveztown. An improvement in 1781 was the arrival of the German physician Franz Rausman who replaced the ineffective Demar. Twenty-two Isleños immediately sought him out, and he stayed as their physician until the end of the Spanish period. Despite this improvement, hardships continued. In 1782 floods wiped out crops everywhere in Lower Louisiana, including Galveztown. The Indians also suffered, and they entered the Galveztown district, searching for food, killing animals, and severely frightening the residents. Intendant Navarro recognized that without rations the Galveztown settlers would desert the community and, in fact, several of them had already done so.[18]

Problems plagued the community through the 1780s. It remained on rations in 1783, costing the treasury 14,000 pesos that year. When government-supplied rations finally terminated in 1786, Governor Miró informed the inhabitants that they could sell their produce wherever they pleased, but they could not abandon the settlement. By early 1787, when Lt. Joseph Petely was temporarily in charge, he described Galveztown as being half abandoned with a number of houses in ruins. Perhaps a few Isleños had moved to their farms in the countryside, although Spanish policy aimed at keeping them in the settlement to reinforce the fort in an emergency. But leaving the community dominated the thinking of the inhabitants and, when Marcos

---

17. Collell to Juan Ventura Morales, Galveztown, May 1, 1781, AGI, PC, leg. 608B; Collell to Bernardo de Gálvez, Galveztown, June 20, 1781, AGI, PC, leg. 2.

18. "Ynstrucción que observará Dn Antonio Maxent, Capn. del Reximiento de Ynfantería de la Luisiana destinado al mando de la nueva Población de Galveztown," New Orleans, June 27, 1781, AGI, PC, leg. 112; Maxent to Martín Navarro, Galveztown, July 3, 1781; AGI, PC, leg. 603B; Navarro to Bernardo de Gálvez, New Orleans, June 16, 1782, AGI, PC, leg. 83; Navarro to José de Gálvez, no. 140, New Orleans, December 4, 1782, AGI, SD, leg. 2609; Maxent to Pedro Piernas, Galveztown, June 16, 1782, in Kinnaird, *Spain in the Mississippi Valley*, 2: 20-21.

DeVilliers soon replaced Petely as commandant, they besieged him with petitions to depart. Some of the petitions were granted in 1787, 1788, and 1789, thus permitting several families to leave for Cuba or, more often, for San Bernardo and, in one case, for anywhere since anywhere was better than Galveztown. In December 1788, DeVilliers painted a distressful image of the community: the houses were in ruins, many of them were vacant with neither windows nor doors and inhabited by animals seeking shelter, and other houses had collapsed into heaps of debris. The Galveztown population continued to decline until the census of 1793 listed only 32 Spanish families of 126 persons residing there. The figure represented less than one-third of the approximately four hundred persons who had gone there fourteen years before.[19]

The decade of the 1790s failed to improve conditions in Galveztown. A hurricane on August 18, 1793, battered it, demolishing cornfields and killing animals. The next year, two hurricanes struck the community, first on August 10 and then again on August 21. Besides destroying fields and drowning livestock, floodwaters stood four feet above the banks that Gálvez once described as high. Every family lost property and, of course, their food supply. DeVilliers stated that the colonists were not any better off now than they had been three years earlier—and he might have added than when they had first arrived in 1779. Nature persisted in treating the Galveztown settlers harshly, and they, in turn, pressed for permission to leave. In early 1796, they repeated their request to the commandant, Capt. Francisco Rivas. They asserted that San Bernardo and Valenzuela fared much better than their miserable settlement and their favorable locations permitted them to trade easily and advantageously with New Orleans. But Rivas and Governor Carondelet refused to recognize the difficulties the Galveztown colonists confronted. As Carondelet wrote about them to Rivas, "It is not right that the king spends money on those lazy and indolent people who are not content in any place except the one

---

19. Maxent to Morales, Galveztown, July 21, 1783, AGI, PC, leg. 608; (Miró) to Maximiliano Maxent, New Orleans, September 3, 1786, AGI, PC, leg. 117A; Joseph Petely to Miró, no. 1, Galveztown, January 30, 1787, AGI, PC, leg. 13. AGI, PC, legs. 13 and 132 contain petitions from Galveztown residents who wanted to leave. Marcos DeVilliers to Miró, Galveztown, December 1, 1783, AGI, PC, leg. 14; Galveztown census, August 16, 1793, AGI, PC, leg. 27A.

in which they are not."[20]

As far as the governor was concerned, the sole key to Isleño success was hard work. But Rivas soon appreciated the obstacles that plagued the settlers. Only a few months later, floods again hit Galveztown, wiping out fields and inundating the village for five days. All the painstaking labor the colonists had performed for the past several months was erased in a matter of hours. That same year, a military report accurately described Galveztown. It declared that the community had been placed too close to the river, which accounted for its repeated flooding, and that low-lying lands (swamps) surrounded it. The population had declined to 21 families composed of 109 persons, who lived "in the depths of obscurity and misery."[21]

Despite the numerous adversities the inhabitants endured, the government steadfastly refused to release the remaining Isleños. Gov. Manuel Gayoso de Lemos, beset by worries of the colony's security, especially after the disastrous Treaty of San Lorenzo (1795) took effect in 1798, regarded the Galveztown fort as indispensible for intercepting enemy forces that might penetrate the province via the Amite River from Lakes Pontchartrain and Maurepas. He advocated rebuilding the fort that was then in a dilapidated condition, and it was done that same year. The Galveztown community served to reinforce the soldiers, and their presence was necessary. But conditions in Galveztown failed to improve as Spain's final years in Louisiana drew to a close. Periodic floods and hurricanes continued and, as if they were not enough, on April 18, 1801, a tornado struck the settlement. Through all the many hardships, the settlers barely succeeded in grubbing out a meager existence.[22]

---

20. DeVilliers to Baron de Carondelet, no. 67, Galveztown, September 7, 1793, AGI, PC, leg. 27A; DeVilliers to Carondelet, Galveztown, September 10 (with attachment) and 25, December 20, 1794, AGI, PC, leg. 30; Francisco Rivas to Carondelet, Galveztown, January 8, 1796, with attached petition of Juan Medina, (undated), AGI, PC, leg. 34; Carondelet to Rivas, New Orleans, January 21, 1796, AGI, PC, leg. 129.

21. Rivas to Carondelet, no. 45, Galveztown, April 27, 1796, AGI, PC, leg. 33; Juan María Perchet report, December 29, 1796, AGI, PC, leg. 2354.

22. Jack D. L. Holmes, *Gayoso: The Life and Times of a Spanish Governor in the Mississippi Valley, 1789-1799* (Baton Rouge: Louisiana State University Press for the Louisiana Historical Association, 1965), 238; Gayoso to the Prince of the Peace (Manuel

Following the retrocession of Louisiana to France and its immediate transfer to the United States, twenty-nine Canary Islander families petitioned the Spanish government for permission to move from Galveztown, which was now in the United States, to Spanish-held lands. While the government told them to wait momentarily, an exodus began and, in 1806, the main portion of the Galveztown Isleños departed for Baton Rouge in Spanish West Florida. They settled in the district that became known as "Spanish Town," where they received lands and houses. By 1807, nearly the entire population had abandoned Galveztown; the Spanish soldiers left the fort in 1804, and it quickly turned into ruins since the Americans had no use for it. Those Canary Islanders who declined to relocate to Baton Rouge and remained in the Galveztown district, preferred to live in the countryside (where some of their descendants still reside today). A few of them, together with small numbers of Acadians and even persons of other nationalities, started a tiny community only two miles southeast of Galveztown that they simply called Galvez. It survived while the former settlement rapidly crumbled. By the mid-nineteenth century, the material remains of Galveztown as well as the fort had vanished from sight, thus removing from view the most unfortunate of the three remaining Isleño settlements.[23]

In contrast, the Valenzuela community emerged successfully after an initial era of reversals and privation. On February 6, 1779, Governor Gálvez ordered his brother-in-law, Gilbert Antoine de St. Maxent, whom he had already appointed commandant, and several others to mark out the site for the future "Villa de Valenzuela." Similar to Galveztown, the

---

Godoy), no. 9 confidential, New Orleans, April 19, 1798, Archivo Histórico Nacional (Madrid), Estado, legajo 3900. On the Treaty of San Lorenzo, see Samuel Flagg Bemis, *Pinckney's Treaty: A Study of America's Advantage from Europe's Distress, 1783-1800*, rev. ed. (New Haven: Yale University Press, 1960); Tomás Estevan to Ramón López y Ángulo, Galveztown, April 28, 1801, AGI, PC, leg. 260.

23. Petition of Josef Pereira *et al.*, (Galveztown), December 14, 1803, AGI, PC, leg. 139; Pedro Cevallos to the Marqués de Casa-Calvo, Aranjuez, January 15 and 16, 1805, AGI, PC, leg. 176B; "Plano de los terrenos destinados para las familias españolas de Galveztown," AGI, Mapas y Planos, Luisiana y Florida, no. 228; and Sidney A. Marchand's two books, *The Story of Ascension Parish, Louisiana* (Baton Rouge: J. E. Ortlieb Printing Company, 1931), 43, and *The Flight of a Century (1800-1900) in Ascension Parish, Louisiana* (Donaldsonville, La.: by the author, 1936), 107.

governor wanted the colonists to live together in a single community and from there work their lands along both banks of the bayou. Valenzuela was placed about four miles below the Mississippi on the left side of Bayou Lafourche (today just below the Ascension Parish line into Assumption Parish, approximately at Belle Alliance). Overall, its communications by water were good and the lands excellent for agriculture. While Valenzuela probably confronted fewer setbacks than any other Isleño settlement, it took time for the community to establish roots.[24]

The first Canary Islanders arrived on Bayou Lafourche in March 1779, and the weary travelers celebrated journey's end by feasting and dancing. More colonists continued to come to Valenzuela until perhaps as many as four hundred Isleños had arrived. As they began their settlement in the spring of 1779, hired men and slaves worked to assist them by constructing cabins of thirty feet by fifteen feet in size and by clearing lands to begin agricultural work immediately. Similar to the other settlements, sickness plagued the new arrivals, but not to the same degree as in Galveztown. In the midst of establishing roots, war came to Valenzuela in August.[25]

In the summer of 1779, Commandant St. Maxent and Sub-Lt. Francisco Corbo, an Isleño, organized the adult males of Valenzuela into a militia company that drilled and stood ready for the anticipated war. In late August, Governor Gálvez alerted his commandants below British Manchac, the southern boundary of British West Florida, that hostilities had broken out. The commandant spent a number of sleepless nights fearful that the enemy might strike the settlement before Gálvez brought his soldiers from New Orleans. When the governor finally assaulted the British posts on the Mississippi River in September, perhaps some of the Valenzuela militiamen saw action but the records are not clear on

---

24. Bernardo de Gálvez, "Ynstrucción que deberá observar el Subteniente Dn. Antonio Maxent, Comandante de la Nueva Población de Valenzuela," New Orleans, May 18, 1779, AGI, PC, leg. 192; Louis Judice to Carondelet, Lafourche des Chetimachas, May 9, 1796, AGI, PC, leg. 212, which recounts the establishment and problems of Valenzuela.

25. (Gálvez to St. Maxent), New Orleans, May 11, 1779; St. Maxent to (Gálvez), Valenzuela, May 3, 1779; Judice to the governor, Lafourche des Chetimachas, March 12, 1779, AGI, PC, leg. 192.

this point. Because fighting on the Mississippi quickly ended, the war only temporarily disrupted Valenzuela's tranquility. By late September 1779, the settlers again turned their principal attention to building the community.[26]

Overall, adjusting to an agricultural way of life on Bayou Lafourche was not as difficult for the Isleños as elsewhere. Nevertheless, life was never serene. A jurisdictional dispute between Louis Judice, commandant at Lafourche des Chetimachas, and St. Maxent, in neighboring Valenzuela, quickly arose. Because the Isleños received land contiguously on the bayou, in order to maintain the road and levees, beginning near Lafourche des Chetimachas where Acadians were already settled, a number of the new arrivals fell into Judice's district and not St. Maxent's. Moreover, the creation of a new jurisdiction immediately adjacent to his post upset Judice, who claimed superior authority over Valenzuela. His complaints and interference greatly vexed St. Maxent, who appealed repeatedly to the government in New Orleans. Although the governor tried to placate the problems between the two districts, the boundary dispute long persisted.[27]

Two years after settling on Bayou Lafourche, only about a third of the Canary Islanders then living in Valenzuela, or sixty-four persons of approximately two hundred, still required rations. What had become of the other colonists is not certain, but it can be surmised that they had abandoned the community to live on their farms. The government attempted to terminate rations in 1781, but several settlers traveled down to New Orleans to protest. The acting governor and the intendant relented and agreed to continue assistance until the harvest (autumn) of

---

26. St. Maxent to the governor, Valenzuela, August 1, 1779; and (Gálvez) to St. Maxent, New Orleans, August 26, 1779; both in AGI, PC, leg. 192; Antonio de Maxent memorial to the King, New Orleans, July 1794, attached to Carondelet to Luis de Las Casas, no. 556, New Orleans, July 15, 1794, AGI, PC, leg. 1443A. The war on the Mississippi is recounted in Caughey, *Bernardo de Gálvez*, 150-55; Eric Beerman, *España y los Estados Unidos en la Guerra de la independencia* (Madrid: Editorial MAPFRE, 1992), 43-65.

27. The origins of the problems between Judice and St. Maxent are in St. Maxent to the governor, Valenzuela, May 3, August 20, and October (n.d.), 1779; (Gálvez) to Judice, New Orleans, May 12, 1779; Judice to the governor, Lafourche des Chetimachas, August 16, 20, and 21, 1779; all in AGI, PC, leg. 192.

1782. That date, too, proved premature for several of the Isleños, mainly widows and orphans, and rations continued until the mid-1780s, when Governor Miró decreed their complete and permanent suspension.[28]

Despite many of the Valenzuela settlers getting off to a good start, nature often failed to cooperate with them. The hurricanes of 1779 and 1780 inflicted harm to their crops. Later, on March 20, 1782, a tornado struck the settlement, destroying four houses and sending debris flying over a six arpent area. The government generously paid for rebuilding the ruined homes. That same year, floods inundated a part of the settlement and high waters, a constant hazard in the lower Mississippi Valley, would recur periodically in the ensuing years.[29]

Keeping roads and levees in a state of good repair was a perennial problem on the bayou and almost everywhere else in the province. Landowners often failed to follow government orders in this matter and, similarly, vacant and abandoned lands had no one to perform the required work. In 1783, flood waters poured in from a crevasse in the Mississippi's bank and damaged a number of Isleño farms from the rear. Levees at this time did not exist everywhere on the Mississippi and, unfortunately, irresponsible persons and absentee landowners compounded the danger from floods. Despite repeated government admonitions that the levees and roads were to be kept in good order, it often did not occur. Those who evaded government decrees frequently were not the small and indigent farmers but the better off landowners who possessed the money and labor for repairs.[30]

In 1784 Commandant Anselme Blanchard took a census that cast light on the condition of the Canary Islanders in Valenzuela. It listed 40 Spanish families, consisting of 154 persons, as residing there. In addition

---

28. Anselmo Blanchard letters to Juan Ventura Morales, Valenzuela, November 12 (with Morales's draft reply on the margin, New Orleans, November 15), November 27, December 19 and 31, 1781; (Morales to Blanchard), New Orleans, December 19, 1781, January 8, 1782; all in AGI, PC, leg. 608B.

29. Blanchard to Morales, Valenzuela, March 21, and May 15, 1782, ibid.

30. Blanchard to (the governor), Valenzuela, December 27, 1782, AGI, PC, leg. 195; Blanchard to Morales, Valenzuela, September 6, 1782, AGI, PC, leg. 608B. Carondelet's orders on repairing roads and levees are in his letter to Nicholas Verbois, New Orleans, October 10, 1794, AGI, PC, leg. 209. The orders also applied to Valenzuela.

six other families of twenty people also lived in the community. The census seems to have counted only those persons living in the settlement; however, it also showed that none of the Isleños owned slaves, that they possessed no cattle or cows, that only a few owned pigs, and that perhaps as many as half of the families did not even have chickens. The families lived from subsistence farming, with 80 percent of them being self-sufficient, growing mainly corn. Most of the Canary Islanders appeared to be living in poverty, and those receiving rations were in the worst condition.[31]

A major change on Bayou Lafourche occurred in 1785 and 1786 with the arrival of the Acadian immigrants from France. A large number settled on the bayou, some of them among the Isleños but more of them received lands for miles farther down the stream, perhaps as far as modern-day Lafourche Parish. The arrival of the Acadians increased the population of the district (which was now often called Lafourche Interior) from about 352 in 1785 to 1,500 in 1788. Although it did not happen immediately, the Acadians would in time engulf many of the Canary Islanders. Intermarriage between the two groups of people occurred from the start, and it has continued down to the present. When Isleño families grew in size and number in the early nineteenth century, they often moved farther down the bayou to Lafourche Parish, where they acquired vacant lands among the Acadians. Here the Acadians often absorbed the Canary Islanders, who retained only their surnames to attest to their origins. Spanish names, however, were sometimes Gallicized.[32]

Because of Valenzuela's proximity to the Church of the Ascension in Lafourche des Chetimachas, the government felt no urgency to build one for the Isleños. These settlers occasionally voiced their need for a place of worship, but Spanish Louisiana suffered from a shortage of priests. When the Acadians took up residence in Lafourche Interior, they asked for a church in their midst since they claimed that Ascension

---

31. Blanchard census, Valenzuela, 1784, AGI, PC, leg. 192.

32. On the coming of the Acadians, see Fernando Solano Costa, "La emigración a la Luisiana española (1783-1785)," *Cuadernos de Historia Jerónima Zurita* 2 (1954): 82-125; Oscar W. Winzerling, *Acadian Odyssey* (Eunice, La.: Hebert Publications, 1981). A published census of Bayou Lafourche is in Albert J. Robichaux Jr., comp., trans., and ed., *Louisiana Census and Militia Lists, 1770-1789*, vol. 1 (Harvey, La.: by the author, 1973), 115-46. Valenzuela censuses can be found in AGI, PC, legs. 202, 213, and 215A.

was too far removed for many of them living far down the bayou. The Canary Islanders of Valenzuela immediately renewed their own request for a church, protesting that since they had arrived first it should be built in their midst. The government, however, delayed in sending a priest to Lafourche Interior. Finally in 1793, Commandant Nicolas Verret of Lafourche Interior received orders to consult all the residents along the bayou on where they wanted the church to be placed since a priest was being sent there. Because there was no consensus as to where to situate the church, Verret and Bernardo de Deva, the priest who arrived in March 1793, made the decision. Initially, Deva used a house for religious services until a church could be built. Before that occurred, Father Joseph de Arazena, the priest at Ascension, died and the governor ordered Deva to minister to both parishes. The order greatly annoyed Deva, who complained about the size of the two parishes, the constant travel required of him, and the difficulty in crossing the bayou and the Mississippi. Nevertheless, Deva reluctantly served both parishes for two years until Father Notario relieved him in Ascension Parish. About 1795, construction on the Assumption church began, and it was placed below Valenzuela, in what is today Plattenville. The Isleños had lost in their effort to obtain their exclusive place of worship. The church building began as a very modest affair, described by Roger Baudier as comparable to a shack. Not until twenty years into the nineteenth century was a more imposing edifice constructed. Deva stayed on as the Assumption priest even after the American era began, dying in 1826.[33]

In the last decade of Spanish rule in Louisiana, various complaints came from Bayou Lafourche. Roads and levees were not always repaired and crevasses in the levees produced floods. Also, as the population grew, greater problems and conflicts arose, necessitating more government officials. In response, Governor Carondelet created the post of syndic

---

33. Petition of Francisco Corbo, *et al.*, to the governor, Valenzuela, March 11, 1787, AGI, PC, leg. 200; Nicholas Verret to Carondelet, nos. 29, 35, 37, and 42, Lafourche Interior, October 30, 1792, April 9, May 1, and June 4, 1793; Bernardo de Deva to Carondelet, Lafourche Interior, August 30, 1793, all in AGI, PC, leg. 208A; Deva to Carondelet, Lafourche des Chetimachas, May 1, and November 12, 1794, AGI, PC, leg. 28 and 30, respectively; statements of Bernardo de Deva, n.d.s, AGI, PC, leg. 538B; Baudier, *Catholic Church in Louisiana*, 221, 236, and 239.

to assist district commandants in resolving problems. Among the first syndics for Valenzuela were Pedro Doncel, a former army sergeant married to Juana Ximénez, an Isleña, and Andrés de Vega, an Isleño and leader among the Spanish settlers. It was not easy to find qualified candidates to serve as syndics among the Canary Islanders, Commandant Verret complained to the governor, since most of them were illiterate. No schools were ever established in the Isleño communities in Spanish times nor does there seem to have been any effort to educate even a part of the population.[34]

In the 1790s, a comparison could be made on how well off the Canary Islanders and the Acadians of Lafourche Interior were. Evidence suggests that the Acadians arrived in Louisiana with greater resources than the Isleños, most of whom were known to have been utterly destitute. As a result of the Pointe Coupée slave conspiracy in 1795, a number of the participants were executed or imprisoned. Governor Carondelet believed it was necessary to compensate the masters who lost slaves, and he ordered all slaveholders to contribute six reales (seventy-five cents) per slave they owned to a fund. The census of slaves on Bayou Lafourche that year revealed that the Spaniards owned only 6 slaves of the total of 253 in the district. Despite the fact that the Acadians owned so many slaves, they and the Canary Islanders protested poverty and the inability to pay the assessment. Carondelet, however, turned a deaf ear to their pleas and ordered them to pay.[35]

The Bayou Lafourche Isleños preferred to have commandants who were Spaniards, or French if they received fair treatment. The settlers claimed that persons of other nationalities did not understand them and tried to abuse them.[36] Such was the case with the American Evan Jones.

---

34. Nicholas Verret note of 1793 in AGI, PC, leg. 208A; Verret to Carondelet, Lafourche Interior, June 10, 1795, with an attachment, both in AGI, PC, leg. 211A.

35. Verret to Carondelet, Lafourche Interior, August 25, 1795; Judice to the governor, Lafourche des Chetimachas, August 31, 1795; Carondelet to Verret, New Orleans, September 5, 1795; all in AGI, PC, leg. 211A.

36. The Spanish commandants at Lafourche Interior (Valenzuela) were Antonio de St. Maxent (who served from late 1778 or early 1779 to May 1781); Anselmo Blanchard (August 1781 to August or September 1784); Nicholas Verret (November 1784 to early 1799); Auguste Verret (April or May to November 1799); Vicente Fernández Texeiro

In 1797, Gov. Manuel Gayoso de Lemos removed Judice as commandant of Lafourche des Chetimachas and replaced him with Jones. His high-handed tactics, however, particularly in repairing roads and levees, irked the Isleños who felt that he regarded them as inferiors and ordered them about with disdain. Because of complaints, Gayoso sent Capt. Francisco Rivas to Valenzuela to investigate. He met with the Isleños in Vega's house on August 23 and listened to their accusations. They claimed that Jones tried to make them repair levees on the Mississippi, where they bore no responsibility and far from their own lands when they were occupied tending to their crops. Moreover, the American, insensitive to their needs, had tried to remove Vega as their syndic, replacing him with a "foreigner" whose language they could not understand. Although the Isleños might have exaggerated, their charges seemed to have been truthful, and Jones resigned before Gayoso could replace him. The governor next sent Lt. Rafael Croquer, a Spaniard, to be commandant of Lafourche des Chetimachas in September 1798. Croquer remained there until the Spanish era terminated.[37]

In 1801 Militia Lt. Tomás de Villanueva, an Isleño from San Bernardo, became Lafourche Interior's last Spanish commandant. He found the district in a state of neglect, particularly in regard to roads and levees. He attempted to remedy the situation by giving out vacant and abandoned lands so their new owners would repair the roads and levees. Villanueva also noted that many of the farmers, and almost all of them were small farmers, had turned to cotton as their major cash crop. In

---

(to June 1800); Auguste Verret (July 1800 to July 1801); and Tomás de Villanueva (to 1804). The commandants at Lafourche des Chetimachas were Louis Judice (1770 to September 1797); Evan Jones (to September 1798); and Rafael Croquer (to 1804).

37. Evan Jones to the governor, no. 15, Lafourche des Chetimachas, April 15, 1798, AGI, PC, leg. 214A; "Lista de los Avitantes de mi distrito," Andrés de Vega, Valenzuela, March 4, 1798; petition of the Isleños, Valenzuela, March 6, 1798, both in AGI, PC, leg. 215A; (Gayoso) to Vega, New Orleans, August 20, 1798; petition of Domingo Escanio et al., Valenzuela, August 28, 1798; petition of Vega to the governor, Valenzuela, August 28, 1798, the three documents in AGI, PC, leg. 44; Jones to the governor, nos. 18 and 19, Lafourche des Chetimachas, September 3, 1798; (Gayoso) to Jones, New Orleans, September 13, 1798, both in AGI, PC 215A; Rafael Croquer to Gayoso, Lafourche des Chetimachas, September 28, 1798, AGI, PC, leg. 50.

addition, they grew vegetables for subsistence and for sale.[38]

In the last years of the Spanish period, several of the Isleños had acquired cattle, horses, and even slaves. Despite periodic protestation of poverty—and probably most of the Isleños remained poor—several had achieved a degree of prosperity. As an example, in 1799 Miguel Suárez, who at one time operated a tavern in Valenzuela, inventoried his possessions prior to their sale. The inventory showed that he owned eight slaves and had personal property worth 2,953 pesos. Also, his land of three arpents of bayou front by forty deep had a house, an exterior kitchen, a warehouse, a stable, two slave cabins, and a garden with fruit trees, all appraised at a modest 500 pesos. Although Suárez's condition was perhaps exceptional, it suggested that some Isleños had prospered moderately and that others were no longer struggling as they had in their early years of settlement.[39]

By the end of the Spanish period, Lafourche Interior had changed considerably. A twentieth century writer, William O. Scroggs, has noted that the *petits habitants* were "settled thickly along Bayou Lafourche... and in 1803 it contained about 2,800 inhabitants, of whom less than 400 were slaves . . . Bayou Lafourche was lined with farms, only one deep, along its banks for a distance of forty miles. . . ."[40] At that time, the Isleños continued to live along the front of the bayou. Not until the 1820s, with the rise of plantations on the bayou, were many of them forced to retire to the interior ridges. There they cleared the land for agriculture by burning off the vegetation, which gave these pockets of settlement their name, *brulées*, and there the Isleños and their descendants preserved their culture and language practically intact over the next century.[41]

38. Tomás de Villanueva Barroso to Manuel Juan de Salcedo, nos. 1 and 3, Valenzuela, August 25, 1801, AGI, PC, leg. 77B; Villanueva to Morales, Valenzuela, August 25, 1801, AGI, PC, leg. 608B.

39. Ascension Parish Records, Courthouse, Donaldsonville, "Land, 1799," 107-16.

40. William O. Scroggs, "Rural Life in the Lower Mississippi Valley about 1803," *Proceedings of the Mississippi Valley Historical Association for the year 1914-15*, vol. 3 (1916): 262-77. The quotation is on p. 268.

41. W. W. Pugh, "Bayou Lafourche from 1820 to 1825," *Louisiana Planter and Sugar Manufacturer* (September 29, 1788); Lilian Crété, *Daily Life in Louisiana, 1815-1830* (Baton Rouge: Louisiana State University Press, 1981), 277.

Although a number of Canary Islanders petitioned the Spanish government to leave Louisiana as the United States assumed dominion over the territory, very few of them actually left. At Galveztown the major exodus occurred and along Bayou Lafourche a handful of Isleños also departed, but both groups traveled only as far as Baton Rouge, where they again came under American control in 1810. The majority of the settlers, however, remained on their farms and at their occupations. They experienced little disruption in their lives by the new authorities. By 1803, the number of Isleños living in Louisiana had again risen to perhaps two thousand, which was the approximate figure for the immigrants who had arrived in the 1778-1783 period. By then, after years of hardship and toil, they had adjusted to life in the bayou country of Louisiana. In the parishes of St. Bernard, Ascension, Assumption, and East Baton Rouge, many of the Canary Islanders continued to reside, and there they preserved their cultural heritage until recent times. Despite the long-held tendency of Louisiana historians to overlook their existence, the descendants of the original Isleños have grown in size until today they number into the tens of thousands. Perhaps because of the recent popularity of genealogy many of them have begun to assert their identity as a separate people, to explore their history and families, and to point out their contributions to the development of Louisiana.

Bibliography

Archives and Manuscripts

Archivo General de Indias, Seville
   Papeles Procedentes de la Isla de Cuba
      Legajos: 1, 2, 6, 13, 14, 22, 27A, 28, 30, 33, 34, 44, 50, 77B, 83, 85, 89, 93, 102, 104A, 107, 109, 112, 114, 115, 116, 117A, 119, 120, 121, 122AB, 138, 139, 174B, 176B, 177A, 192, 195, 200, 202, 208A, 209, 211A, 212, 213, 214A, 215AB, 217, 233B, 247, 260, 360, 534B, 538B, 568, 576, 593, 595A, 600, 601, 603B, 606, 608AB, 614A, 674, 689, 1146, 1232, 1393, 1425, 1443A, 2317B, 2352, 2354, 2360, 2361, 2363, 2364, 2365, 2368?, 2374, 2547,
   Audiencia de Santo Domingo
      Legajos: 2543, 2548, 2550, 2580, 2589, 2609, 2611, 2617, 2661

Archivo Histórico Nacional, Madrid
   Sección de Estado
      Legajos: 3884, 3885, 3885bis, 3886, 3888, 3888bis, 3889, 3890, 3891, 3893, 3893bis, 3894, 3894bis, 3895, 3895bis, 3896, 3898, 3899, 3900, 3901

Bancroft Library, University of California, Berkeley
   Louisiana Documentary Collection

Biblioteca Nacional, Madrid
   Sección de Manuscritos
      Documentos de la Florida, 2 vols.
      Documentos de la Luisiana, 3 vols.

Museo Naval, Madrid
   Sección de Manuscritos
      Manuscrito 569

Books, Articles, and Dissertations

Acosta Rodríguez, Antonio. *La población de Luisiana española (1763-1803)*. Madrid: Gráficas Condor, S.A., 1979.

———. "Overview of the Consumption of Food and Goods by *Isleño* Immigrants to Louisiana." Translated and Edited by Paul E. Hoffman. *Louisiana History* 22 (Summer 1981): 299-306.

American National Biography. 24 vols. New York: Oxford University Press, 1999.

Bacarisse, Charles A. "Baron de Bastrop." *Southwestern Historical Quarterly* 58 (January 1955): 319-30.

Ballesteros Gaibrois, Manuel. "La Misión Gardoqui." PhD diss., Universidad de Madrid, 1930.

Beerman, Eric. *España y la independencia de los Estados Unidos*. Madrid: Editorial MAPFRE, 1992.

Bekkers, Rev. B. J. "The Catholic Church in Mississippi during Colonial Times." *Publications of the Mississippi Historical Society* 6 (1902): 351-57.

Bemis, Samuel Flagg. *Pinckney's Treaty: America's Advantage from Europe's Distress, 1783-1800*. rev. ed. New Haven: Yale University Press, 1960.

———. *The Diplomacy of the American Revolution*. 1957. Reprint, Bloomington: University of Indiana Press, 1965.

Bergerie, Maurine. *They Tasted Bayou Water: A Brief History of Iberia Parish*. New Iberia: by the author, 1962.

Bolton, Herbert Eugene. *The Spanish Borderlands: A Chronicle of Old Florida and the Southwest*. New Haven: Yale University Press, 1921.

Brackenridge, Henry Marie. *Views of Louisiana*. 1817. Reprint, Chicago: Quadrangle Books, 1962.

Brasseaux, Carl A. *The Founding of New Acadia: The Beginnings of Acadian Life in Louisiana, 1765-1803*. Baton Rouge: Louisiana State University Press, 1987.

———. "*Scattered to the Wind*": *Dispersal and Wanderings of the Acadians, 1755-1809*. Lafayette, La.: Center for Louisiana Studies, 1991.

Brasseaux, Carl A. and Richard E. Chandler. "The *Britain* Incident, 1768-1770: Anglo-Hispanic Tensions in the Western Gulf." *Southwestern Historical Quarterly* 87 (April 1984): 357-70.

Browne, Patrick W. "Salamanca and the Beginnings of the Church in Florida." *The Ecclesiastical Review* 84 (1931): 581-87.

Burns, Francis P. "The Spanish Land Laws of Louisiana." *Louisiana Historical Quarterly*

11 (October 1928): 557-81.

Burson, Caroline Maude. *The Stewardship of Don Esteban Miró, 1782-1792*. New Orleans: American Printing Company, 1940.

Carter, Clarence E., ed. "A Projected Settlement of English Speaking Catholics from Maryland in Spanish Louisiana, 1767, 1768." *American Historical Review* 16 (January 1911): 319-27.

Cantillo, Alejandro de. *Tratados, convenios y declaraciones de paz y de comercio...desde el año de 1700 hasta el día*. Madrid: Alegría y Charlain, 1843.

Carondelet, Francisco Luis. "Carondelet on the Defense of Louisiana, 1794." Translated by W. F. Giese. *American Historical Review* 2 (April 1897): 474-505.

Caughey, John Walton. *Bernardo de Gálvez in Louisiana, 1776-1783*. Berkeley: University of California Press, 1934.

Chapman, Charles Edward. *Colonial Hispanic America: A History*. New York: Macmillan, 1933.

Chávez, Thomas. *Spain and the Independence of the United States: An Intrinsic Gift*. Albuquerque: University of New Mexico Press, 2002.

Coker, William S. "The Bruins and the Formulation of Spanish Immigration Policy in the Old Southwest, 1787-88." In *The Spanish in the Mississippi Valley, 1762-1804*, edited by John Francis McDermott, 61-71. Urbana: University of Illinois Press, 1974.

Cox, Isaac Joslin. "The New Invasion of the Goths and Vandals." *Proceedings of the Mississippi Valley Historical Association* 8 (1914-1915), 176-200.

Coutts, Bryan E. "Flax and Hemp in Spanish Louisiana, 1777-1783." *Louisiana History* 26 (Spring 1984): 129-39.

Crété, Lilian. *Daily Life in Louisiana, 1815-1830*. Baton Rouge: Louisiana State University Press, 1981.

Cunningham, Charles H., ed. "Financial Reports Relating to Louisiana, 1766-1788." *Mississippi Valley Historical Review* 6 (December 1919): 381-97.

Curley, Michael. *Church and State in the Spanish Floridas (1782-1822)*. Washington, DC: Catholic University Press, 1940.

Darby, William. *The Emigrant's Guide to the Western and Southwestern States and Territories*. New York: Kirk and Mercein, 1818.

Dawdy, Shannon Lee. *Building the Devil's Empire: French Colonial New Orleans*. Chicago: University of Chicago Press, 2008.

Din, Gilbert C. *The Canary Islanders of Louisiana*. Baton Rouge: Louisiana State University Press, 1988.

———. "Empires Too Far: The Demographic Limitations of Three Imperial Powers in the Eighteenth Century Mississippi Valley." *Louisiana History* 50 (Summer 2009): 261-92.

———. *Francisco Bouligny: A Bourbon Soldier in Spanish Louisiana*. Baton Rouge: Louisiana State University Press, 1993.

———. "Lieutenant Raimundo DuBreüil, Commandant of San Gabriel de Manchac, and Bernardo de Gálvez's 1779 Campaign on the Mississippi." *Military History of the West* 10 (Spring 1999): 1-30.

———. *Louisiana in 1776: A Memoria by Francisco Bouligny*. New Orleans: Louisiana Collections Series, 1977.

———. "Protecting the '*Barrera*': Spain's Defenses in Louisiana, 1763-1779." *Louisiana History* 18 (Spring 1978): 183-211.

———. *Spaniards, Planters, and Slaves: The Spanish Regulation of Slavery in Louisiana, 1763-1803*. College Station: Texas A&M University Press, 1999.

Ekberg, Carl J. *Colonial Ste. Genevieve: An Adventure on the Mississippi Frontier*. Gerald, Mo.: Patrice Press, 1985.

Fabel, Robin. *The Economy of British West Florida, 1763-1783*. Tuscaloosa, Ala.: University of Alabama Press, 1988.

Faragher, John Mack. *A Great and Noble Scheme: The Tragic Story of the Expulsion of the French Acadians from Their American Homeland*. New York: W. W. Norton, 2005.

Fletcher, Mildred Stahl. "Louisiana as a Factor in French Diplomacy from 1763-1800." *Mississippi Valley Historical Review* 17 (December 1930): 367-76.

Forman, Samuel S. *Narrative of a Journey down the Ohio and Mississippi in 1789-90*.

Cincinnati: R. Clarke and Company, 1888.

Fortier, Alcée. *A History of Louisiana*. 4 vols. New York: Goupil and Company, 1904.

Frederick, Julia C. "Luis de Unzaga and Bourbon Reforms in Spanish Louisiana, 1770-1776." PhD diss., Louisiana State University, 2000.

French, Benjamin Franklin, ed. *Historical Collections of Louisiana*. 5 vols. New York: Lamport, Blakeman and Law, 1846-1853.

Gayarré, Charles. *History of Louisiana*. 4 vols. New Orleans: Armand Hawkins, 1885.

Gerow, Most Rev. Richard O. "History of the Catholic Diocese of Natchez." *Catholic Action of the South*. Centennial Edition, Vol. 5. New Orleans, October 14, 1937.

Haarmann, Albert W. "The Spanish Conquest of British West Florida, 1779-1781." *Florida Historical Quarterly* 39 (October 1960): 107-34.

Hall, F. R. "Genêt's Western Intrigue, 1793-1794." *Journal of the Illinois State Historical Society* 21 (October 1928): 359-81.

Haman, Rev. Thomas L. "Beginnings of Presbyterianism in Mississippi." *Publications of the Mississippi Historical Society* 10 (1909): 203-21.

Hatcher, Mattie Austin. "The Louisiana Background of the Colonization of Texas, 1763-1803." *Southwestern Historical Quarterly* 24 (January 1921): 169-94.

Holmes, Jack D. L. "The Abortive Slave Revolt at Pointe Coupée, Louisiana, 1795." *Louisiana History* 11 (Fall 1970): 341-62.

———, ed. "The Calcasieu Promoter: Joseph Piernas and His 1799 Proposal." *Louisiana History* 9 (Spring 1968): 163-67.

———, ed. *Documentos inéditos para la historia de la Luisiana, 1792-1810*. Madrid: Ediciones José Porrua Turanzas, 1963.

———. "*Dramatis Personae* in Spanish Louisiana." *Louisiana Studies* 6 (Summer 1967), 149-85.

———. "Father Francis Lennan and his Activities in Spanish Louisiana and West Florida." *Louisiana Studies* 5 (Winter 1966): 255-68.

———. *Gayoso, The Life of a Spanish Governor in the Mississippi Valley, 1789-1799*.

Baton Rouge: Louisiana State University Press for the Louisiana Historical Association, 1965.

———. *Honor and Fidelity: The Louisiana Infantry Regiment and the Louisiana Militia Companies, 1766-1821*. Birmingham, Ala.: by the author, 1965.

———. "Irish Priests in Spanish Natchez." *Journal of Mississippi History* 29 (August 1967): 169-80.

———. "Joseph Piernas and a Proposed Settlement on the Calcasieu River, 1795." *McNeese Review* 13 (1962): 59-80.

———. "Some Economic Problems of Spanish Governors of Louisiana." *Hispanic American Historical Review* 42 (November, 1962): 521-43.

———. "Some Irish Officers in Spanish Louisiana." *The Irish Sword* 6 (Winter 1964): 234-47.

Houck, Louis. *A History of Missouri from the Earliest Explorations and Settlements until the Admission of the State into the Union*. 3 vols. Chicago: R. R. Donnelley and Sons, 1908.

———, ed. *The Spanish Régime in Missouri*. 2 vols. in 1. 1909. Reprint, New York: Arno Press and New York Times, 1971.

Ingersoll, Thomas N. "Old New Orleans: Race, Class, Sex, and Order in the Early Deep South, 1718-1819." PhD diss., University of California, Los Angles, 1990.

Jacobs, James Ripley. *Tarnished Warrior: Major-General James Wilkinson*. New York: Macmillan, 1938.

Johnson, Cecil. "Expansion in West Florida: 1770-1779." *Mississippi Valley Historical Review* 20 (1934): 481-96.

Kapp, Friedrich. *Life of William Frederick von Steuben, Major-General in the Revolutionary War*. New York: Mason Brothers, 1859.

Kinnaird, Lawrence. "American Penetration into Spanish Louisiana." *New Spain and the Anglo-American West*. 2 vols. Los Angeles: privately published, 1932. 1: 211-27.

———, ed. *Spain in the Mississippi Valley, 1764-1794*. 3 Parts (Washington, DC: GPO, 1949.

Kuethe, Allan J. *Cuba, 1753-1815: Crown, Military, and Society*. Knoxville: University of Tennessee Press, 1986.

LaChance, Paul. "The Growth of the Free and Slave Populations." In *French Colonial Louisiana and the Atlantic World*, edited by Bradley G. Bond, 204-243. Baton Rouge: Louisiana State University Press, 2005.

Lauvrière, Émile. *Histoire de la Louisiane Française, 1763-1939*. Paris: G.-P. Maisonneuve, 1940.

Leavell, Z. T. "Early Beginnings of Baptists in Mississippi." *Publications* of the Mississippi Historical Society 4 (1901): 246-52.

Liljegren, Ernest R. "Jacobinism in Spanish Louisiana, 1792-1797," *Louisiana Historical Quarterly* 22 (January 1939): 47-97.

Linklater, Andro. *An Artist in Treason: The Extraordinary Double Life of General James Wilkinson*. New York: Walker Publishing Company, 2009.

Lowry, Robert and William H. McCardle. *A History of Mississippi*. 1891. Reprint, Jackson, Miss.: Power and Barksdale, 1964.

Marchand, Sidney A. *The Flight of a Century (1800-1900) in Ascension Parish, Louisiana*. Donaldsonville, La.: by the author, 1936.

———. *The Story of Ascension Parish, Louisiana*. Baton Rouge: J. E. Ortlieb Printing Company, 1931.

Martin, Fontaine. *A History of the Bouligny Family and Allied Families*. Lafayette, La.: Center for Louisiana Studies, 1990.

Martin, François-Xavier. *The History of Louisiana, from the Earliest Period*. 1827-29. Reprint, New Orleans: James A. Gresham, 1882.

McMichael, Andrew. "The Kemper 'Rebellion': Filibustering and Resident Anglo American Loyalty in Spanish West Florida." *Louisiana History* 43 (Spring 2003): 136-38.

Mitchell, Jennie O'Kelly and Robert Dabney Calhoun. "The Marquis de Maison Rouge, the Baron de Bastrop, and Colonel Abraham Morhouse—Three Ouachita Valley Soldiers of Fortune." *Louisiana Historical Quarterly* 20 (April 1937): 289-462.

Moody, V. Alton. "Early Religious Efforts in the Lower Mississippi Valley." *Mississippi*

Valley Historical Review 22 (September 1935): 161-76.

Moore, John Preston. "Antonio de Ulloa: A Profile of the First Spanish Governor of Louisiana." *Louisiana History* 7 (1967): 189-218.

———. *Revolt in Louisiana: The Spanish Occupation, 1766-1770*. Baton Rouge: Louisiana State University Press, 1976.

Nasatir, A. P., ed. *Before Lewis and Clark: Documents Illustrating the History of the Missouri, 1785-1804*. 2 vols. St. Louis: St. Louis Historical Society, 1952.

———. "Jacques Clamorgan: Colonial Promoter of the Northern Border of New Spain." *New Mexico Historical Review* 17 (April 1942): 101-12.

Navarro Latorre, Juan, and Francisco Solano Costa.*¿Conspiración española? 1787-1789: Contribución al estudio de las primeras relaciones históricas entre España y los Estados Unidos de Norteamérica*. Zaragoza, Spain: Editoriales Librería General, 1949.

Nunemaker, J. Horace. "Francisco Bouligny's Absence from Louisiana." In *Research Studies* 10. Pullman: State College of Washington, 1942: 198-201.

———, ed. "The Bouligny Affair in Louisiana." *Hispanic American Historical Review* 25 (August 1945): 339-63.

Otken, Charles H. "Richard Curtis in the Country of the Natchez." *Publications* of the Mississippi Historical Society 3 (1900): 147-53.

Perez, L. M. "French Immigrants to Louisiana, 1796-1800." *Publications of the Southern History Association* 11 (1907): 106-12.

Powell, Lawrence N. *The Accidental City: Improvising New Orleans*. Cambridge: Harvard University Press, 2012.

Power, Maj. Steve. *The Memento: Old and New Natchez, 1700 to 1897*. Natchez, Miss.: Myrtle Banks Publisher, 1984.

Pugh, W. W. "Bayou Lafourche from 1820 to 1825." *Louisiana Planter and Sugar Manufacturer*, September 29, 1878.

Ribes,Vicent. *Comerciantes, esclavos y capital sin patria*. Valencia, Spain: Artes Gráficas Soler, 1993.

Rice, Howard C. *Barthélemi Tardiveau: A French Trader in the West*. Baltimore: Johns

Hopkins University Press, 1938.

Robertson, James Alexander, ed. *Louisiana Under the Rule of Spain, France, and the United States, 1785-1807: Social Economic, and Political Conditions of the Territory in the Louisiana Purchase*. 2 vols. Cleveland: Arthur Clark Co, 1911.

Robichaux, Jr., Albert J. Compiler, Translator, and Editor *Louisiana Census and Militia Lists, 1770-1789*. Vol. 1. Harvey, La.: by the author, 1973.

Rozier, Fermin A. "Rev. James Maxwell, Missionary at St. Genevieve." *The United States Catholic Historical Magazine* 1 (1887): 283-86.

Savelle, Max. "The Founding of New Madrid, Missouri." *Mississippi Valley Historical Review* 19 (June 1932): 30-56.

———. *George Morgan, Colony Builder*. New York: Columbia University Press, 1932.

Scramuzza, V.M. "Galveztown: A Spanish Settlement of Colonial Louisiana." *Louisiana Historical Quarterly* 23 (1930), 553-609.

Scroggs, William O. "Rural Life in the Lower Mississippi Valley about 1803." *Proceedings of the Mississippi Valley Historical Association for the year 1914-15*. Vol. 3 (1916): 262-77.

Serrano y Sanz, Manuel. *El Brigadier Jaime Wilkinson y sus tratos con España para la independencia del Kentucky*. Madrid: Tip. de la "Revista de arch., bibl. y museos," 1915.

Shepherd, William R. "Wilkinson and the Beginnings of the Spanish Conspiracy." *American Historical Review* 9 (April 1904): 490-506.

Siebert, Wilbur H. "The Loyalists in West Florida and the Natchez District." *Mississippi Valley Historical Society Proceedings* 8 (1914-15): 102-22.

Solano Costa, Fernando. "La emigración acadiana a la Luisiana española (1783-1785)." *Cuadernos de Historia Jerónimo Zurita* 2 (1954): 85-125.

———. "La fundación de Nuevo Madrid." *Cuadernos de Historia Jerónimo Zurita* 4-5 (1956): 91-108.

Stewart, George Rippey. *American Place-Names: A Concise and Selective Dictionary for the Continental United States of America*. New York: Oxford University Press, 1970.

Stoddard, Amos. *Sketches, Historical and Descriptive, of Louisiana*. Philadelphia: Mathew Carey, 1812.

Swem, E. G. "A Letter from New Madrid, 1789." *Mississippi Valley Historical Review* 5 (December 1918): 342-46.

Texada, David Ker. *Alejandro O'Reilly and the New Orleans Rebels*. Lafayette, La.: Center for Louisiana Studies, University of Southwestern Louisiana, 1970.

Torres Ramírez, Bibiano. *Alejandro O'Reilly en las Indias*. Seville: Escuela de Estudios Hispano-Americanos, 1969.

Turner, Frederick Jackson. "The Origin of Genêt's Projected Attack on Louisiana and the Floridas." *American Historical Review* 3 (July 1898): 650-71.

Viles, Jonas. "Population and Extent of Settlement in Missouri before 1804." *Missouri Historical Review* 5 (July 1911): 189-213.

Vilette, E. M. "Early Settlements in Missouri." *Missouri Historical Review* 1 (October 1906): 38-52.

Villeré, Sidney Louis. *The Canary Islands Migration to Louisiana, 1778-1783: The History and Passenger Lists of the Isleño Volunteer Recruits and Their Families*. Baltimore: Genealogical Publishing Company, 1972.

Weddle, Robert S. *Changing Tides: Twilight and Dawn in the Spanish Sea*. College Station: Texas A&M University Press, 1995.

"West Florida: The Capture of Baton Rouge by Gálvez, September 21, 1779." *Louisiana Historical Quarterly* 12 (1929): 255-65.

Whitaker, Arthur Preston. "The Commerce of Louisiana and the Floridas at the End of the Eighteenth Century." *Hispanic American Historical Review* 8 (May 1928): 190-203.

———. *The Mississippi Question, 1795-1803: A Study in Trade, Politics, and Diplomacy*. 1934. Reprint, Gloucester, Mass.: Peter Smith, 1962.

———. "Spain and the Retrocession of Louisiana." *American Historical Review* 39 (April 1934): 454-76.

———. *The Spanish American Frontier: 1783-1795: The Westward Movement and the Spanish Retreat in the Mississippi Valley*. 1927. Reprint, Gloucester, Mass: Peter

Smith, 1962.

Willey, George. "Natchez in the Olden Times." In *Mississippi, as a Province, Territory and State*, by J. F. H. Claiborne. Jackson, Miss.: Power and Barksdale, 1880.

Winzerling, Oscar W. *Acadian Odyssey*. Eunice, La.: Hebert Publications, 1981.

World Almanac. New York: American Heritage Press, 1967.

Yela Utrilla, J. F. *España ante la independencia de los Estados Unidos*. 2nd ed. 2 vols. Lérida, Spain: Gráficos Academia Mariana, 1925.

Index

A

Acabannoosa District, 7
Acadiana, 6
Acadian Coast, 4, 7n16
Acadians: assistance to, 4-6, 19-20, 29, 65, 67-68; in Attakapas, 6-7, 25n5; in Bayou Teche region, 29-32, 34; in Galvez, 168; immigration, vii, 1, 3, 7-8, 10, 12, 18-19, 21, 23, 39-40, 64, 67-68, 108, 129, 168, 170, 172-74; in Lafourche, 157, 170, 172-174; in Opelousas, 6-7, 9, 25n5
Adams, Calvin, 116
Adams-Onis Treaty, 150
African slaves. *See* slaves
agriculture, 7, 10, 15, 17, 24, 30, 34, 37, 45, 68, 70, 157, 161, 169-70, 176
Alicante, Spain, 23
Amable María, 108
Amat de Tortosa, Andrés, 13, 19, 154-55
American era, 173
American frontier, 84, 87, 89-90, 92. *See also* American West
Americanization of Upper Louisiana, 130
American Protestants, vii, ix, 51, 64, 69, 81-82, 122, 143
American Revolutionary War, 41, 44, 67. *See also* American War for Independence and War for American Independence
American War for Independence, 1, 13, 23, 63, 65, 79, 133. *See also* American Revolutionary War and War for American Independence
American West, 44-45, 49-50, 55, 57, 59-61, 65, 76-77, 80, 84, 86-87, 93-94, 102, 106, 112, 114
Americans: in Galveztown, 14, 111, 168; immigration, ix, 43-44, 50-51, 56, 59-61, 63-64, 66-67, 69, 76-78, 81, 83, 91-92, 94, 102-103, 105-107, 110, 115, 118-19,124-27, 128-31, 133, 140, 143, 149; in Natchez, 117, 119, 121, 124, 147; in Texas, 61; in West Florida, 21, 41, 82; use of the Mississippi River, 46-48, 85, 87, 89-90, 139
Amite-Manchac waterway, 162
Amite River, 107, 157-58, 164, 167
Anderson, Richard, 54, 97
Andrés, Bishop of Salamanca, 135-36
Anglican, viii
Anglo-Americans, 42, 46, 112; in Natchez, 44-46, 72, 76, 81-82, 85, 134, 137, 140
Anglo-Saxon residents, 21, 137; in West Florida, 82
Appalachian Mountains, 64
Aranda, Conde de, 44-47, 81-82, 84, 102, 111
Aranjuez, Spain, viii, 47
Arazena, Father Joseph de, 173
Arkansas, 140
Artache family, 34
artisans, 10, 17, 75, 85, 115, 157, 162
Ascension Parish, 169, 173, 177
assimilation, 64, 85, 133, 143, 151. *See also* Hispanization
Assumption church, 173
Assumption Parish, 169, 177
Atlantic Ocean, 21, 40, 88
Attakapas territory, 6-7, 27, 30, 141
Audiencia of Quito, 123

Audrain, Pedro, 111
Avoyelles, La., 115

B

Baptists, 144-45, 147
Barataria, La., 14, 153, 158-59, 164
barrera, ix, 1, 6, 10, 22
Bastrop, Philip Hendrik Nering Bögel, baron de, 120-23; immigration plan, 121-23
Baton Rouge, La., 20, 32, 134, 141, 145, 148, 150, 163, 168, 177
Baudier, Roger, 173
Bayou de los Ecores, 20. *See also* Thompson Creek
Bayou Lafourche (La Fourche), 14, 157, 169-70, 172-74, 176-77
Bayou Manchac, 6, 157
Bayou Pierre, 140
Bayou Sara, 138
Bayou Têche, 17, 27-29, 31
Bayou Terre-aux-Boeufs, 158, 161
Belle Alliance, La., 169
Benedictine order, 110
Berviquet (Berwick), Thomas, 35
Biloxi, Miss., 2
Blanchard, Anselme, 20, 171
Blount, William, 124
Bodkin, John, 142
Bolls, John, 146
Bordeaux, France, 68
Borme, Césaire, 8
Bouligny, Dominique, 37
Bouligny, Francisco, x, 10, 16-18, 23-24, 26-35, 37
Bouligny Memoria, 154
Brady, Father John, 142-43, 148, 150
Breard, Augustus de, 115, 121
Breckenridge, Henry Marie, 29
Britain, 8
British: army, 67; inhabitants of West Florida, 41, 83; posts, 32, 158, 169; territory, 14; threat in Louisiana, 9, 24
British Canada, 119
Bruin, Bryan, 68-70
Bruin, Peter Bryan, 69-70, 70n16
brulées, 176
Brunete, Friar Mariano de, 160
Bryan, Jonathan, 118
Burke, Charles, 140-41, 150
Butler Memorial, 117-18
Butler, William, 70-71

C

Cádiz, Spain, 16, 26, 135-37
Cahokia settlement, 4
Calcasieu River, 116
California, vii, ix, 2, 9, 25, 41, 64, 120, 154
Canada, 118, 126; immigrants from, 12, 25
Canary Islanders: in Barataria, 159; in Galveztown, 14, 160, 162, 165, 168; immigration, vii, 25, 40, 64-65, 153-54, 156, 177; in Lafourche, 169; in New Iberia, 36n38; in Pensacola, 15; in San Bernardo, 160, 162; in Valenzuela, 160, 162, 170, 172-74
Canary Islands, 13-14, 19, 25, 157
Caracas, Venezuela, 156
Caribbean, 3, 156
Caribbean Islands, 3, 13
Carmelite, 142
Carondelet, Francisco Luis Héctor, baron de: and Galveztown, 166; and immigration, 109-12, 114-116, 119-24, 128; immigration policy, 61, 106-107; and Irish missionaries, 141; and Protestants, 146; and slavery, 174; trade policy, 113
Casa-Calvo, marqués de, 123, 127-28
Catholic: Acadians, 8, 40, 10; Americans, 65-66, 69, 83n8, 85n16;

Canadians, 12; conversion, viii, 42, 56, 74, 81-83, 105, 125, 134, 137, 143-44 (*see also* Catholicism and Irish missionaries); Dutch, 108, 115-16; English, 6; French, 10, 40; Germans, 8, 10, 12, 25, 40, 108; immigrants, 1, 6, 11-13, 39, 42, 46, 67, 122; immigration policy, 1, 11-13, 42, 94, 125-26; Irish, 10, 12, 42, 65, 67-68, 116; Italians, 25; marriage, 147; public worship, 85, 95n44, 134, 144; seminaries, viii

Catholicism: conversion to, viii, 64, 77, 81-83, 105, 144, 151; public worship, 42-43, 46, 51, 64, 77, 95

Caughey, John, 36-37

Central America, 154

Chapman, Charles, 130

Chouteau, Auguste, 4

churches: Assumption, 173; Cole's Creek, 138, 148; Cole's Creek (Protestant), 144-45; Natchez, 54, 138, 149; San Bernardo, 14, 161

Church of the Ascension, 157, 172

Clamorgan, Jacques, 112-13

Clark, George Rogers, 47

Cloud, Reverend Adam, 145

Clouet, Alexandre de, 30

Coleman, James, 140-41, 149-50

Cole's Creek, La., 43, 137-38, 140-41, 145, 148. See also Villa Gayoso, La.

Collell, Francisco, 158, 163-65

commerce, 5, 9-10, 24, 27-28, 45, 52, 82, 88-90, 117, 130

Company of the Indies, 2

Company of the West, 2

Concepción, La., 159. See also San Bernardo, La.

Concepción, 71

Congregational Church, 144

Continental Army, 75

Convent of St. Peter, 136

Corbo, Francisco, 169

cotton, 123, 176

Council of State, 117

Council of the Royal Treasury, 122

Court (Spanish), viii, 21, 39-40, 43-53, 65-66, 68, 71, 75-76, 79, 82-84, 86-96, 98-100, 102, 107, 111, 114-17, 121, 127, 139

Creek Indians, 118

Creole French rebellion, 7-8

Croquer, Rafael, 175

Crozat, Antoine, 2

Cruzat, Francisco, 12

Cuba, 9, 15, 67, 71, 91, 156, 161, 166

Cumberland District, 63, 92, 99

Curtis, Patrick, 135

Curtis, Reverend Richard, Jr., 144-45

D

d'Argès, Pierre Wouves, xi, 5, 44-45, 47-50, 52-54, 79-82, 84-90, 92-103, 139; commission, 54, 57, 92-93, 99; immigration proposal, 44-47, 53, 58, 81n3, 83-84, 95

DeLassus, Carlos DeHault, 111-12

Delaware, 109

Delfin, 156-57

Demar, Antonio, 163, 165

Deva, Bernardo de, 173

DeVilliers, Marcos, 165-66

Didier, Friar Josef, 110

disease, 162-64

Dominican order, 136

Donaldsonville, La., 157

Doncel, Pedro, 174

dropsy, 163. *See also* disease

Dutch, 11, 72, 120; immigration, 108, 115-16

E

East Baton Rouge Parish, 177

East Florida, 109, 136, 142, 149-50

education, 11, 43, 51. *See also* schools

Ellicott, Andrew, 146
Elliot, James, 138
El Jasón, 154. See also *Santísimo Sacramento*
El Sagrado Corazón de Jesús, 155. See also *Natural*
England, 4, 68, 117
English: in Caribbean, 156; colonials, 154; colonies, 6-7; in Pensacola, 15; immigration, 11, 125; royalists, 67; in West Florida, 5, 9
English Atlantic colonies, 3
Escambé region, 15
European: Catholics, 39, 63, 68, 105, 107; colonists, 1; immigrants, 4, 108, 115
Ezpeleta, José de, 67, 71

F

Falls of the Ohio, 44. See also Louisville, Ky.
Feliciana District, 71
fever, 162-63. *See also* disease
Filhio, Juan, 123
Fitzgerald, William, 66-67
Fixed Louisiana Infantry Battalion, 23, 40, 154
Fixed Louisiana Infantry Regiment, 13, 32, 37, 141, 154
Flanders, 118
flax, 11-12, 16, 24, 26, 30, 37, 40
Flemish immigrants, 107-108, 111, 114-16
floods, 36, 158, 165-67, 171, 174
Florida, 118
Floridablanca, Conde de, 47-48, 82, 84-87, 91-92, 97, 99, 101-102
Florida, French threat to, 113
Ford, Philip, 8
Forstall, Nicholas, 18, 35
Fort Chartres settlement, 4
Fort at Galveztown, La., 162, 165, 167-68
Fort Graham, 164
Fortier, Alcée, 153
Fort Panmure, 95, 147
Fort Pitt, 89
Fort San Gabriel, 6
Fowler, Alexander, 107
France, 1, 2, 4, 44, 79, 102, 106, 117, 119, 129-30, 161, 168, 172
Franciscan order, 143
free blacks, 11
free mulattoes, 11
French, 174; army, 65; *émigrés*, 110, 125; immigrants, 3, 10, 12, 14, 25, 28, 108, 111, 116, 125, 129; militia, 113; missionaries, 82; navy, 142; priests, 46; republicans, 115; royalists, 108, 115; threat to Louisiana, 113
French Antilles, 7
French Canadians, vii, 1, 4, 12, 40, 126
French Creole rebellion, 23
French Creoles, 5n9, 113, 116
French era, 2-4, 12
French Revolution, 61, 101, 107, 111, 141-42

G

Gallipolis, 110, 112; immigrants, 111
Gálvez, Bernardo de, 11-14, 16, 24-25, 27, 31-37, 41-42, 134, 154-55, 157, 163-166, 168; campaign against the British, 17, 32, 169; immigration policy, 12-13, 25
Galvez community, 168
Gálvez, José de, Marqués de Sonora, 16, 24, 27, 47, 82, 85, 90, 136, 154
Gálvez, Matías de, 154
Galveztown, La., 14, 27, 111, 153, 158, 162-69, 177
Galveztown, 49, 87-88, 91
Gardoqui, Diego de, 46, 48-49, 53, 55-56, 63-67, 70-73, 75, 86-93,

Index

95-96, 99, 101-102
Gayarré, Charles, 153
Gayoso de Lemos, Manuel, 37, 60, 85, 123, 125-26, 128, 143, 145-46, 147, 175; and the Isleños, 167, 175; immigration policy, 122, 124-26; in Natchez District, 48, 143
Genet, Edmond, 113
German: agriculture, 116; in Bayou Manchac, 8; in Bayou Teche, 29; immigration, vii, 4, 10, 12, 25, 28, 40, 75, 107-108, 111-12, 114-16, 125, 130; in Kentucky, 44; missionaries, 82; in New Iberia, 18, 32, 34, 36; priests, 46
German Coast, 4
Godoy, Manuel, 117-19, 124, 127, 130
Granada, 26, 40; immigrants, 16, 18
Grand-Pré, Carlos de, 52, 70, 95, 115
Great Britain, 1-2, 4, 41, 144; war with Spain, 9, 13, 17, 23, 32, 35, 37, 102, 118-19, 126, 133, 154, 161, 163-64
Grevemberg, Juan Bautista, 28
Grevenberg, François, 34
Grimaldi, Marqués de, 6
Guadarrama Mountains, 24
Guarico (Cap Français, Saint-Domingue), 99
Guatemala, 149
Guinea, 7
Gulf Coast, 2, 28, 149
Gulf of Mexico, 116

H

Hannon, Barton, 147
Hassett, Thomas, 142, 149
Havana, Cuba, viii, 13, 15, 59, 67, 91, 95, 123, 136-37, 141, 155-56
hemp, 11-12, 16, 24, 26, 30, 37, 40
Hispanization, 61, 105, 125. *See also* assimilation
Holland, 117. *See also* Dutch
Holston River, 63
House of the Venerables, 136
Hurricane Katrina, 162
hurricanes, 158, 163-64, 166-67, 171

I

Iberville, La., 142
Iberville River (Bayou Manchac), 8, 27
Illinois, 100
illness, 163, 169. *See also* disease
immigration agents, xi, 52-53, 56, 75-76, 78, 82, 96, 109, 139
immigration tax, 100
Indian raids, 110
Indians, 2, 27-28, 30, 44, 61, 80, 118, 123, 165
Ingersoll, Thomas, 2
Innes, Harry, 120
Ireland, viii, 135, 141, 150
Irish: agriculture, 116; immigration, vii, 10, 12, 23, 28, 40, 65, 67-68, 107-108, 115-16, 125; missionaries, viii, xi, 42-45, 51, 64, 82, 134, 138-39, 147-48, 150-51; priests, 42-43, 46, 51, 78, 83, 85, 133, 135, 137, 139-45, 151
Irish College of the University of Salamanca, 140-41
Irujo, Carlos Martínez de, 124
Isleños, xi, 18, 155-57, 176; at Barataria, 153, 158-59; at Bayou Lafourche, 174-75, 177; at Bayou-Terre-aux-Bouefs, 153, 158; early assistance to, 14, 19; at San Bernardo, 159-62; at Galveztown, 14, 153, 158, 162-65, 167; at New Iberia, 153; at Pensacola, 15; at Valenzuela, 14, 153, 159, 169-74
Isle of Orleans, 2
Italian, immigrants, 12, 25

J

Jacobins, 113, 115
Jáudenes, José de, 108-109, 117-18
Jefferson, Thomas, 105-106
Jerningham, Henry, 6
Jesuit missionary order, vii
Jones, Evan, 174-75
Judice, Louis, 157, 170, 175
Jung, Andrés, 158

K

Kaskaskia settlement, 4, 110
Kennedy, James, 68
Kentucky, 46, 60, 66, 77, 121, 127n53; d'Argès proposal, 44, 49, 79-80, 82, 84-89, 91-93, 95, 97, 99, 101-103; Wilkinson proposal, viii, 51-54, 57-59, 75-7685, 94, 97, 120, 140; separatists, 58, 76, 99n59, 120, 140
King Carlos III, vii
Kingdom of New Spain, 1. *See also* Mexico

L

La Coruña, Spain, 86-87
Lafourche: church parish, 142, 148; Parish, 139, 172
Lafourche des Chetimachas, 157, 170, 172, 175
Lafourche Interior, 172-76
La Guaira (port), 156
Lake Barataria, 158
Lake Maurepas, 167
Lake Pontchartrain, 167
La Luisiana, 148
Lamar, Friar Agustín, 160
Lamport, Michael, 135-38
l'Ance à la Graisse, 54-55, 73, 100. *See also* New Madrid
Las Casas, Luis de, 59
La Victoria, 154

Law, John, 2
Leamy, John, 71-72
LeClède, Pierre Liguest, 4
Lennan, Father Francis, 140-41, 143, 146, 150
levees, 170-71, 173-75
Leyba, Fernando de, 12
Libro Maestro, 163
Lille Sarpy Colsson and Company, 123
London, England, 67
Lonergan, Patrick, 142
López y Ángulo, Ramón de, 123, 128
Louisiana: defense of, 11, 64, 94, 113-14, 119, 139; French transfer to Spain, 1, 2, 39; French transfer to United States, 129, 162, 168, 177 (*see also* Louisiana Purchase); military, 116, 157; Spanish transfer to France, 106n3, 127, 131, 149
Louisiana Creoles, vii
Louisiana Purchase, 131, 149
Louisville, Ky., 80, 99
Louis XVI, 113
Lower Louisiana, 14, 25, 31-32, 71, 76, 100, 107, 111, 119, 124, 129, 158, 165
Lunney, Bernard, 136
Lydia, 71

M

Macarty, Agustín, 65
Mackay, James, 125
MacKenna, Constantine, 135-38
Madrid, Spain, vii-viii, 6, 24, 47, 79, 82, 94, 106, 119, 137
Maguire, John, 142, 150
Maison Rouge, Marquis de, 114-16, 120-21
Málaga, Spain, 16, 18, 26-27, 40
Malagueños: agriculture, 16, 34-35; assistance to, 16, 18, 28, 33; immigration, 16-18, 19n51, 26-26,

Index 197

31, 64, at New Iberia, 17-18, 26-36;
Malvina (Falkland) Islands, 9
Manchac, 20, 41, 134, 150, 158, 163;
 British post at, 32, 163, 169
Mangan, Patrick, 140-41, 150
mange, 162-63. *See also* disease
Maramec River, 107
Margarita, 15, 156
Marigny de Mandeville, Pierre de, 14, 158, 161
market, 70, 77, 94, 161
Martin, François-Xavier, 153
Martinique, 54, 80, 98
Maryland, 6-8, 66
Maxwell, James, 142
merchants, 10; American, 108; English, 9; Irish, 68
Methodists, 147
Mexico, 9, 42, 60-61, 94, 114, 117, 126-27, 131, 150. *See also* Kingdom of New Spain
Mexico City, Mexico, 134
Migas y Vida family, 34
military posts, 3, 32, 119, 163, 169
militia: and Bouligny, 11, 32; Galveztown, 162-63; Louisiana, 109, 113, 161; Natchez, 113; Natchitoches, 8; Valenzuela, 169
Minor, Stephen, 137
Miró, Esteban: d'Argès proposal, 44-45, 48, 52-54, 80-83, 86, 91, 103; Galveztown, 165; immigration policy, 21, 42-44, 51-53, 59, 61, 63-72, 74, 78, 136-37, 139; Morgan proposal, 55-57; religion, 42-43, 45, 51, 64, 140, 144, 148; Valenzuela, 171; West Florida, 133-137; Wilkinson proposal, 50-51, 57, 59, 75-7
missionaries: French, 82; German, 82; Irish, vii, xi, 42-45, 51, 64, 81-82, 134-35, 138-40, 142, 144, 147-50, 160

Mississippi basin, 3, 85
Mississippi River: Spanish commercial policy, 46-47, 49, 53, 64, 69, 81, 83-85, 87-90, 92-94, 102, 114, 118
Mississippi Valley, 45, 63, 81, 84-85, 102, 117-18, 130, 171
Missouri River, 125
Mobile, Ala., 2, 37, 41, 43, 137-38, 140-41, 150, 164
monopoly companies, 2
Morales, Juan Ventura, 121-22, 126, 128
Morgan, George, 55-57, 72-75, 102n66; immigration proposal, 56-57
Morhouse, Abraham, 122-23
mulatto slaves, 11
Murcia, Spain, 11, 24
Murphy, George, 140-41
Murray, William, 119-20; immigration proposal, 120

N

Napoleon Bonaparte, 129, 131
Natchez: Anglo-American settlers, 44-46, 72, 76, 81-82, 85, 134, 137, 140; British post, 32, 33n27, 41, 163; Catholicism in, 43, 135, 137-38, 141-44, 148; defense, 45, 121; Protestantism in, 145-47; transfer to Spain, 42; transfer to United States, 97, 143-44, 146-47
Natchez District, 41, 43-44, 60n53, 140, 143-44, 146-47
Natchez revolt of 1797, 119, 124
Natchitoches, 2, 8
Natural, 155. *See also El Sagrado Corazón de Jesús*
Navarro, Diego Joseph, 156
Navarro, Martín, 16, 18-20, 35-36, 43-44, 51-53, 80-81, 102, 159-60, 165

New Bourbon, La., 111-12
New Feliciana, 143, 148, 150
New Iberia, La.: and Bouligny, 28n14, 36, 30-35, 37; floods, 31-32, 36; Isleños at, 153; Malagueños at, 17, 26, 31, 33-36
New Madrid, 55-56, 72, 74-75, 107, 110-11, 114-15, 121, 125, 140. *See also* l'Ance à la Graisse
New Orleans, La.: religious services, 160; Spanish acquisition of, 2-3; trade, 118, 166
New Orleans Cabildo, 161
New Orleans theater of war, 156
New Spain, 10
Nogales (Vicksburg), 111, 140-41
North America, ix, 46-47, 63, 78-79, 102, 154
North Carolina, 92
Notario, Father, 173
Nova Scotia, 3, 19
Novelas de Miguel Cervantes, 86
Nowland, Mauricio, 67-68
Nowland project, 67
Nuestra Señora de los Dolores, 156
Nueva Gálvez, La., 159. *See also* San Bernardo, La.

O

oath of allegiance, 47, 51, 67, 124, 134
Ohio River, 54, 70, 73, 100
Ohio River basin, 139
Ohio River Valley, 45, 79, 125
Oneida County, N.Y., 75
O'Neill, Arturo, 15
Opelousas territory, 6-7, 7n16, 9, 30
Order of St. Louis, 44, 49, 79
O'Reilly, Alejandro, 8-9, 23; immigration policy, 9
Ouachita district, 27, 28n14, 114-16, 119, 121-23

P

Pacheco, Rafael Martínez, 8
Paris, France, 44-45, 79-81, 84, 100
Paulus, Peter, 72
Peleagonzalo, Tirso de, 161
Peñalver, Bishop Luis, 143, 149
Pennsylvania, 72, 143
Pensacola, 15, 37, 41, 140-42, 149-50, 156, 158, 164
Petely, Joseph, 165
petits habitants, 176
Peyroux de la Coudrenière, Henri, 40, 108-109
Philadelphia, Penn., viii, 71, 75, 99, 108-109, 111-12, 116-18, 124, 162
Piernas, Pedro, 12, 116
Piernas, Joseph, 116
planters, 9
Plaquemine, La., 29
Plattenville, La., 173
Pointe Coupée, La., 148, 150, 174
Pointe Coupée slave insurrection, 113, 174
Portell, Thomas, 115
Port Tobacco, Md., 8
Prados family, 34
Presbyterian, 146-47
Prévost, François, dit Collet, 31
Princesa de Asturias, 16, 26
Protestants: conversion, viii, xi, 82, 85, 133-34, 141, 143-44; in East Florida, 142; immigration policy, ix, 39, 42, 44, 51, 64, 67, 77, 82; marriage, 147-48; ministers, 46, 83, 144-46, 151; in Natchez, 137, 140; in New Orleans, 140; in West Florida, 21, 42, 133-34, 139, 143-44;
Protestant Episcopal Church, 146
Puerto Rico, 26, 66, 156

R

Rausman, Franz, 165

Index

religion: and assimilation, 11, 42, 45-46; freedom of, 44, 48, 55, 72, 74-75, 80, 92, 94, 95n43; and immigration policy, 51, 55-56, 67, 72, 126; public worship, 21, 42, 46, 77, 83, 85, 95n44, 134, 144-47
Rendón, Francisco, 121
Rivas, Francisco, 166-67, 175
Rome, 117
Ronde, Pierre de la, 161
Royal College of Irishmen, 135

S

Sabine River, 116
Sagrado Corazón, 15
Salamanca, 43, 136, 140
Salcedo, Manuel Juan de, 127, 129
San Agustín de Ahumada, Tex., 8
San Bernardo, La., 14, 159-61, 166, 175. *See also* Concepción, La., Nueva Gálvez, La., and Tierra de Bucycs, La.
San Carlos, 156
San Ignacio de Loyola, 155
San Ildefonso de La Granja, Spain, viii, 24, 84
San Josef, 16, 26
San Juan Nepomuceno, 136, 155
San Lorenzo de El Escorial, Spain, viii
San Pedro, 156
Santa Catalina Creek, 43. *See also* St. Catherine Creek
Santa Cruz de Tenerife, 13, 19, 155
Santa Faz, 155
Santa Theresa, 16, 26n7
Santísima Trinidad, 156
Santísimo Sacramento, 154-55, 157. See also *El Jasón*
Santo Domingo, 54, 66
Savage, William, 135-38, 143
schools, 42, 46, 73, 116, 135, 174
Scioto Company, 110

Scroggs, William O., 176
scurvy, 163. *See also* disease
Sebastian, Benjamin, 57, 120
Second Creek, 43, 137
separatist movement, 49, 92, 94
Seven Years' War, 1-3, 39
Seville, Spain, viii, 135
slaves: for agriculture, 12, 123; ban on the importation of, 113; in Bayou Lafourche, 174, 176; French era, 2, 3; with immigrants, 58, 66; in Galveztown, 162; importation of, 24, 67-68; insurrections, 113, 115, 122, 174; in Natchez, 43n12, 70; in New Iberia, 17, 28-31, 34-35; population, 11; in San Bernardo, 161; in Valenzuela, 169, 172
smallpox, 163. *See also* disease
South Carolina, 145
Spain: acquisition of Louisiana, 1-2, 4, 5n9, 21; French relations, 113, 118-19; immigration, 1, 26, 40; immigration policy, 13, 23, 69; laws, 56, 77, 95, 144-46; military, 14, 32, 78, 113, 160, 168; Mississippi River policy, 46, 64, 102; priests, 143; retrocession of Louisiana, 129-31; U.S. relations, 83-84, 117, 148; war with Great Britain, 9, 13, 17, 32, 118-19, 154, 163
Spanish Conspiracy, 50
Spanish Empire, 51, 73, 93, 95, 131, 150
Spanish Floridas, 118
Spanish Illinois, 4, 7. *See also* Upper Louisiana
Spanish Town, Baton Rouge, La., 168
speculation, 120
Stampley, Jacob, 145
Stampley, John, 145
St. Andrew on the Missouri River, 125
St. Augustine, 109

St. Bernard Parish, 162, 177
St. Catherine Creek, 137, 146. *See also* Santa Catalina Creek
Ste. Genevieve, Mo., 4, 142
St. Louis, Mo., 4, 7, 112
St. Mary's County, Md., 66
St. Maxent, Gilbert Antoine de, 28, 165, 168-170
Suárez, Miguel, 176
Suárez, 15
sugar, 68
Supreme Council, 5n9, 42-43, 53, 85-87, 135
Swayze, Reverend Samuel, 144

T

Tardiveau, Barthélemi, 110-12
tariff on immigrants, 96
Tenerife, Canary Islands, 154
Tennessee, 46, 63, 77
Tensas settlement, 140
Tensas River, 137-38, 148
Terre-aux-Boeufs, La., 153, 159. *See also* Tierra de Bueyes, La. and San Bernardo, La.
Texas, 8, 61, 89, 123, 129, 131
Thompson Creek, 20. *See also* Bayou de los Ecores
Tierra de Bueyes, La., 14. *See also* Terre aux Beoufs, La. and San Bernardo, La.
Tinzas settlement, 43
tobacco, 30, 34, 58, 60, 77
Tombigbee settlement, 138, 140-41, 148-49
tornados, 167, 171
Tortosa, Andrés Amat de, 13, 19, 154, 156
trade, 43, 114, 120, 166; with Americans, 48; with English, 10; with Indians, 123; with Kentucky, 100; posts, 2, 4
trans-Appalachia, 1, 4

Treaty of Paris 1763, 2, 4
Treaty of Paris 1783, 41, 82, 133
Treaty of San Lorenzo, 117-19, 146, 148, 167
Trudeau, Zenon, 125-26

U

Ulloa, Antonio de, 3-8; assistance to immigrants, 3, 5; immigration policy, 7
United States: acquisition of Louisiana, 37, 123, 129, 131, 149, 162, 168, 177; acquisition of Natchez District, 119, 138, 146-48; acquisition of East and West Florida, 150; settlers in Louisiana, 21, 39, 44, 47, 65, 67, 70, 107, 110, 121, 126-27, 130, 133; Spanish relations, 83, 92, 130, 151; western separatists, viii, 47, 57, 76, 84, 96, 120, 140
University of Salamanca, 135. *See also* Irish College of the University of Salamanca
Unzaga, Luis de, 9
Upper Louisiana, 4, 7, 12, 47, 55, 76, 98, 107-108, 110, 112-13, 125-26, 130, 142. *See also* Spanish Illinois

V

Valdés, Antonio, 47, 85, 102
Valencia, Spain, 11, 24
Valenzuela, La., 14, 20, 153, 157, 159-60, 165-66, 168-76. *See also* Bayou La Fourche
Vega, Andrés de, 174-75
Venezuela, La., 156
Verret, Nicolas, 173-74
Viar, José Ignacio de, 108-109
Vilemont, Luis de, 116-17
Villa Gayoso, 140. *See also* Cole's Creek

Index

Villanueva, Tomás de, 175-76
Villaprovedo, Father José de, 160
Virginia, 68-69
Volunteers of the Mississippi, 161
Von Steuben, William Frederick, 75

W

Walker, Jacobo, 6
Walsh, Patrick, 140-41, 149
War for American Independence, 139
Washington, George, 105
West Florida: British, 1, 5, 9, 10, 17, 23-24, 32, 157-58, 163, 169; conversion efforts, 83, 134-36, 138-39, 141-45, 150-51; immigration, ix, xi, 21, 23-24, 32, 43, 63, 76-78; Isleños in, 168; Protestant residents, 41-42, 69, 82, 85, 94, 106, 133-35, 136, 138-39; Spanish acquisition of, 20; Treaty of San Lorenzo, 119, 148; United States acquisition of, 149
wheat, 30, 111, 114, 121-22
White, Gregory, 135-139, 143, 148
White, Henry, 85
White, James, 49, 92, 99
Wilkinson, James, viii, 50-51, 53-54, 57-60, 70, 75-76, 93-97, 100-101, 103, 120, 139-40; immigration plan, 50-53, 96, 99, 120, 139
Wooster, Thomas, 109

X

Ximénez, Juana, 174

Y

Ybáñez family, 34
Ynfante, 66